A Laboratory
On The Open Fields

Ignorance

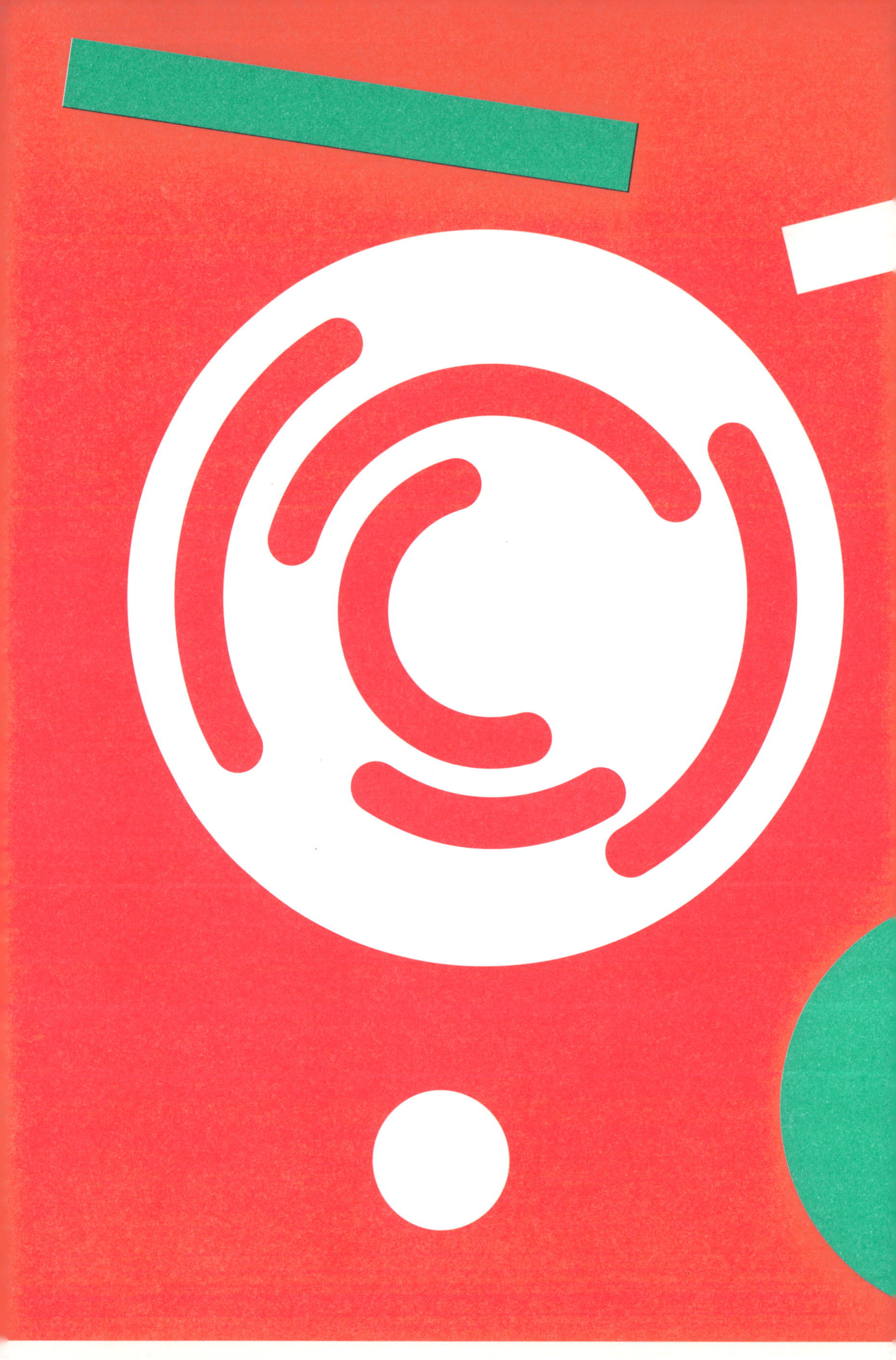

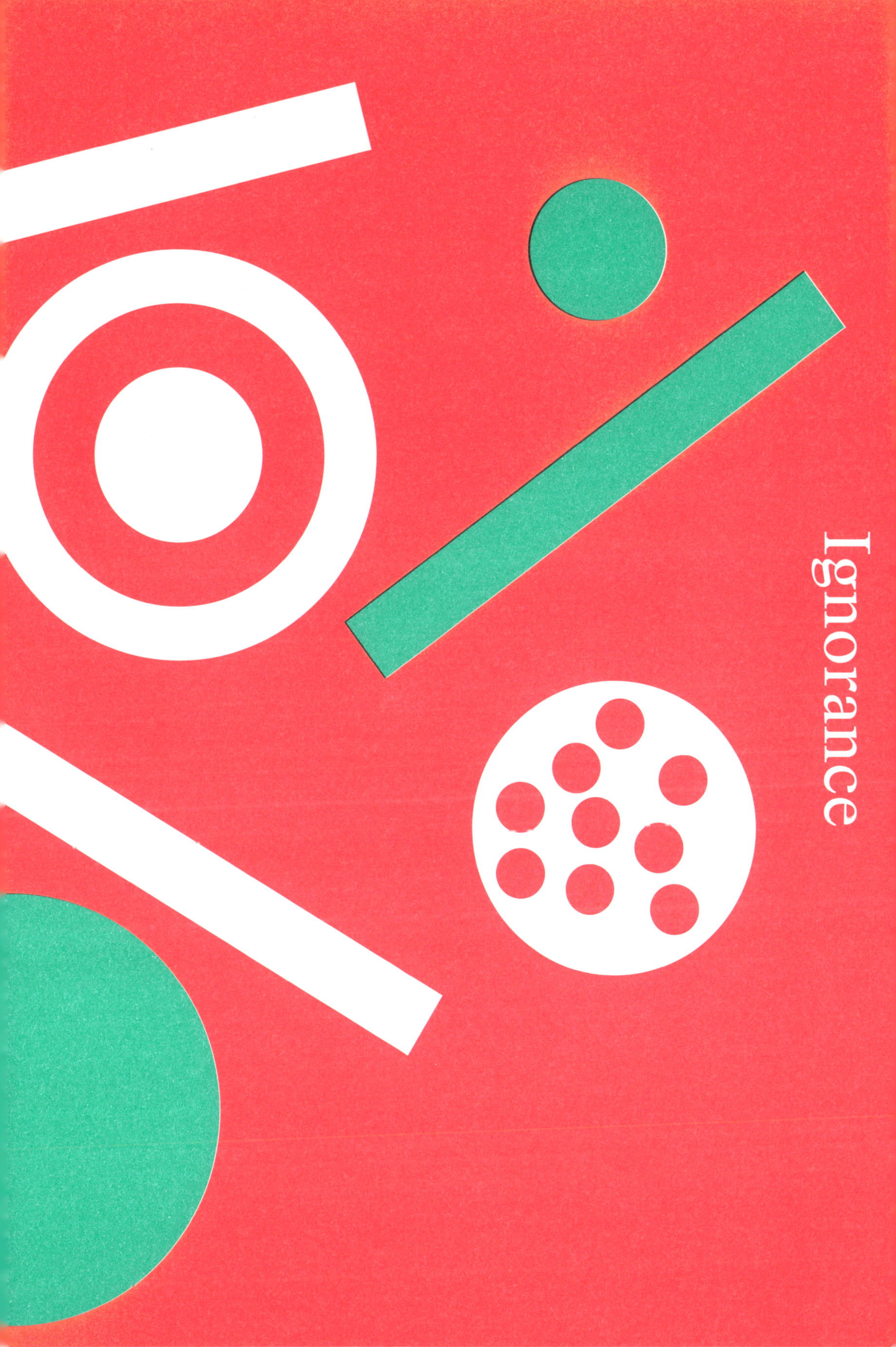
Ignorance

EDITORIAL

When media artists become actively involved in publishing, one automatically would expect a more open and free attitude towards the *medium*. But twice over the last five years it proved to be a hard task to get away from a conventional idea of what a publication can do, and how it could be used in novel ways today. The initiative *Time Inventors' Kabinet* [1] ended with a box filled with loose papers and an extensive table of contents. Within this context the editor's task is to keep the gate open, and to reformulate over and over again the nature of the endeavour, and fight the cultural trends for functionalism, formalism, conventionalism. On the other hand, one wants to remain visible within the context that art is providing. Between these two *forces* all choices are out of balance, in contradiction, escaping reason. Finally, or should it be 'initially', there is the monster called *Aesthetics*. There are very few discussions about it nowadays, everyone being afraid to mention it. It is more than beauty, it comes together with structure and content, skill, and the deviant attitude of the particular artist, breaking the imitation and repetition, moulding something of an original nature. And so *a publication* is not a catalogue, not a portfolio, not a photobook, not a collection of essays, not a novel, not a poem, not a print, not a website, not a . But *something derivative*, possibly including all of it, along the lines known and at the same time questioning exactly that, producing something different, something that was not there before.

Ignorance, after: "*The ecology of ignorance*" by Niklas Luhmann, and "*ignorance more frequently begets confidence than does knowledge*." by Charles Darwin.

Ignorance started in *a wiki*, a so-called collaborative and online hypertext environment, existing already for at least 20 years. When we set out to work on the concepts for the longer term initiative '*A Laboratory On The Open Field*' (abbreviated as ALOTOF) [2], the artists involved began to put their documentation in it, their ideas and resources, their technical set-ups, their problems and findings, tests, failures, successes. Over time it became a common place where the making of creative works could be followed. After two years, there was the need for a round-up, a sort of bringing together what we had done, and also to fill the gaps: what is imagined but not there yet.

Convergence was a related small festival, in the fringe of bigger cultural events in Brussels, Nantes, Saint-Nazaire, Praha, Hranice, …

But how to bring all of this really together, in something that lasts, something that can be read again, revised, corrected and commented on its relevance after the facts? *A publication*, in whatever form that is possible today, bringing the story of how things are being made while making them, how they are presented then differently, is for sure a daring task. For *ecologically concerned* artists, a print is never the solution, it is too expensive for what it is yielding, while the digital environment only is missing part of the audience, part of where one positions him/herself next to the rest of culture or art.

This book is *a compilation* of all 3 things mentioned above: how the making of art can be organized, how art is gradually being made, DIY and collaborative, and finally how it can be presented. Maybe we are the last of the media art mohicans, working over longer periods of time in *an experimental way*, taking all the time that is needed to think about the things that matter for us in this world. On the other hand, we are only anecdotal. Whatever it be, it includes *a sensitive* under the surface attitude of being anti-project, anti-formal, and anti-conform, anti-designed.

So it includes this *reflection* and at the same time the working out of something realistically perceivable. Reading through it all, maybe this is the way things can be done today, *experimentally*, different in character one from another, but disparate as the whole seems, there are strong internal connections between people, ideas, creative expressions. From the theoretical poetic computer poems, the personal poetic reflections, the connection with research and the sciences, the explorative and inventive spirit in constructing certain objects, the attention for the environment, the intractable walking away …

This *printed book* is part of another book, an *online book*, and that is part of another book, still to be written, and maybe there is yet another one, parallell, and only imagined, still to be printed, or not anymore. This book, *these books*, want to jump around, turn things upside down, fly away. Maybe the first move, is a *collective notebook* wondering about the mechanisms for how to make the first step. And then slide forward to a different nature, for *creativity and ecology*. Think about it, and hop along.

Gívan Belá.
20150530.

1   Time Inventors Kabinet – TIK, 2009-2012:
http://timeinventorskabinet.org/
2   www.alotof.org

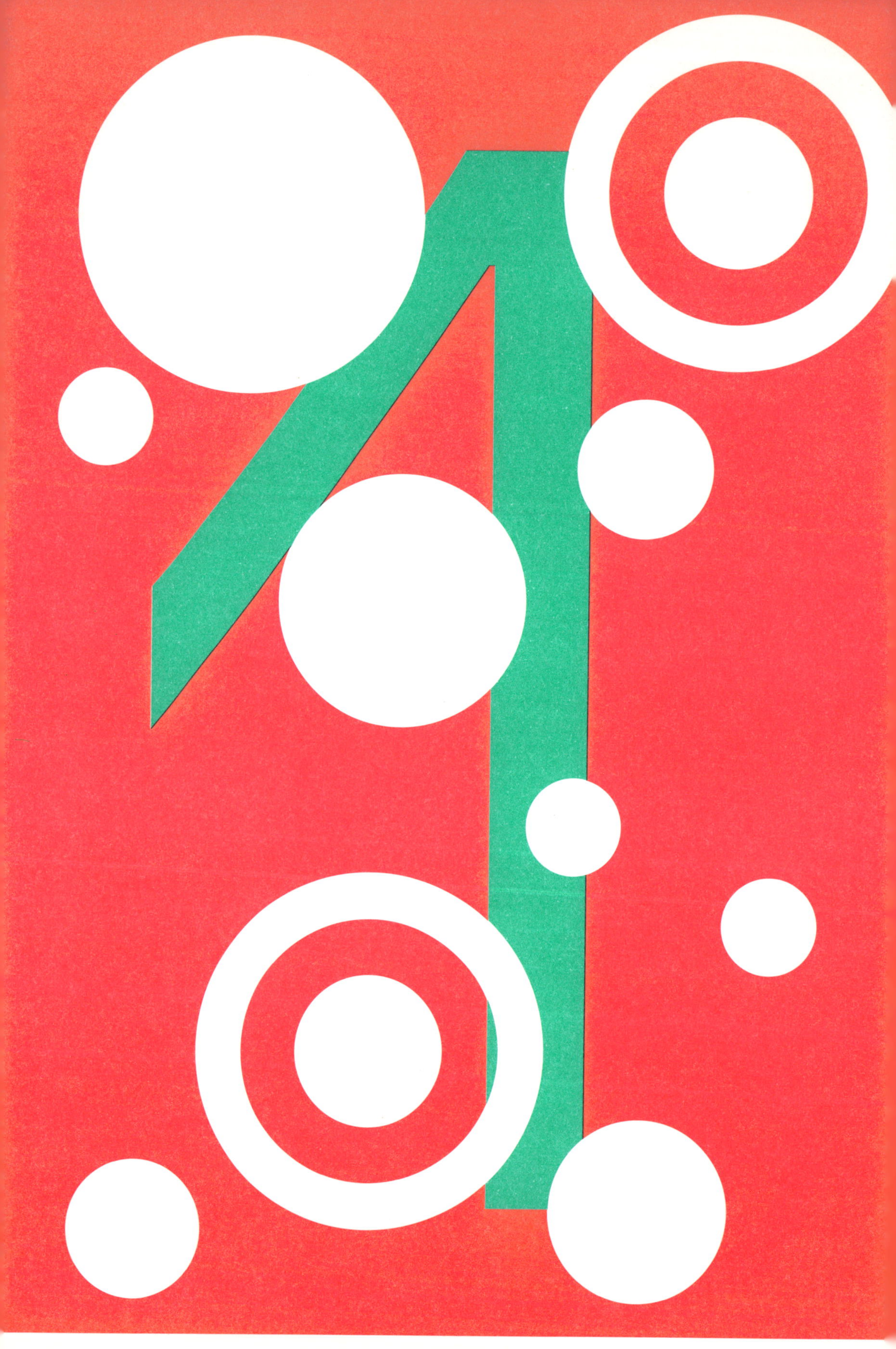

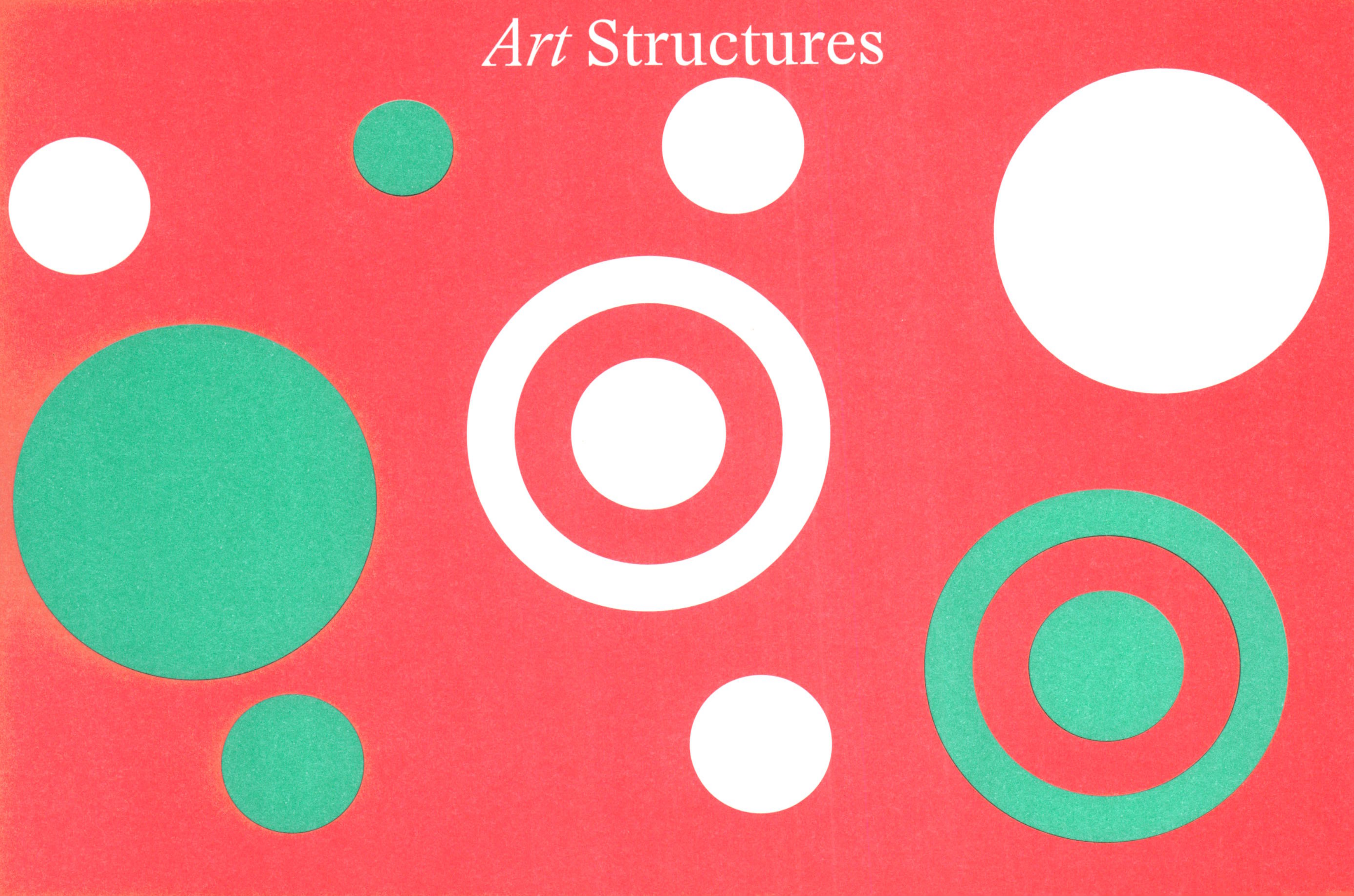
Art Structures

OKNO – A Laboratory On The Open Field: Looking Back to Look Forward?

*Gívan Belá
& AnneMarie Maes*

In the world today, where everything that is not an object (and ready for sale) is being tagged as a 'project', more complex forms of creativity are often invisible since they simply don't meet the requirements for being evaluated. Okno as an organisation was started ten years ago by artists to support collaborative, DIY and open source work. It has remained experimental ever since, and was always, rather on purpose, on the verge of invisibility. Over the years, there have been changes in people's lives, attitudes, characters, and so, too, in organisations. The slow drift toward critical ecological content certainly meant an irreversible departure from mainstream media art. The events and projects became larger initiatives, running over several years and starting up different, often contradictory, processes. The *Time Inventors' Kabinet* (TIK, 2009-2012), turned artists in ecological clockmakers, dreaming up a non-linear wind time, monitoring bees, thinking about slow art. In many ways *A Laboratory on the Open Field* (ALOTOF, 2013-2015) was a continuation that tried to take a radical step further into the dark. The question '*What if we go outdoors and make media art in a natural environment?*' will never be definitively answered, but it certainly provides an interesting starting point for creating new instruments and discovering new ways of perceiving and communicating.

In Brussels during the days of the *Convergence festival*, it is only at first glance that we find media art works as expected: Franziska Windisch's corroding copper discs, the 'talking' holes in Gert Aertsen's building, the outdoor objects and audiovisuals by David De Buyser, Anti-Delusion Mechanism's earth energy sonification, AnneMarie Maes' sound beehives, and Gívan Belá's solaramps. But there is more to it. Each of the presented works was certainly influenced by the open development style by which the workshops, presentations and meetings were set up. Parts were made in locations abroad provided by the ALOTOF partners, often together with local artists in those locations. And there is still more to it. To bring about the connectedness of the events in Brussels, Saint-Nazaire, the Atlantic Coastline, Prague and Hranice,

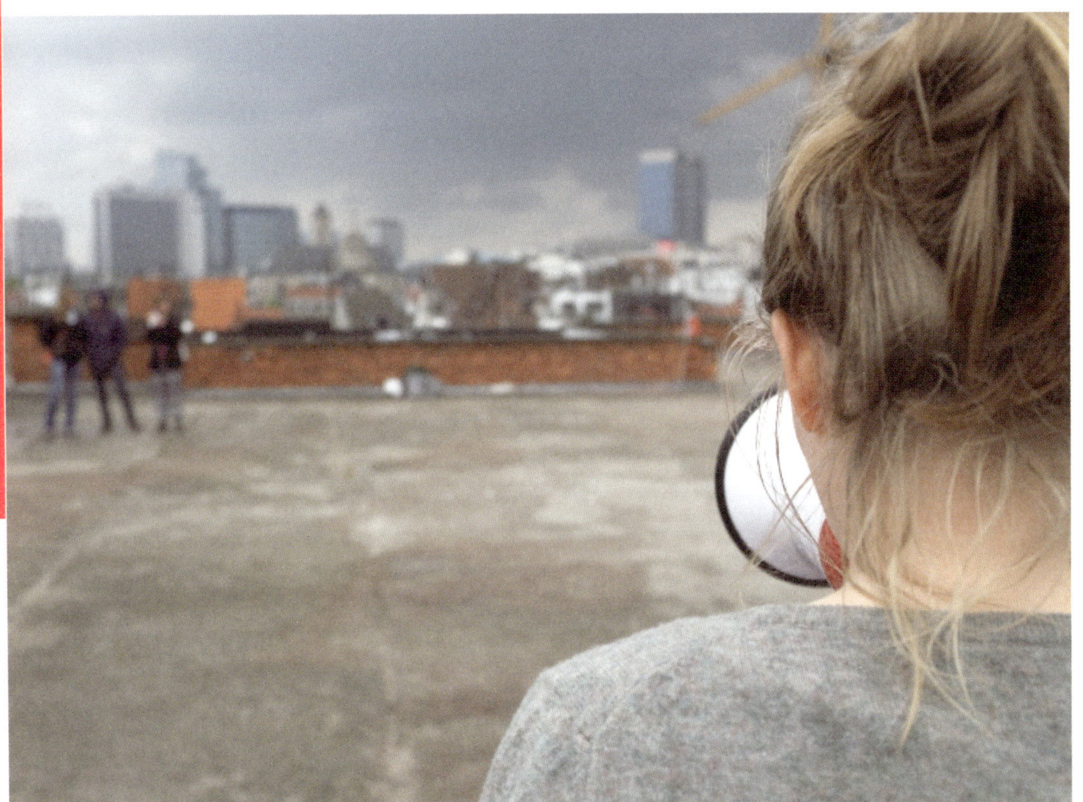

✖ 1. Convergence festival, *Brussels*

an online system was programmed. PVC, or People's Vision Collector shows all events in parallel on the different locations. Every artist elsewhere will be around, somehow.

Maybe the only merit of ALOTOF was to bring together artists who were compatible for working together on quite diverse themes and content, but deeply rooted in an ecological background. No way are we claiming here to have solved anything. For each environmental issue more than a lifetime would be needed. But at least, in recent years, we were setting up camp together to discuss, make, present sonifications, visualisations, and systems for communicating environmental information. At the same time, not — it was sometimes too speculative for serious artistic research, and yes — often there was silence while people investigated things that were too difficult to understand intuitively. Altogether its outcome was unpredictable, coming from a mix of uncertain and, at first sight, unrelated subjects: walks, bees, gardens, technology, music, visuals, installations, writing, solar cells, greenhouses, bikes, and the like.

Yes, it was important to be inspired by Jan Kostolansky's and Martin Janíček's installations, or Jan Poupě's kites, the countryside visits to Periférne Centrá and other places. Also, by not making distinctions among technicians, scientists, gardeners, artists, children, and other creative people like the rest of us, working alongside Peter Hanappe's concept of community greenhouses was important. The dream of a collective look through Balt De Tonnac's app, a remote glimpse of Fabrice Gallis' islands, or a shaky ride in Luc Kerléo's DIY open source bike, as well as the ungovernable walking by Various Artists, surfaced more than often, even if the remote sensors that Dom Leroy and Jef Rolez are developing need another version and more time to really use easily. Still, at least there is a beginning, one to build on, and in a different direction than one would consider when working alone. Scientists around the world warn us of a pending ecological catastrophe, a spiral down that has already started in many ways. Still, we continue living a lifestyle that is largely incompatible with how nature itself deals with waste, pollution, regeneration. Despite all the political and industrial propaganda, it is obvious that the seas and rivers are in a worse state than 50 years ago, that in general the soil and air quality has not improved in the last century, probably the contrary is the case. For each of us, it seems only obvious to work on reversing this trend, changing many aspects of the way we live. Still we see a lot of changes in media, but art itself — despite all activism in galleries — seems to be quite persistent in producing, on average, the same things it gave us half a century ago, and even longer. Maybe in general artists are too pragmatic for a change that would double-cross this. Maybe ALOTOF won't change this, either. Maybe a different agenda for aesthetics, or a new non-prescriptive poetica, based on renewable materials, nature-friendly processes, that requires other tools, media, instruments, ideas, but mostly, another kind of assessment, is just the dream of a few. We hope to have worked with them here.

Maybe after *Convergence* only *Ignorance* will be left.

—

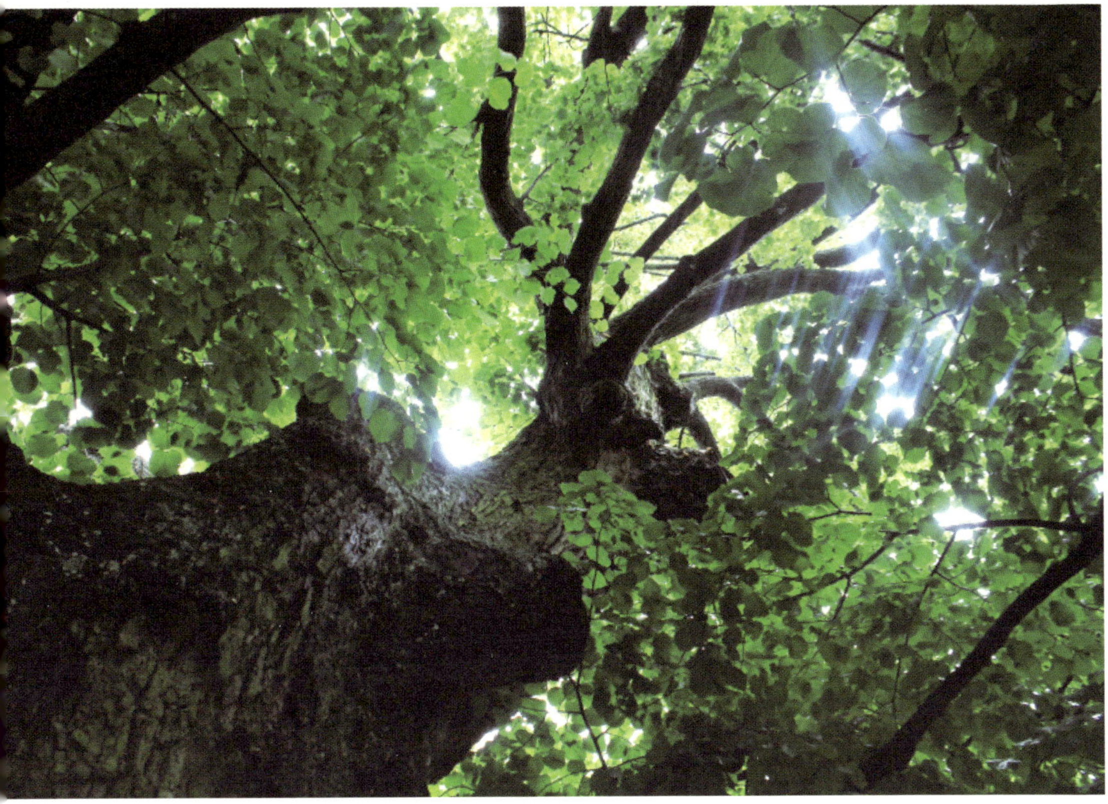

2. Lípa – 750 years old

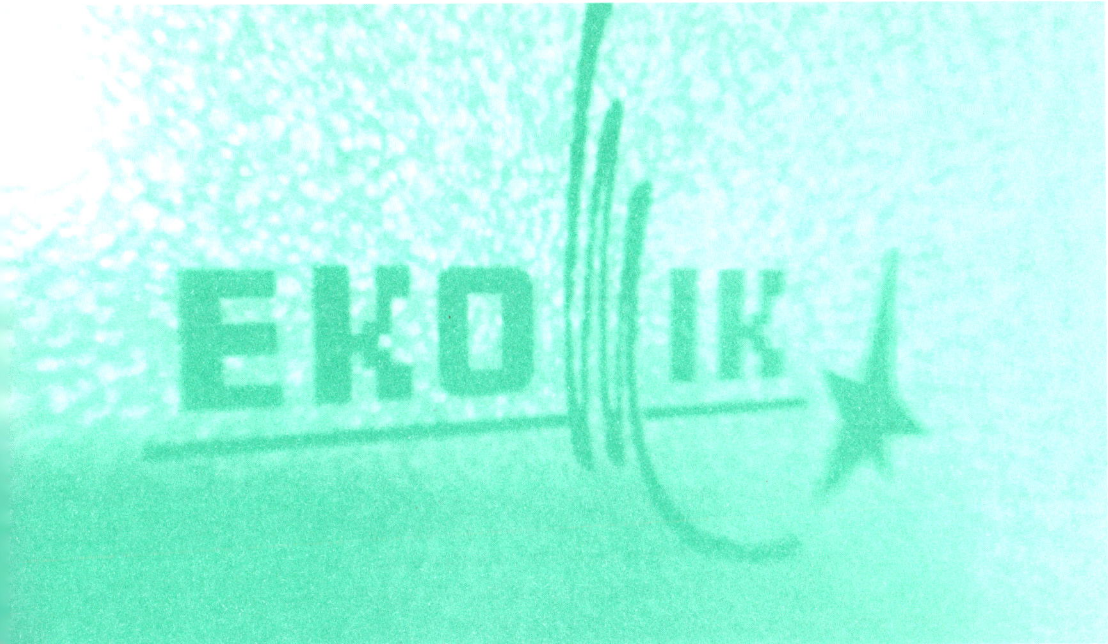

3. Sign of the times

ECOS
◉ *Dominique Leroy*
& Marina Pirot
& Guillaume Ertaud

n+1) Portraits on the motif

We can draw shared stories, document fictional presents, make sketches of working artists. This would be like portraits of the motif, a stop-motion of the elusive art work in progress; arborescent working zones infiltrating the "real" by contagion.

ALOTOF is becoming a lot of artists, a network of projects itself conceived as a rhizomatic form, with multiple identities and outside the boundaries. ECOS is embedded in this plural laboratory and engages in diverse research projects, with areas of exploration so open that we cannot grasp its unity, only its dimensions and shifting directions, its criss-crossing lines; a multiplicity of projects that evolve within this plural laboratory.

They make their own working objects by infiltrating such invested contexts where transmission mixes with diffusion and where the sharing of time creates time. Le déjeuner sur l'herbe [2] (Luncheon on the Grass) is a socio-active process that associates the inhabitants of a neighborhood with the making of multifunctional mobile units for picnicking and gardening, as well as cooking workshops for convivial times, and strolling-harvesting in the city. These diverse occurrences over a two-year period may enable tools or re-appropriation of notices, with the challenge of "*participation*", for users who have already become co-constructors of the utopias sketched out in this way.

The proposed spaces for artistic meeting are in this way confusing: They make their own fleeting workshops of specialised activities (or artistic works) where tools are exchanged, where sharing and inventing is "common" — often technological; this laboratory time, as with the experimentation undertaken, is already active and takes on board partners, artists and participants. And what does it cover? So many projects in genesis, a kaleidoscope of a reality with empty promises, a sort of inversion of the broader concept of art or of one of its legacies.

The Entomosolar project [3] presented during Posedy [4] — a public event using hunters' hides which were reinvested by artistic proposals held in the summer of 2014 in the Czech Republic — was able to create a disturbance by creating a dubious diffusion of synthetic grasshopper sounds, through intensifying the sound of one of the real grasshoppers active in the environment. This sort of identity splitting questions the artist's position and the degree of re-appropriation of aestheticism through inversion, where the utopia of art is merely passing through. The Bee Monitoring Project [5], as it was called, traces the ecosystem of the life of bees into a living sculpture project that captures and transmits interconnecting, poeticised scientific data. In the artist-generators, the guests and the drifting protocols, we notice the political effects of this artistic praxis, implying the social and political dimensions of these invested contexts. In the layers of trans-boundary projects, the context becomes a terrain for artistic activities, engaging the "real" within the realm of art until this, too, becomes muddled.

Offshore expeditions prepared a landing on a fantasy island, the Island project [6], mapping the crossing of Default [7], following random longitudes, the course of sunlight captured in a rock cleft, as in Refrain [8]. The building of the mobile bike Velosynth [9] up

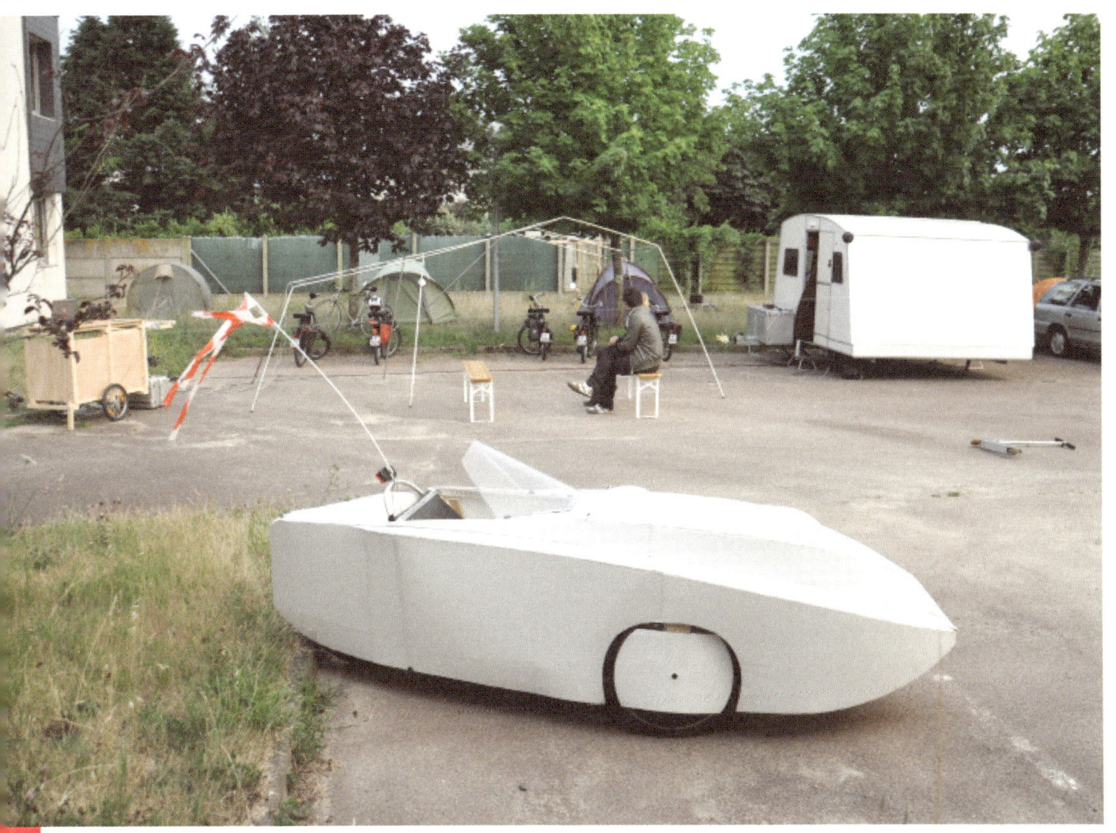

⠏ 4. Caravan-Lab and VeloSynth,
Saint-Nazaire

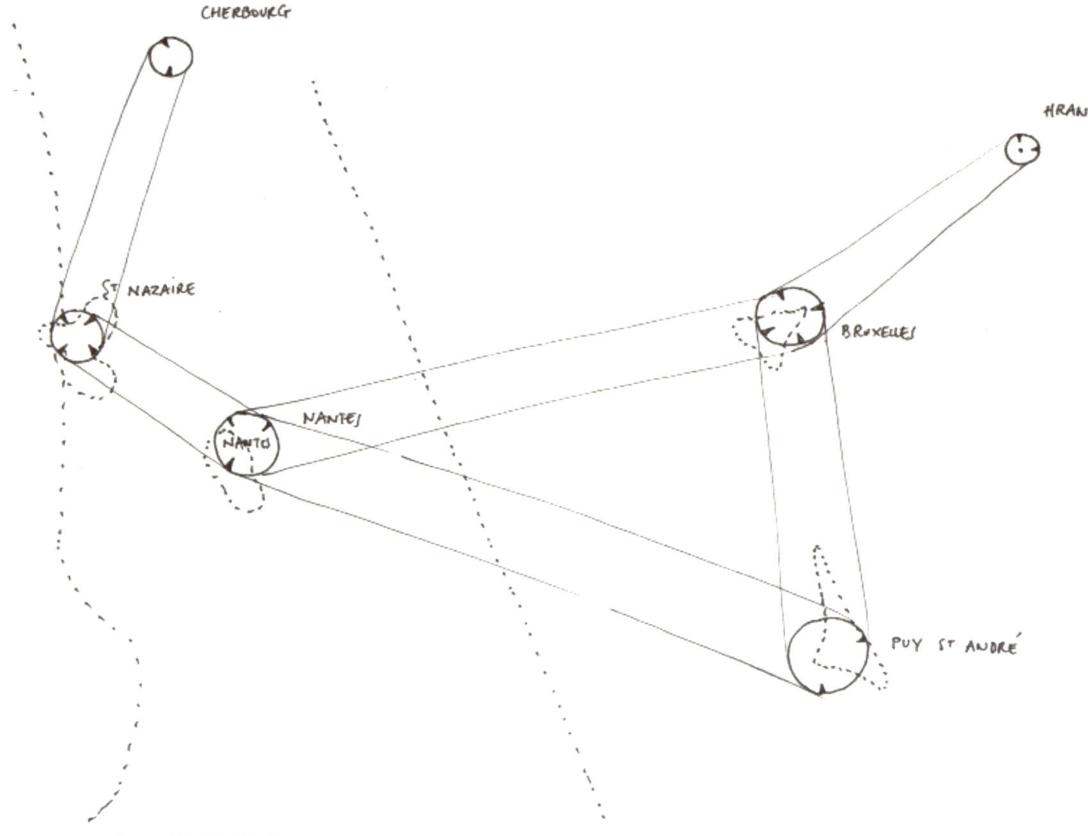

▓ 5. ALOTOF parcours

to the prototype stage, is shared with a community of inventors and makers, displays awareness of the revival of various modes of transport. Or in the nomadic workshop (n)A [10], conceived according to the potential of the context of its construction using many collaborative devices which actively involved artists and participants on the world stage. All these processes are shattering borders and entangling their own particular creative threads in these open fields.

ECOS, like many ALOTOF partners, have based their artistic research on issues of autonomy, ecology, exchange, sharing and re-appropriation (DIY), in addition to allowing time for workshops at Valldora, Hranice, and Brussels, where the artists' networks covered various modes of appropriation (such as peer to peer and greenfablab).

Artistic actions such as the boats for the Island project involved the creation of research teams where these meetings, in turn, created the method. Like the landscape artist Cécile Mercat, with

Uni-de-uni [11], who underscores potential uses of disinvested urban spaces, which can then be transformed by another vision of public space and by merely passing through, these artist practice forms prospectively that involve participants in various projects.

The research by ALOTOF artists is both technical and technological. They share a kind of wild thinking, a hybrid between makers and engineers. Studio production looks like an outdoor performances, where the game returns to the relative autonomy of the artist through composite methods, without abstracting economic or ecological issues. It constitutes an esthetic resolution to the stark questions that the artists of the ALOTOF network take on and develop, the heirs of artistic movements that elevate life to the level of art.

Many projects capture environmental variables and reinvest this data through various engineering projects, replaying the "real" and duplicating it. A poetics is thus born of such work processes that stretch from the time of creation, the projects are composed of adventures or the life of the artists, to beyond their time of production and exhibition. They are auto-generated or become transmitters, or smugglers. By contagion, the "real" reinforces itself with projective aesthetic traversals, and one can see there a kind of contributory democracy being invented.

Far from a reclusive laboratory in a corner of the world, ALOTOF and its emergences propose a platform for collaborative and collective production, an open experience that never ceases to remind us that, *"there is no common world, it needs to be composed"*.

Marina Pirot
March 2015

1   Schemes for discussing, Dominique Leroy, 2014-2015, more drawings at http://photos.dominiqueleroy.info/index.php?/category/15

2   "Le déjeuner sur l'herbe" : http://alotof.org/w/DEJEUNER_SUR_L%27HERBE

3   Entomosolar : http://alotof.org/w/CARAVANLAB-sonifications

4   Posedy :http://yo-yo-yo.org/en/posedy-lovci-a-zvireci-stezky/

5   Article "Sound Beehive" : http://urbanbeelab.okno.be/doku.php?id=sound_beehive

6   ISLAND :http://alotof.org/w/Islands lien vers ISLAND/ and http://alotof.org/w/ISLAND

7   Default : http://nadine.be/project/peregrini/default-1-more-information

8   Refrain : http://alotof.org/w/REFRAIN

9   Velosynth :http://alotof.org/w/AlotofVelosynth

10 Ateliers arborescents :http://alotof.org/w/LES_ATELIERS_ARBORESCENTS

11 Uni-de-uni : http://alotof.org/w/UNI-DE-UNI

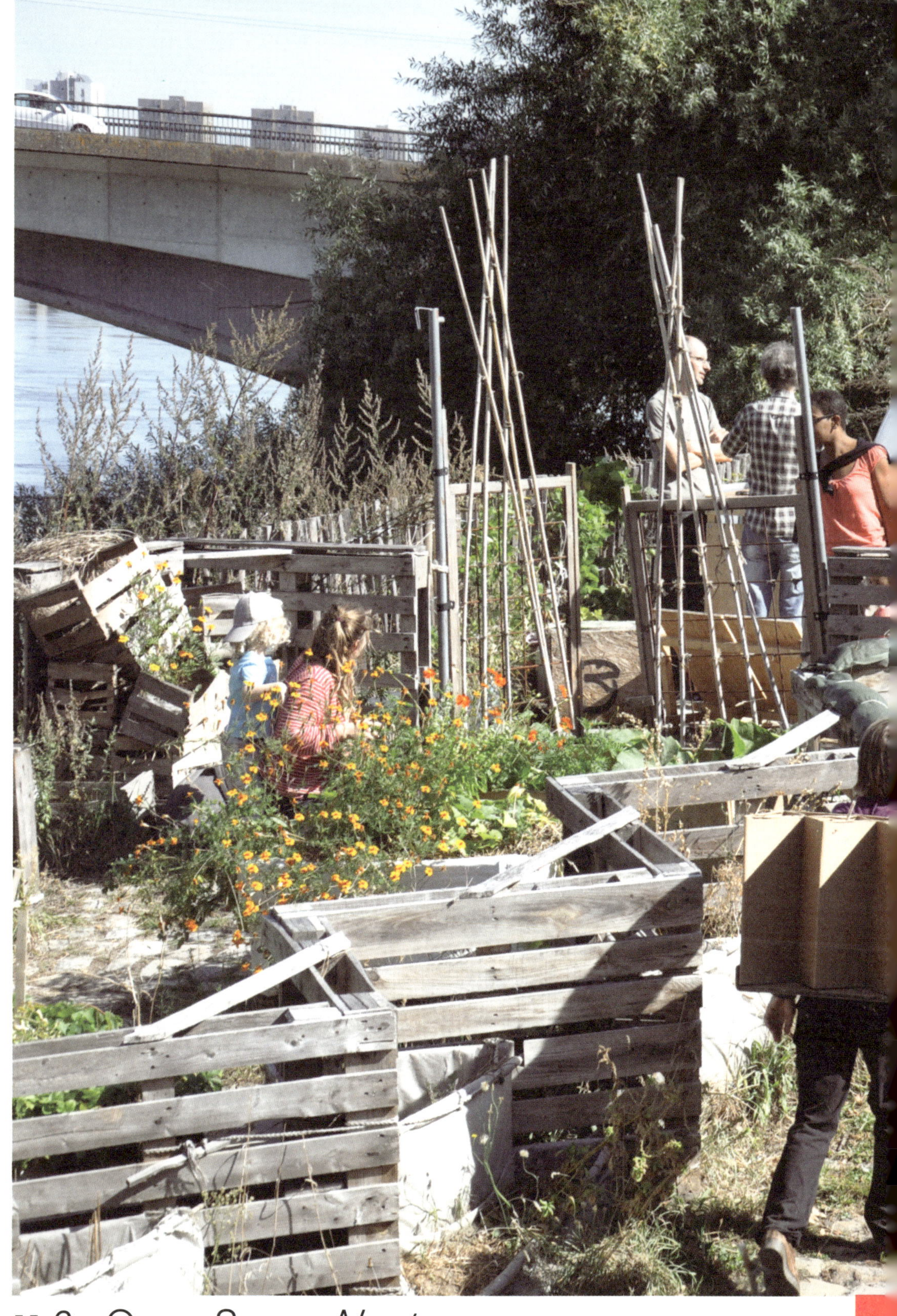

❖ 6. Open Serre, *Nantes*

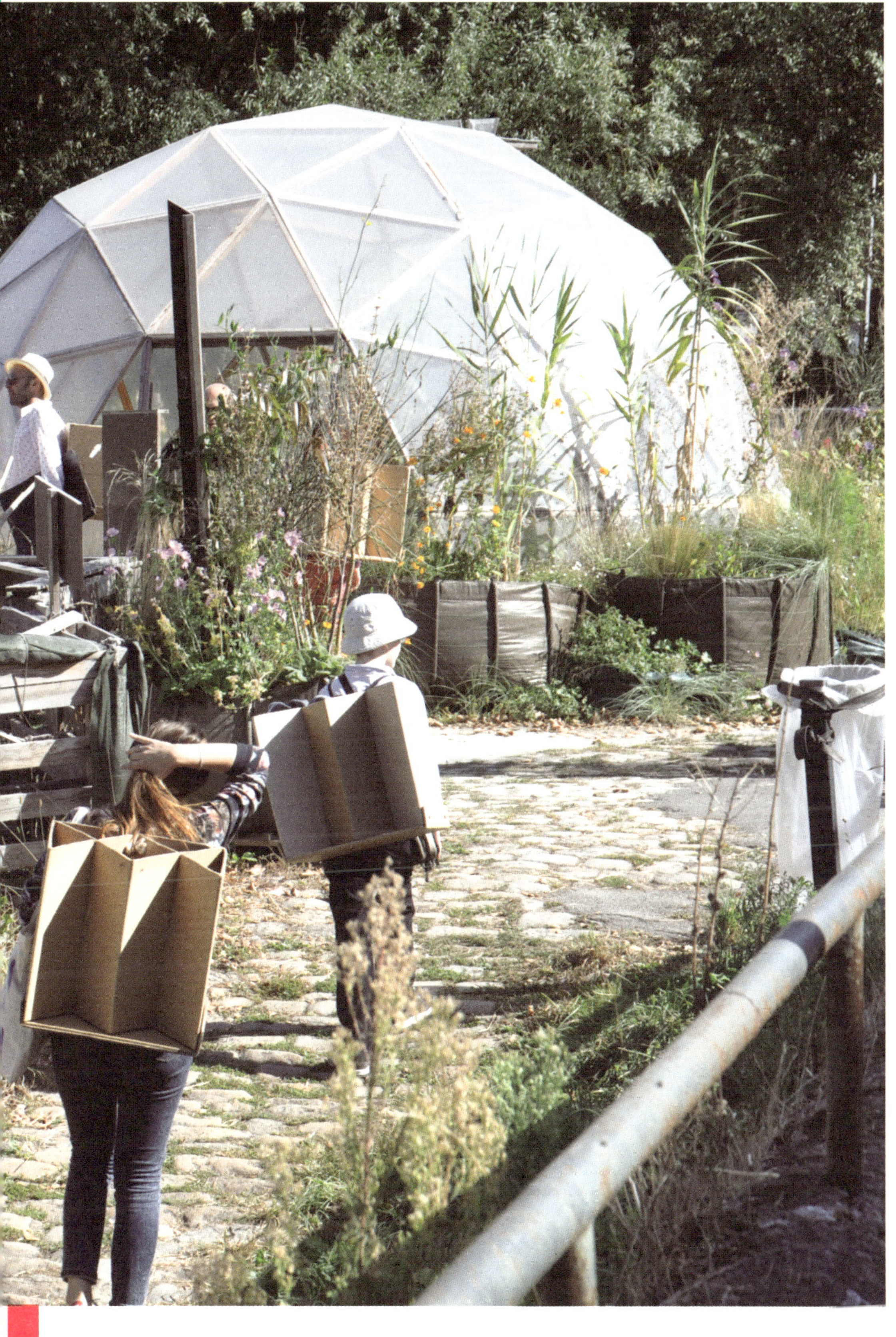

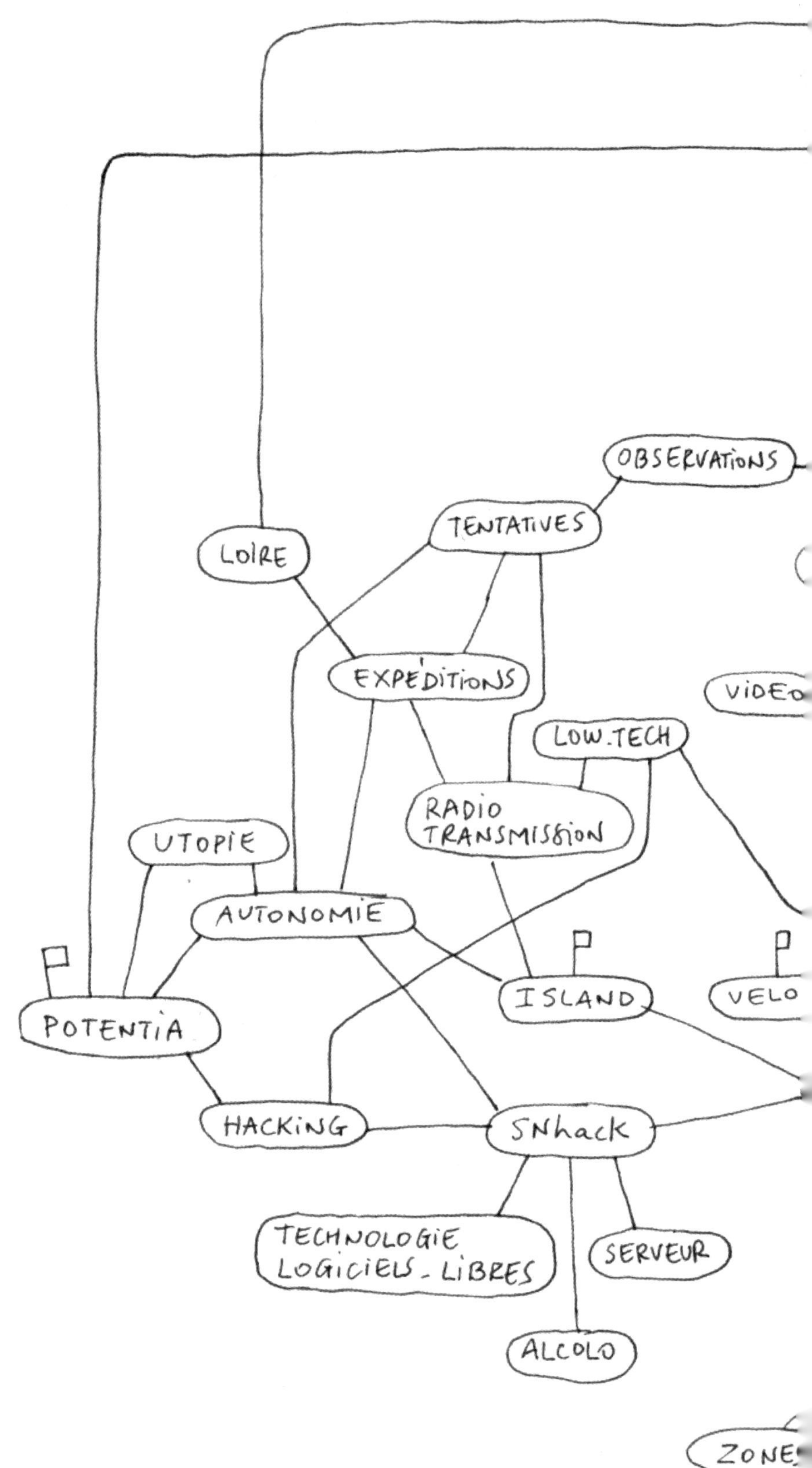

7. ECOS schema

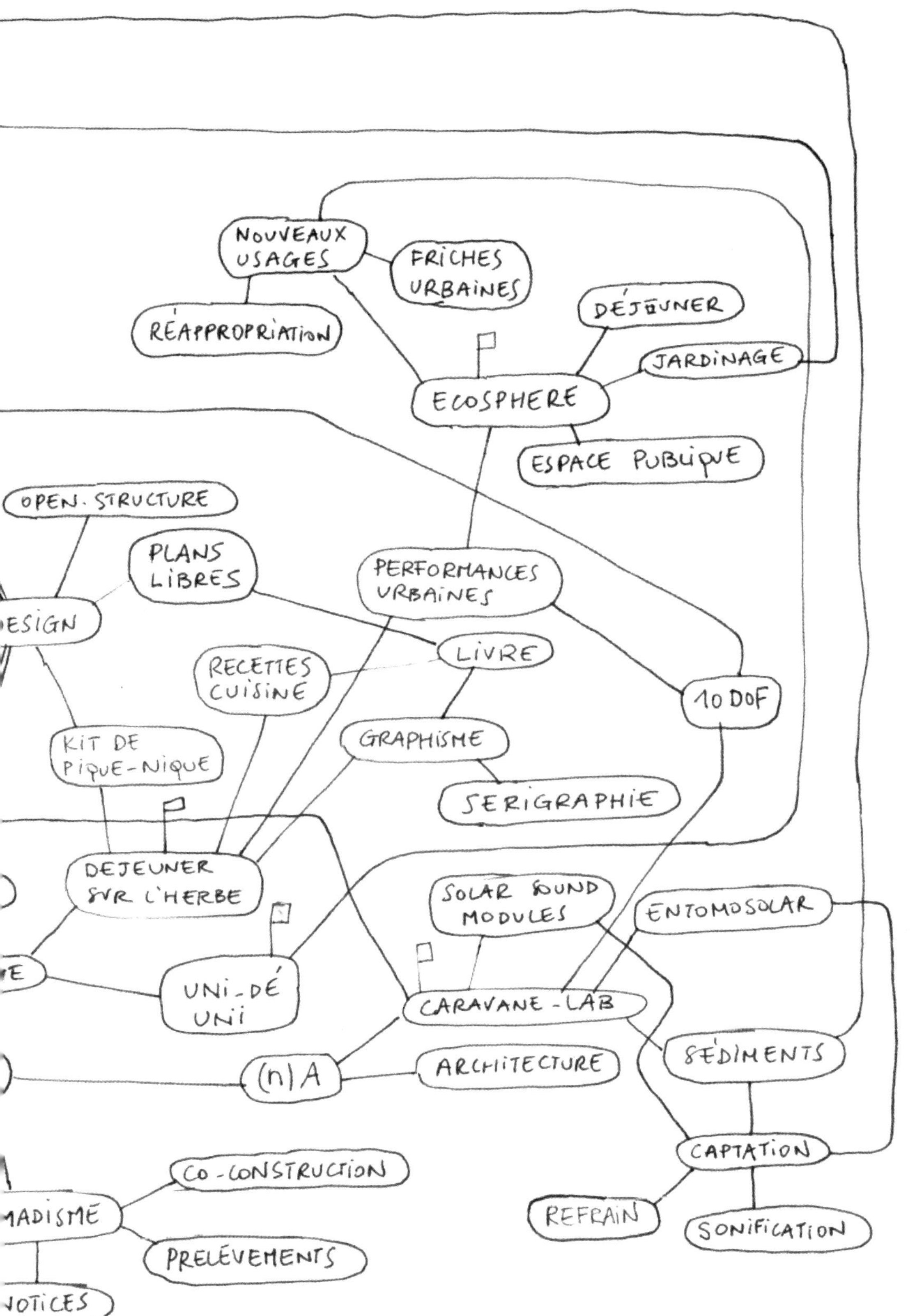

NOUVEAUX USAGES
FRICHES URBAINES
RÉAPPROPRIATION
DÉJEUNER
JARDINAGE
ECOSPHERE
ESPACE PUBLIQUE
OPEN. STRUCTURE
PLANS LIBRES
DESIGN
PERFORMANCES URBAINES
RECETTES CUISINE
LIVRE
10 DOF
KIT DE PIQUE-NIQUE
GRAPHISME
SERIGRAPHIE
DEJEUNER SUR L'HERBE
SOLAR SOUND MODULES
ENTOMOSOLAR
UNI-DÉ UNI
CARAVANE-LAB
SÉDIMENTS
(n)A
ARCHITECTURE
CO-CONSTRUCTION
CAPTATION
MADISME
REFRAIN
SONIFICATION
PRELEVEMENTS
NOTICES

KRA – Kravín Rural Arts as a Garden Laboratory
◉ *Lenka Dolanová*

The location is the foundation! – a former cowshed (in Czech: kravín) on the periphery of a village, Hranice u Malče, is home to KRA: *Kravín Rural Arts*, established in cooperation with Yo-yo. The name given to this site and the organisation itself does not only refer to the building's former use, but also to melting icebergs (in Czech: kra) as a symbol of environmental crisis. An iceberg, a solitary sanctuary floating in the ocean, characterises this site both visually and symbolically. This tall two-storey building, a rare example of a late-baroque manorial farm in this district and formerly part of a seigniorial estate, stands out with its scale and significance. We want to take up its rich history in a modified form. KRA should function as an island for artistic, cultural and environmental initiatives, a place for gatherings and a range of creative and social activities. And finally there is a reference to the raven's croak: KRAA-KRAA. Ravens are apparently one of only a few wild animals who make their own toys. In mythology the raven is a trickster who breaks rules, ignores convention and acts unpredictably. For us the raven symbolises art, playfulness and creativity.

Since July 2014 KRA has hosted a number of activities as part of the ALOTOF (*A Laboratory On The Open Fields*) project, organized by Yo-yo. I shall attempt to outline these activities' repeated rituals, visitors and models for action, discussion and creativity. The first question was how the garden could be used for art work, and here we interpreted "garden" in the broadest possible sense. According to Murray Bookchin's Ecology and Revolutionary Thought, the entire countryside can be seen as a garden, and "*the land must be cultivated as though it were a garden*". In using this rural garden we have taken modest excursions into solar energy, made use of the wind, worked with soil, seeds and plants, and we have also learned something about water. These activities have involved neighbours, musicians, filmmakers, children, gardeners, cooks, hunters (and game), beekeepers and artists. We have continued our work on establishing a rural network of allied initiatives in the form of *RurArtMap*, a printed and online map.

For our first event, *SolarKRA* (3-7 July 2013), we invited a German artist, Ralf Schreiber, who works with minimalist robotics.

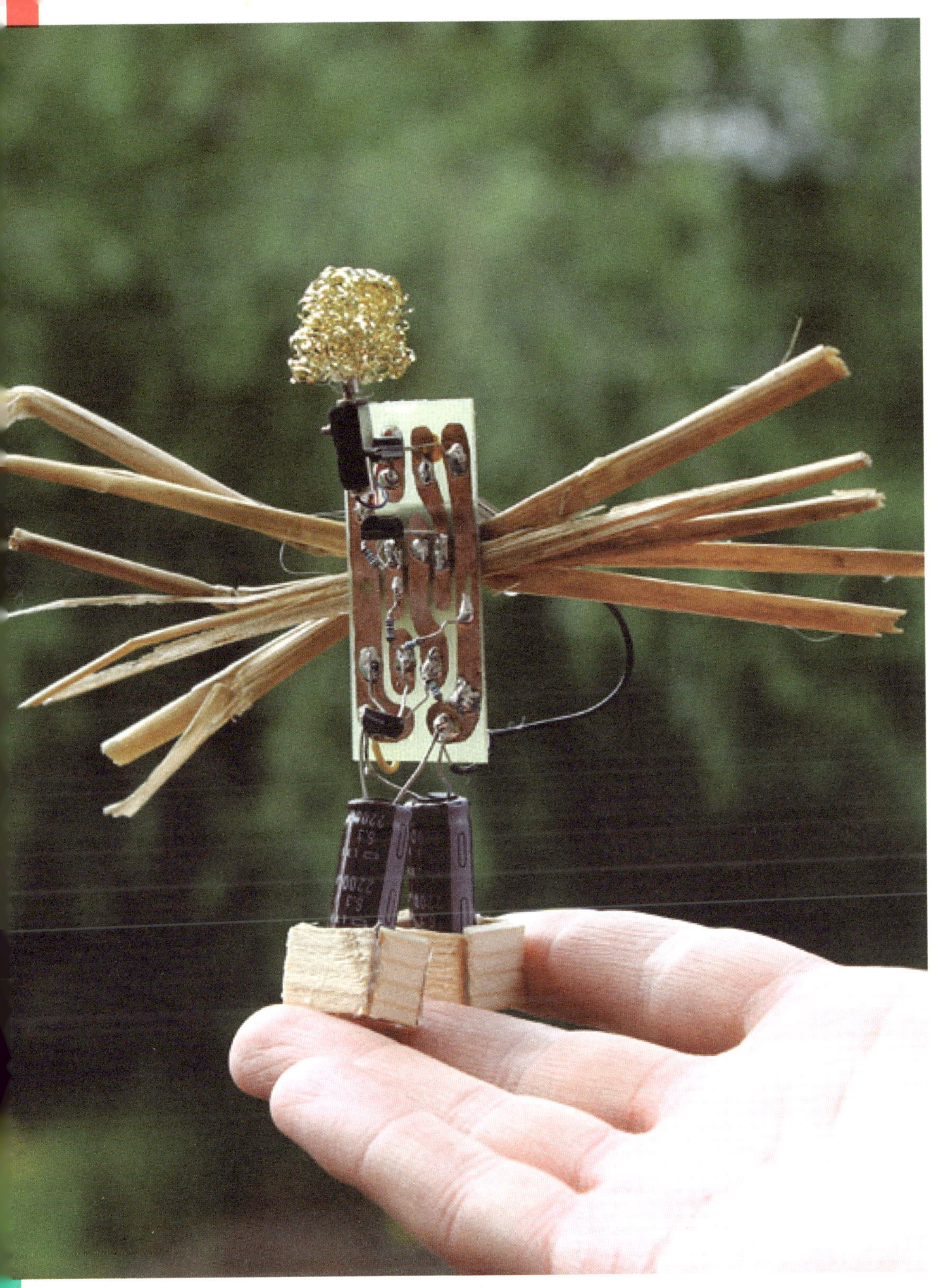

❖ 8. SolarKRA, *Hranice*

He makes self-sustaining sound installations that use a small amount of energy to produce sound and motion. During the workshop we assembled small solar-powered kinetic sound sculptures in preparation for the potential future use of more complex solar-powered systems, e.g. for monitoring bee colonies. These sculptures variously combined motion with sound that resembled most of all the chirping of crickets. People slept in tents in the garden and washed in solar-heated showers.

In autumn we tidied up the *KRAlab garden* and planted trees and bushes, and then to celebrate spring we went to Dúbravica in Slovakia, where Periférne Centrá had organised a month-long event called *Fruit of Art* (5 April – 4 May 2014), a celebration of spring and creative work. This included fruit-growing courses (cutting and grafting fruit trees) led by the gardener and artist Martin Bendžela. Periférne Centrá is trying to cultivate a wild, overgrown orchard in a site named Čo (after a sculpture by the French artist Benoit Lazaro that has been installed here since 2012). Other gardening activities included beekeeping courses and digging new beds. Dávid Turčáni gave a lecture on the work of his beekeeping organisation, Včelí kRaj. Those of us from Yo-yo presented RurArtMap, our map of rural art centres. For Kunstdorf Oto Hudec created a new structure, DBSP 01 (Dúbravica Beekeepers' Space Programme), combining an apiary, library and reading room.

For our spring-summer working weekend we had planned to build a greenhouse and children's playground with sandpit and raised beds, but this proved too much for a single weekend. We managed to finish the raised beds and later plant them with crops from Gengel and seeds from Marek Kvapil, who presented a short course on seeds and taught us how to cultivate them, emphasising the free pollination of rare and old varieties. Our Polish partners organised the *Nowina Land Art Festival* (20–22 June 2014), a small village event that included performances, happenings, dancing and painting an old bus.

The idea behind *Stands, Hunters and Animal Paths* (18–24 August 2014) was to expand beyond our garden and explore potential sites for creative work. We were also interested in the theme of hunting: Czech hunters have recently been included in the intangible cultural heritage list. In spring we issued an invitation to produce temporary art projects that could be implemented in hunting stands, and we received replies from artists from the nearby town of Chotěboř, and also from Slovakia and Amsterdam. Nine artists and groups took part in reworking stands in various ways. In the meadow below the stands there was an exhibition of Kamila Musilová's photographs of stuffed animals. On a walk around these stands marking the culmination of this week-long event, the artists presented their projects and there were sound performances and presentations by Dominique Leroy (who used microphones mounted on fishing rods that extended from a stand above the meadow to "hunt" ambient sounds), Martin Janíček (who wrapped a stand in flexible tubes fitted with game calls) and the duo Anti-Delusion Mechanism (who made an installation with several miniature stands, fitted with amplifiers and placed in various locations in the woods and meadows; one of them generated sounds from underground). The walk ended with an animal dance. In the winter of 2015 documentation from this project was presented at the Stands exhibition at the Vysočina Regional Gallery in Jihlava (23 January – 8 February 2015).

We presented Yo-yo's activities under ALOTOF during the *Open Studios festival*, when artists from the Vysočina Region opened their studios to display their work (4–5 October 2014). In mid-October we organised Singing Kites, when under the guidance of artist and kite maker Jan Poupě we tried to construct kites that would sing as they flew. However, kite flying was only briefly possible – it was a rare windless day – and only a few photographs were taken. The kites are still waiting to sing. To be continued!

This was followed in November by an exhibition and discussion with urban beekeepers Urban Beeing / Bees in the City (official opening 20 November, discussion 21 November 2014), when we expanded into the city and occupied *Communication Space Školská 28* in Prague. The discussion investigated some of what is said about beekeeping in the city, such as whether urban bees give more honey, and whether bee pasturage is more diverse in cities than in the countryside. We were also interested in urban beekeepers' experience and motivation, and how the local beekeeping communities operated, and the pros and cons of the coexistence of people and bees. We invited beekeepers from various societies, mostly based in Prague, including beekeepers from Prague Zoo, the roof of Chodov Shopping Centre and the airport, and also from London and Brussels. Also represented was the *Bee Research Institute* in Dol, and biodynamic beekeeping was covered too. The conclusions can be quickly summarized: in all probability there are no fundamental differences between bees, bee pasturage

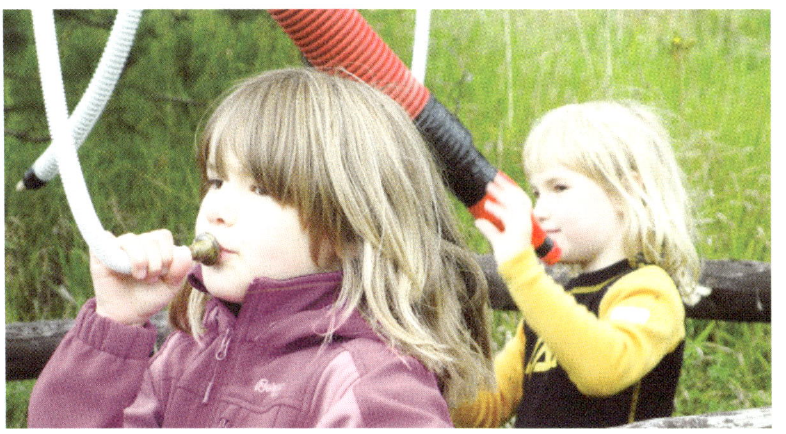

✥ 9. Posedy, *Hranice*

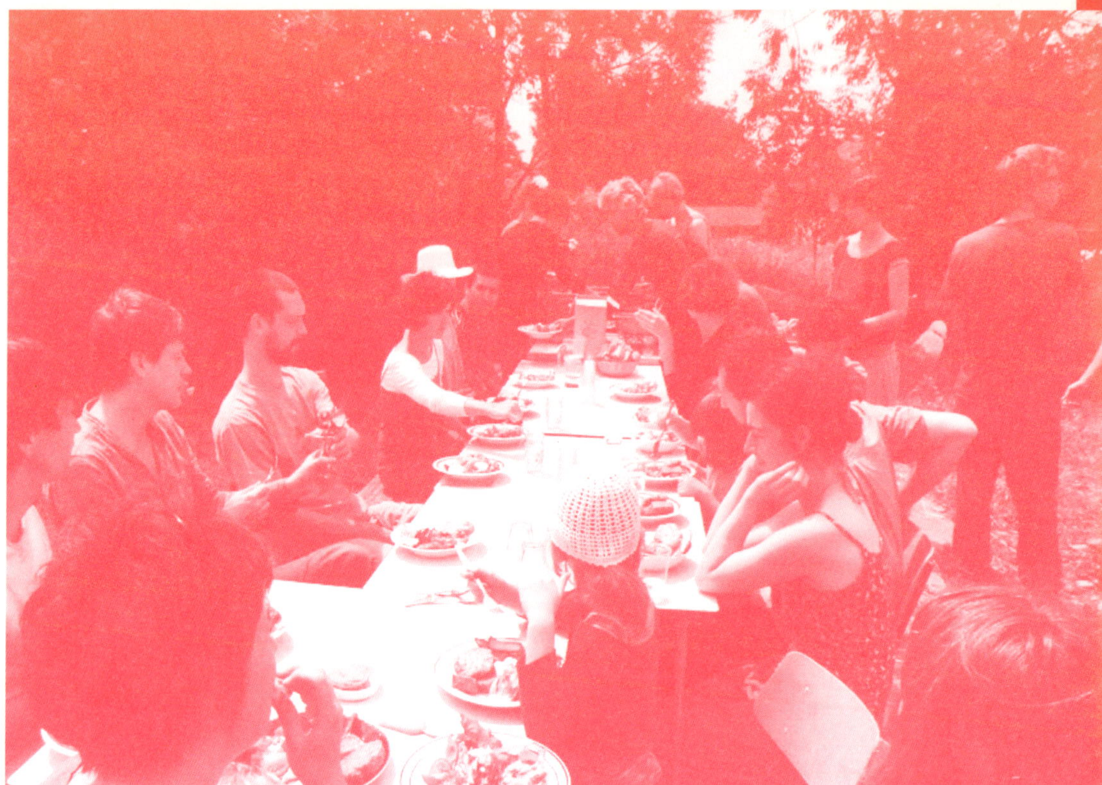

✖ 10. Kravín Festival Lunch

and honey in the countryside and in the city. Urban beekeeping is currently in vogue, but it is nothing new. Interestingly the speakers and the audience agreed that we should return to more natural beekeeping methods: accepting the swarming instinct as something natural, using natural hives (built by bees), and letting bees spend the winter with stores of honey, rather than sugar. A highly inspirational gathering!

In March 2015, to celebrate spring and World Water Day, there was a prelude to the Convergence permaculture gardening festival, looking at water resources in the countryside and in the garden under the guidance of Zelený čaroděj. Part two, looking at edible gardens, will follow in April.

Other Activities

RurArtMap is an affiliated Yo-yo activity that is part of the ALOTOF project. This is a map of rural centres for art, ecology and related areas. Since 2012 we have published a printed map with a programme for the summer months, and last year we launched an online version that should serve as a workspace for rural organisers, as well as a discussion forum and a portal for planning journeys.

Our partners have opened up other inspirational areas for us. Filip Kavka Smiggels from the Mlsná Kavka restaurant in Karlín

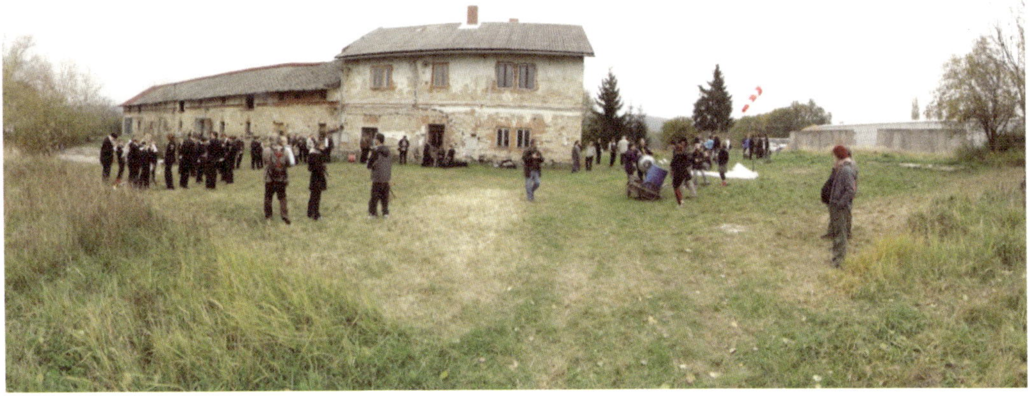

11. Vítr for Marching Bands

in Prague has already cooked for two of our events. He treats his cooking, using local ingredients, as a form of education, and introduces participants to new recipes. We published our Honey Cookbook in collaboration with him. Similarly another partner, Lucie Pelouchová, comes from the Zastráň vegetable farm just over the hill, where we buy fresh vegetables. Also related to food are our mushroom walks with mushroom aficionado Ivan Kidles from a nearby village, Víska. The Kino Na Beton cinema is a traditional venue for film screenings.

Another regular theme is walking, and old and new paths through the countryside. In the summer the Various Artists group from Brussels organised a walking performance, *Périphérique.0*, treading out an entirely new path around part of the garden. To be continued next time.

And Finally: What Next?

Our activities comprise a less popular, more experimental parallel to rural events such as hunt balls, children's carnivals, beekeeping meetings and annual gardening shows. We did not manage to do nearly as much as we had planned. The garden is gradually changing and for 2015 we plan to establish a natural permaculture garden. Perhaps more interesting are our options for the future. Implementing our initial ideas came up against the harsh reality that public gatherings for artists are time-consuming in terms of organisation, arranging accommodation, food and transport and adapting the venue, and this leaves little time for creative work. So far we have always tried to operate somewhere between working encounters – in the form of (open) workshops – and events and exhibitions for the public. We still need a lot of time to truly turn the garden into a place for the activities described above. We are planning to build a greenhouse in line with *OpenStructures principles*, as well as observation hives and a children's nature playground. In 2015 we will look at soil, and in 2016 our subject will be house and courtyard, and village storytelling…

Wandering Arts Biennial: Platform For Artistic Mobility
◉ *Loes Jacobs*

Nadine Mission

The ability to travel has shaped cultures fundamentally throughout history, be it through trade, war, pilgrimage, migration, private or state-sponsored explorations. Many journeys recurred annually or were linked to the seasons, such as cattle herders' migrations between summer pastures and winter shelter, extended families coming together at anniversaries of births, deaths and marriages, itinerant merchants and entertainers traveling between markets and festivals. Since the industrial age these slow peregrinations have given way to mechanical efficiency, where the primary reason for traveling is to arrive at the destination A.S.A.P.

The impact of our ever faster A-to-B travels is enormous; climate change, globalisation, tourism, to name just a few. The search for slow mobility is increasing, and a lot of people are exploring alternative modes of and reasons for traveling. Among them, there are a lot of creative thinkers and artists, who use mobility or nomadism as a tool or creative method in their artistic practice.

To support and collect the diverse mobile practices of artists, we created the platform Wandering Arts Biennial or WAB. WAB is a platform for creative meandering/wandering, and explores ways to re-establish the journey itself as the aim of travel, connecting with the landscape and its inhabitants along the way. WAB taps into the mobile potential of our contemporary cultures and technologies to seek out and experiment with resilient modes of cultural travel, including biking, hiking and other locomotion, powered by renewable sources, both elemental and muscular in origin.

WAB supports mobile artistic practices by offering a platform to present, share and communicate in an autonomous context. Mobility refers here to artistic work in a particular environment; to the movement that is performed (such as art walks, or performative walking projects and one public); and to artistic research where movement and landscape are the tools or working methods in order to come to new artworks. WAB projects focus on different interpretations of mobile arts practices — performance in public space — nomadism as artistic research method — the public space as a meeting and experience space — mobile temporary/alternative studio. > http://wab.nadine.be

During the European project ALOTOF, WAB supported several nomadic projects. From 2013 to 2015 the artistic laboratory nadine co-produced co-creative and collective research travels, performances, and formats in the framework of ALOTOF exploring artistic nomadism using the platform WAB to share these projects with a wider public. The projects are almost all serial and will continue in the future of WAB.

1. Default

Default is a journey of discovery for artists, designers, technologists and collectors working while traveling by bike through Europe along a straight line from North to South.

A fold in a map. Default are wandering strangers and itinerant artists/collectors who embarked on a bicycle expedition following the core concept of industrial travel, the straight line. The folds of a European train map are our guides. These arbitrary lines are a limitation, an absolute rule, but also a score that would help the artists explore their given territory — a 25 km-wide strip along the fold — without hesitation, second thoughts, or prejudice.

Overcoming tourism. Following the invisible vector of a fold in the map is an invitation for a joint in-situ improvisation with a multitude of personalities, rather than the line being the most straight and efficient way to reach the end node. People are invited to suggest ways to connect to the landscape and the journey, to investigate and explore the ways artists and adventurers can form a portable, nomadic creative studio powered by sun, wind and muscles.

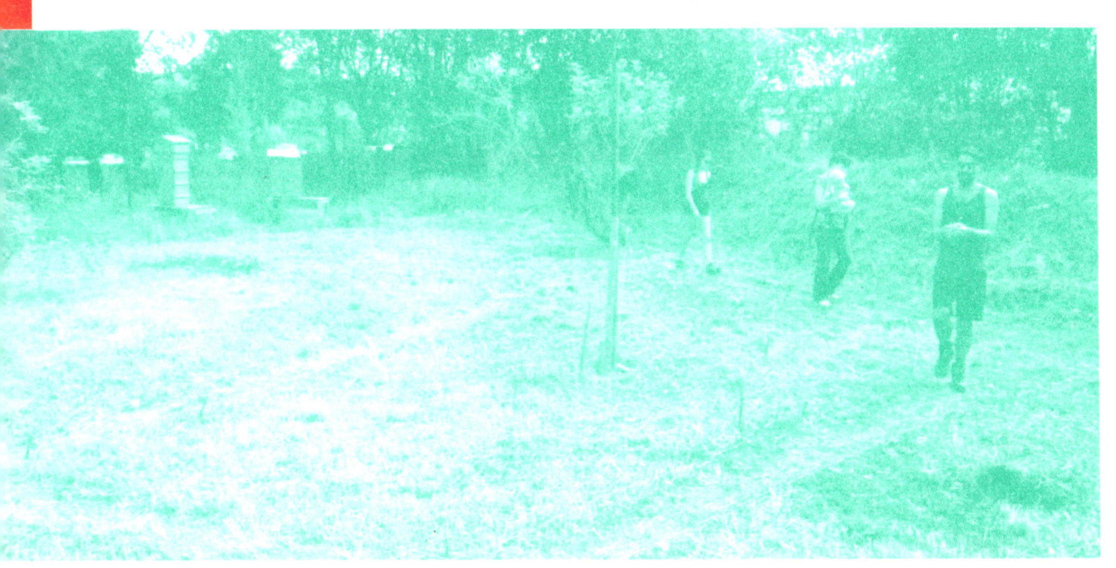

⊠ 12. Peripherique, *Hranice*

Nomadic studio and technology. In the aftermath of the last major ice age, early Europeans traveled north following the receding permafrost through an unknown landscape. In Default, a group of cyclists moves south, during what many see as the prelude to another major climatic shift. Every fold is an experiment in the sustainable mobility of cultural practices, framed by the environmental, social and economic challenges our future societies may be facing – such as the unpredictability of fuel prices or the wastefulness of overconsumption, tourism included. While on the road we explore how artists come together in fragile research processes, and how they can break out of static, heavy-handed approaches to production. How flexible is the artistic process of co-creation when it is disconnected from the power grid? What existing and emerging technologies could meet these challenges? And what communication channels are most suited for maintaining contact with the wider world when artists move off the grid in small, nomadic communities for long periods? The experience can result in numerous works, from sculptures made and installed on the road, to maps, video performances and blogs. This constrained journey proves to be a valuable format in which people can explore and enrich their creative practices in alternate ways. For many participants this experience instigates new approaches and nomadic working methods.

Default is a project by the Brussels-based artistic organisation nadine and is part of WAB and the European project ALOTOF. The journey took place from 15 August to 15 September 2013.

2. Buratinas, nadine

Buratinas is a solar powered boat, and an artistic project developed to question contemporary issues like renewable energy, slow mobility, public space and waterways in the city and countryside. Buratinas offers a mobile platform to artists who want to create while moving slowly. It is also a local Brussels-based project that looks into waterways through public interventions, workshops, meetings and open discussions. > http://buratinas.be

3. Circling Around Without Taking Off, Bruno de Wachter

Circling Around are performative walks around airports. Airports all over the world look very similar. Regional differences are reduced to the souvenirs that you can buy in the gift shop. In terms of the geographic landscape, they are non-places. However, the immediate vicinities of airports differ greatly. The airport cuts a hole in the landscape. That is why it is represented as a shaded area on the map. Bruno De Wachter invites people to walk along the roads and trails that are close to the airport. In August 2014 Bruno and invited artists circled around two airports - Charleroi Brussels South (BE) and Paris Charles de Gaulle (FR) - as part of the Alotof project. The journey is documented with photos and short pieces of text.

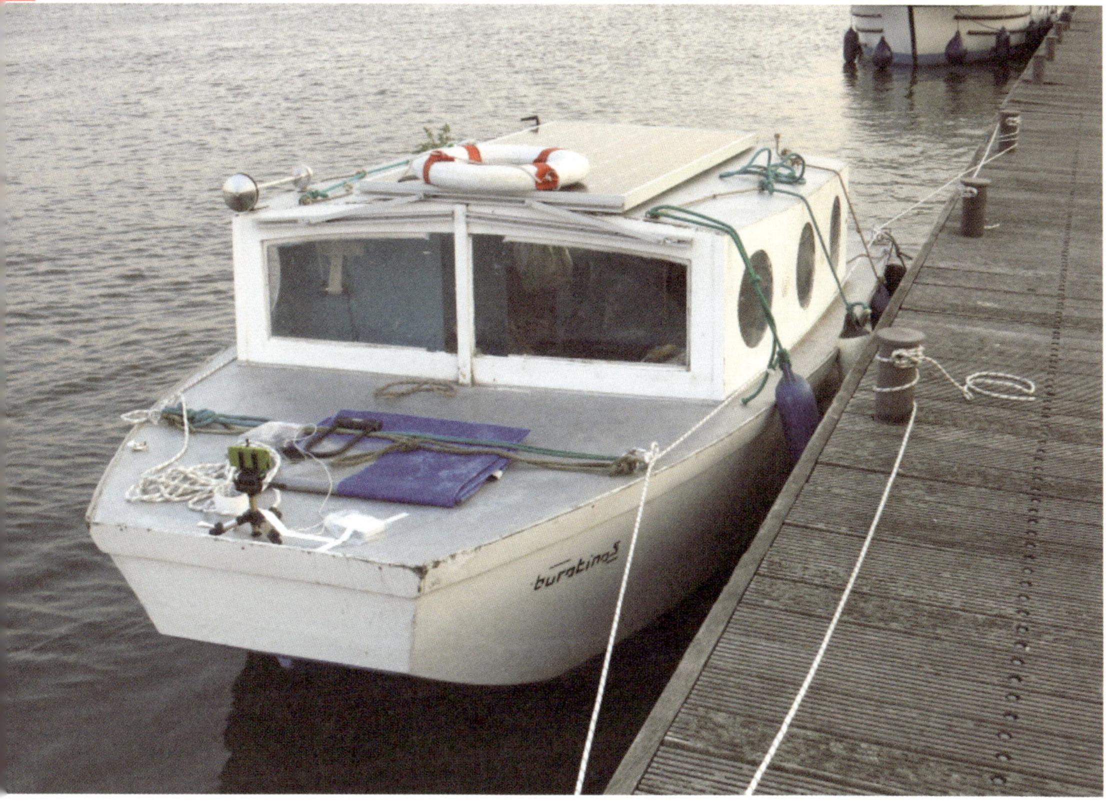

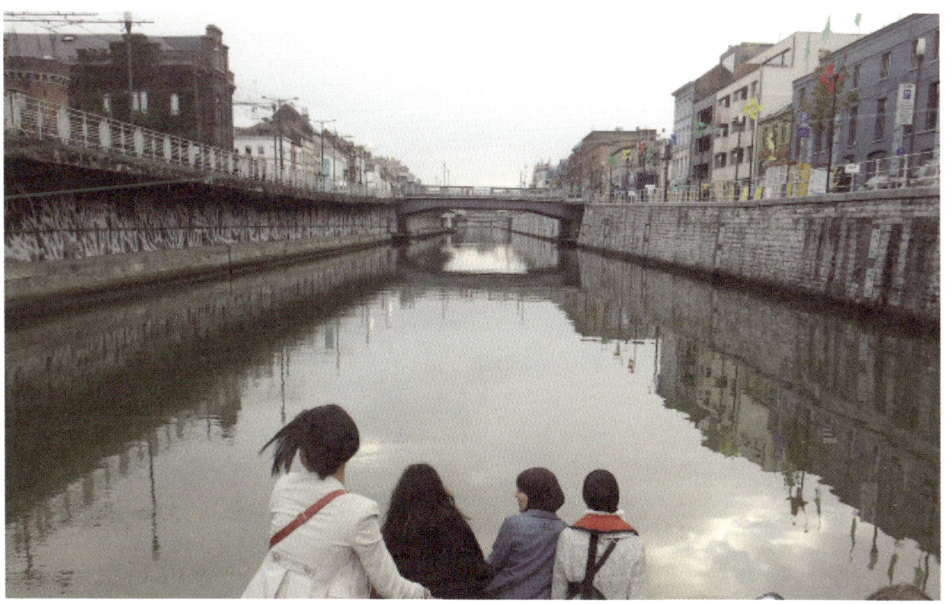

:: 13. Buratinas, *Brussels*

:: 14. Buratinas, *Canaltrip*

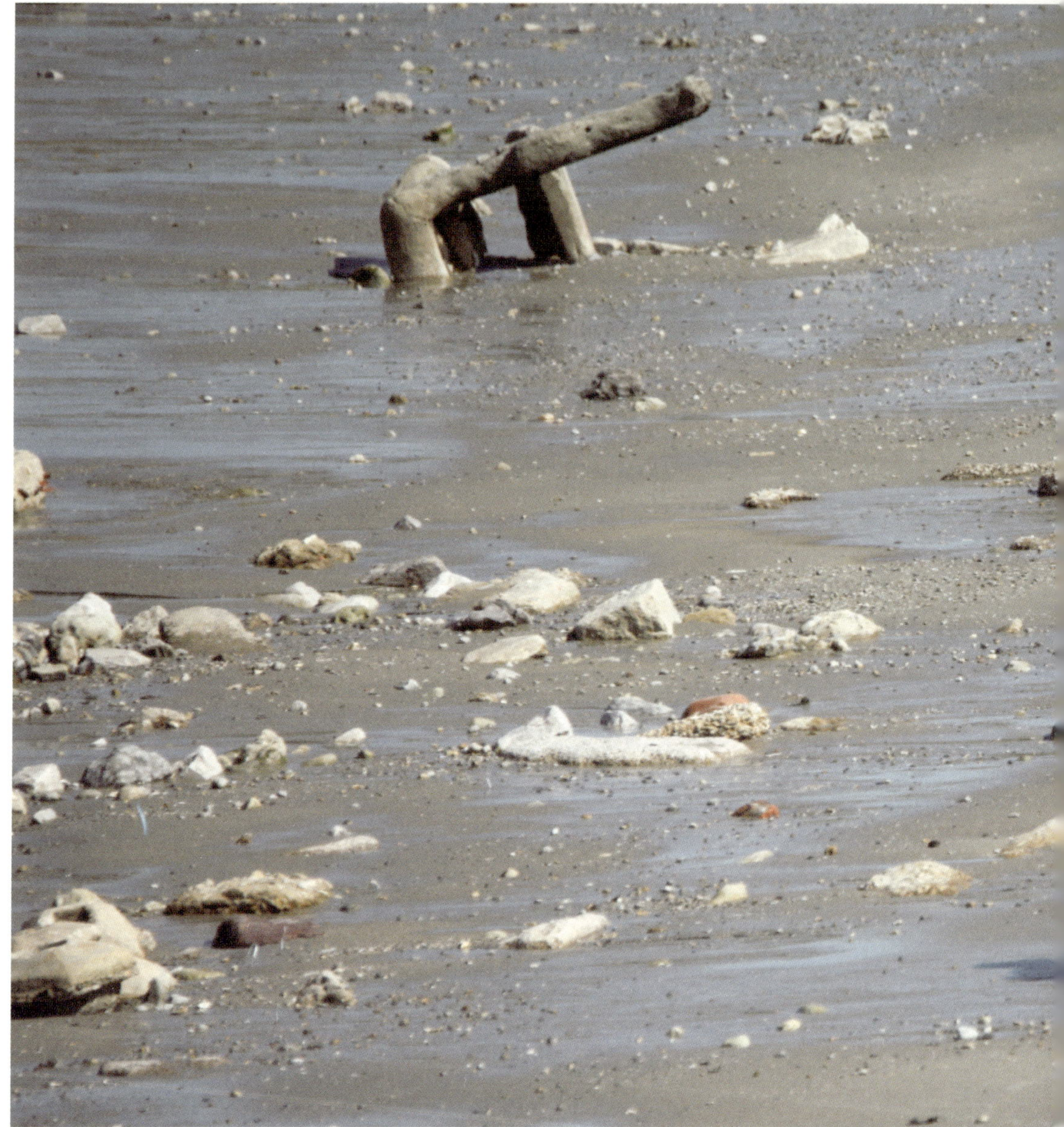

✖ 15. Various Artists

4. Peripherique.0, n0dine

Périphérique.0 is a land-art performance that took place in Hranice in August 2014. During three days, four people walked for 8 hours making a path around a lot of 30m^2 (pun not intended). The small piece of land offers a place to reflect about private and public space, the use and appropriation of land, etc. The public was invited to join the performance and share their thoughts. How can artists appropriate public space in urban and rural settings? How can their works or projects encourage other users to use that space differently and not merely as a transit zone? How do we avoid a public place that is occupied by private initiatives?

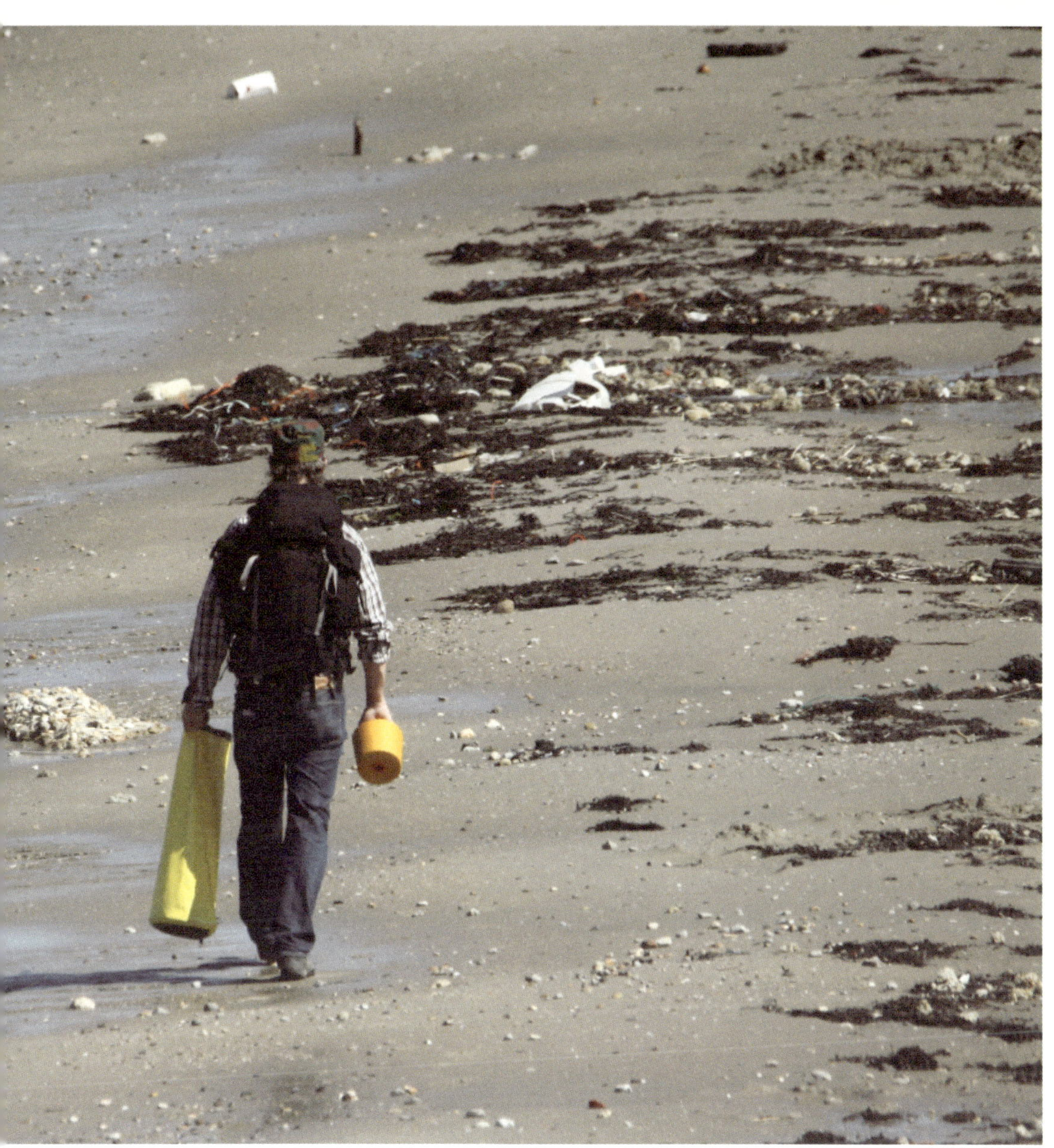

5. Camino Welt, Various Artists

Camino Welt is a project by Various Artists, where one physical artist undertakes a walk following the coastline from Santiago de Compostela to Ostend. This (anti)-pilgrimage brings Various Artists into a state of constant temptation, and contamination. Camino Welt is a reversed pilgrimage set up as a mobile production studio. The concept is to produce as much work on the road as humanly possible. Various Artists will collaborate, sabotage, and influence each other into a frenzy of overproduction. The project is spread over several years, and in April 2015, the first two-week walk from Bilbao to San Sebastian was undertaken.

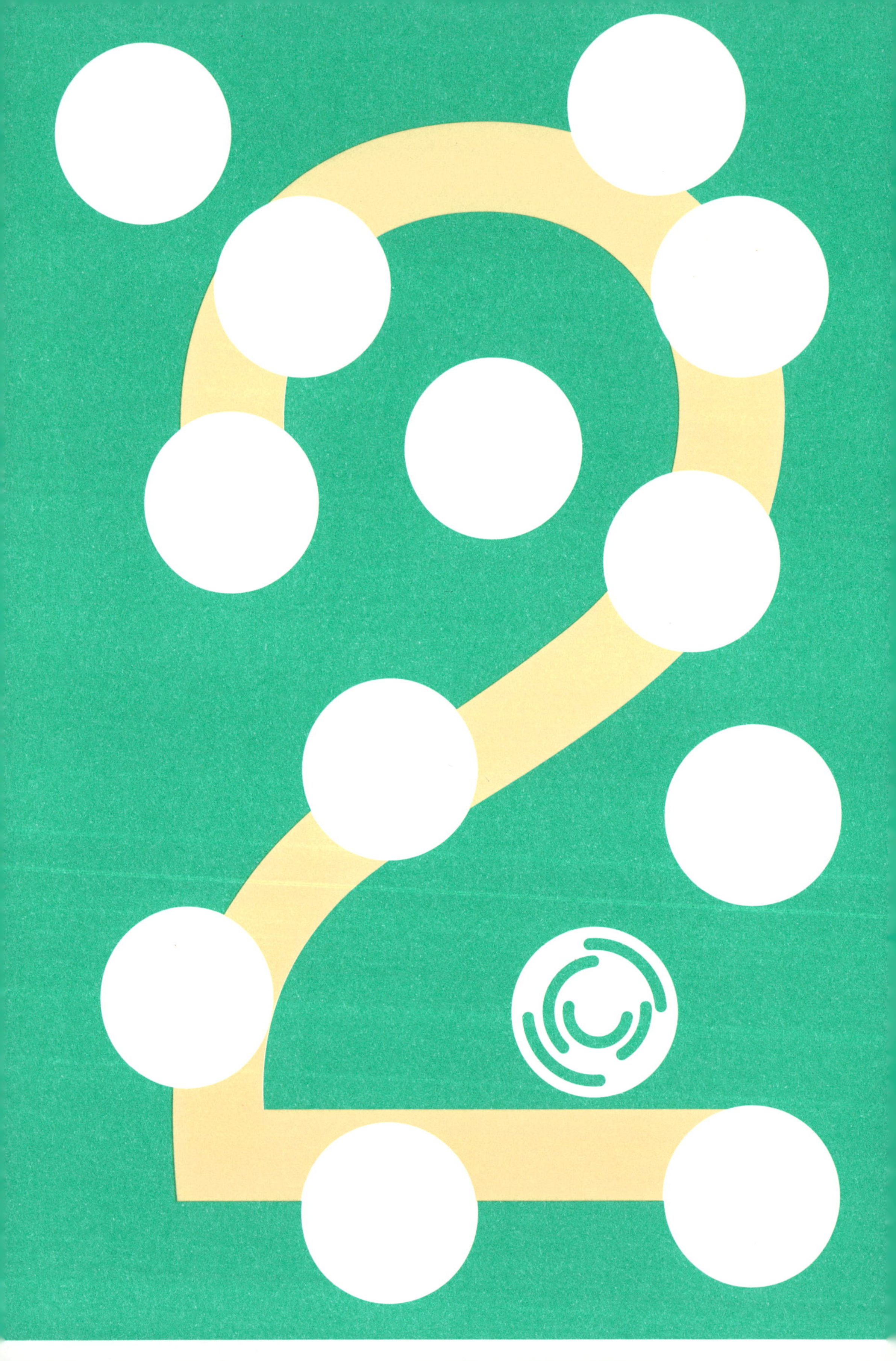

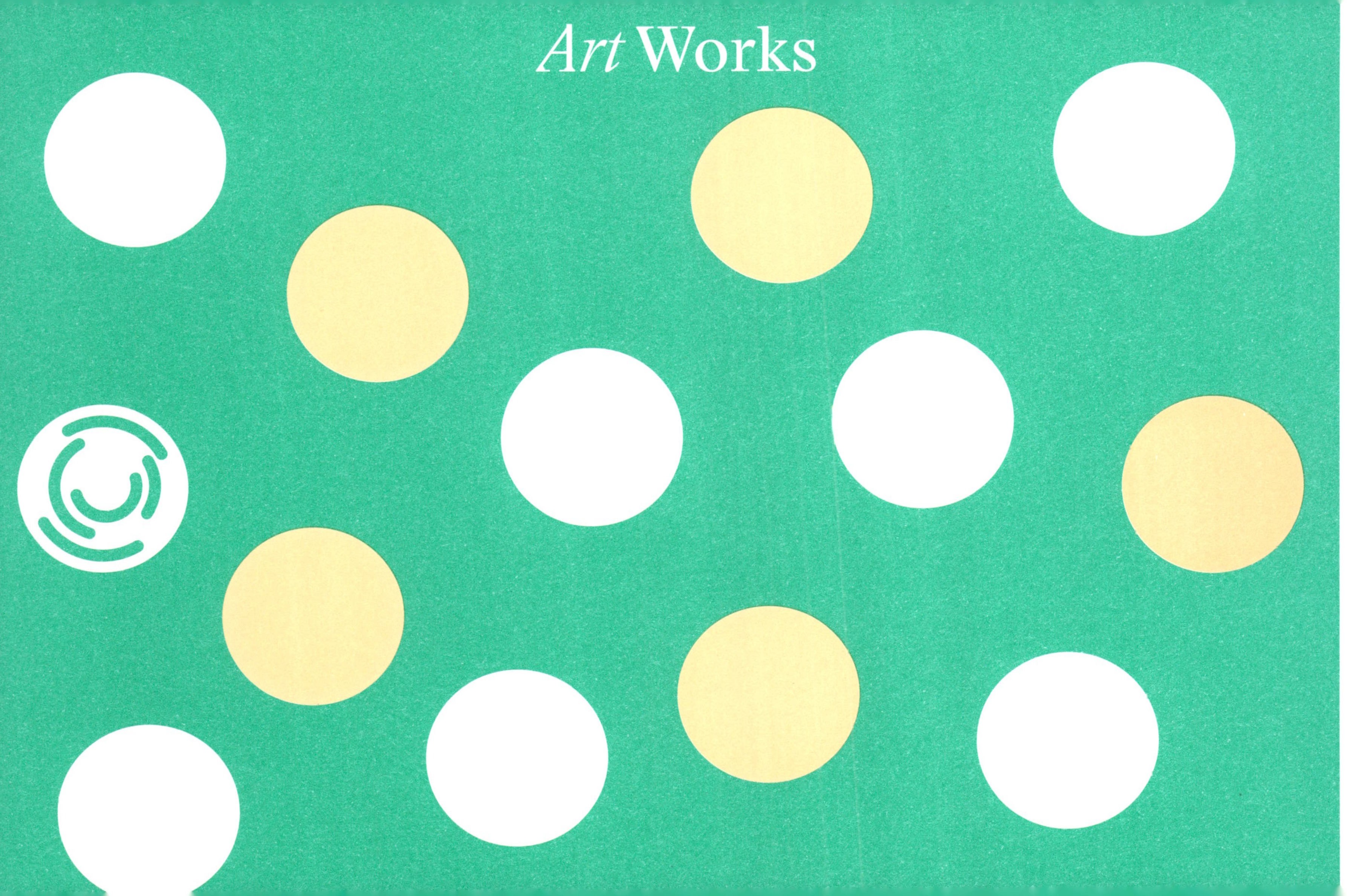
Art Works

About the notions Experimental and Ecology

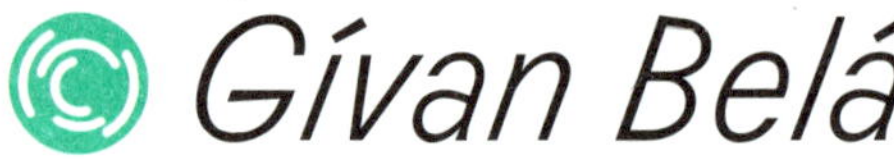

Gívan Belá

Dedication

Je sais aussi, dit Candide, qu'il faut cultiver notre jardin. Vous avez raison, dit Pangloss; car, quand l'homme fut mis dans le jardin d'Éden, il y fut mis ut operaretur eum, pour qu'il travaillât; ce qui prouve que l'homme n'est pas né pour le repos.Travaillons sans raisonner, dit Martin, c'est le seul moyen de rendre la vie supportable.

THE NOTION OF THE EXPERIMENTAL

1. the situation, a sketch of the arts, and other things around

75 the, 52 and, 43 of, 36 jazz, 31 a, 30 in, 27 to, 23 is, 13 be, 13 are, 12 an, 11 with, 11 this, 11 that, 11 more, 11 it, 11 as, 10 but, 10 art, 9 we, 9 at, 9 about, 8 science, 8 for, 7 sciences, 7 on, 7 media, 7 can, 7 between, 7 artists, 6 what, 6 seems, 6 by, 6 all, 5 way, 5 there, 5 other, 5 from, 5 both, 5 arts, 5 also, 4 would, 4 were, 4 was, 4 traditional, 4 talking, 4 situation, 4 rather, 4 one, 4 not, 4 making, 4 lets, 4 knowledge, 4 here, 4 free, 4 experimental, 4 culture, 3 you, 3 years, 3 within, 3 who, 3 ways, 3 us, 3 up, 3 too, 3 today, 3 these, 3 some, 3 social, 3 so, 3 see, 3 say, 3 same, 3 own, 3 only, 3 obvious, 3 new, 3 many, 3 latter, 3 its, 3 interested, 3 humanities, 3 hand, 3 exact, 3 everything, 3 different, 3 differences, 3 could, 3 content, 3 common, 3 being, 3 already, 3 academic, 2 yet, 2 where, 2 west, 2 universities, 2 understanding, 2 turn, 2 though, 2 think, 2 their, 2 than, 2 terms, 2 take, 2 styles, 2 still, 2 smaller, 2 since, 2 should, 2 set, 2 seen, 2 scientist, 2 scientific, 2 rock, 2 reality, 2 real, 2 ragtime, 2 quite, 2 possible, 2 outcomes, 2 or, 2 objects, 2 notion, 2 no, 2 music, 2 multidisciplinarity, 2 mostly, 2 mentioned, 2 make, 2 major, 2 maintaining, 2 like, 2 larger, 2 kind, 2 kansas, 2 itself, 2 interesting, 2 individual, 2 indicate, 2 including, 2 if, 2 how, 2 history, 2 have, 2 has, 2 handling, 2 gypsy, 2 gradually, 2 go, 2 genres, 2 first, 2 even, 2 end, 2 emerging, 2 economy, 2 each, 2 did, 2 dance, 2 cultures, 2 creativity, 2 create, 2 coast, 2 city, 2 bridge, 2 books, 2 blues, 2 becoming, 2 beauty, 2 around, 2 after, 2 aesthetical, 2 activities, 2 50.

2. the ontology of the experimental

105 the, 72 of, 52 and, 49 a, 43 is, 42 to, 34 experimental, 30 in, 25 it, 25 an, 20 that, 19 for, 19 are, 18 as, 17 this, 15 or, 15 be, 13 not, 11 model, 10 what, 10 representation, 10 but, 9 which, 9 we, 9 rheinberger, 9 from, 8 would, 8 systems, 8 on, 7 with, 7 use, 7 things, 7 there, 7 models, 6 system, 6 scientific, 6 science, 6 research, 6 epistemic, 6 can, 6 by, 6 also, 6 all, 5 yet, 5 where, 5 way, 5 one, 5 more, 5 knowledge, 5 its, 5 i, 5 history, 5 first, 5 at, 5 activity, 4 unexpected, 4 traces, 4 some, 4 see, 4 reality, 4 only, 4 notion, 4 into, 4 here, 4 he, 4 further, 4 exactly, 4 different, 4 both, 4 being, 4 again, 4 about, 3 within, 3 usually, 3 using, 3 used, 3 us, 3 time, 3 they, 3 these, 3 their, 3 than, 3 technical, 3 spaces, 3 so, 3 sense, 3 seems, 3 scientist, 3 results, 3 producing, 3 out, 3 nothing, 3 new, 3 media, 3 maybe, 3 machine, 3 level, 3 language, 3 interesting, 3 his, 3 has, 3 general, 3 future, 3 existing, 3 epistemology, 3 data, 3 considered, 3 between, 3 2, 2 "of, 2 "epistemological", 2 "epistemic", 2 writing, 2 world, 2 work, 2 will, 2 when, 2 were, 2 validity, 2 up, 2 units, 2 understand, 2 transformations, 2 toward, 2 tools, 2 theory, 2 then, 2 text, 2 test, 2 term, 2 talking, 2 szallasi, 2 surely, 2 states, 2 special, 2 sort, 2 something, 2 social, 2 ship, 2 set, 2 seen, 2 seem, 2 same, 2 rheinbergers, 2 representing, 2 relating, 2 recently, 2 rather, 2 quite, 2 productive, 2 process, 2 point, 2 physical, 2 philosophy, 2 part, 2 our, 2 ontological, 2 often, 2 no, 2 mostly, 2 making, 2 longer, 2 local, 2 limited, 2 like, 2 leading, 2 knows, 2 kittler, 2 interconnectedness, 2 instrumental, 2 institutional, 2 instance, 2 individual, 2 imagination, 2 hope, 2 have, 2 graphematic, 2 geertz, 2 game, 2 friedrich, 2 flusser, 2 experiments, 2 experiment, 2 example, 2 events, 2 else, 2 does, 2 difference, 2 descriptions, 2 describing, 2 definition, 2 cultures, 2 creation, 2 conventional, 2 continue, 2 conform, 2 concepts, 2 clarify, 2 call, 2 because, 2 arts, 2 artists, 2 artist, 2 art, 2 activities, 2 2006, 2 1997.

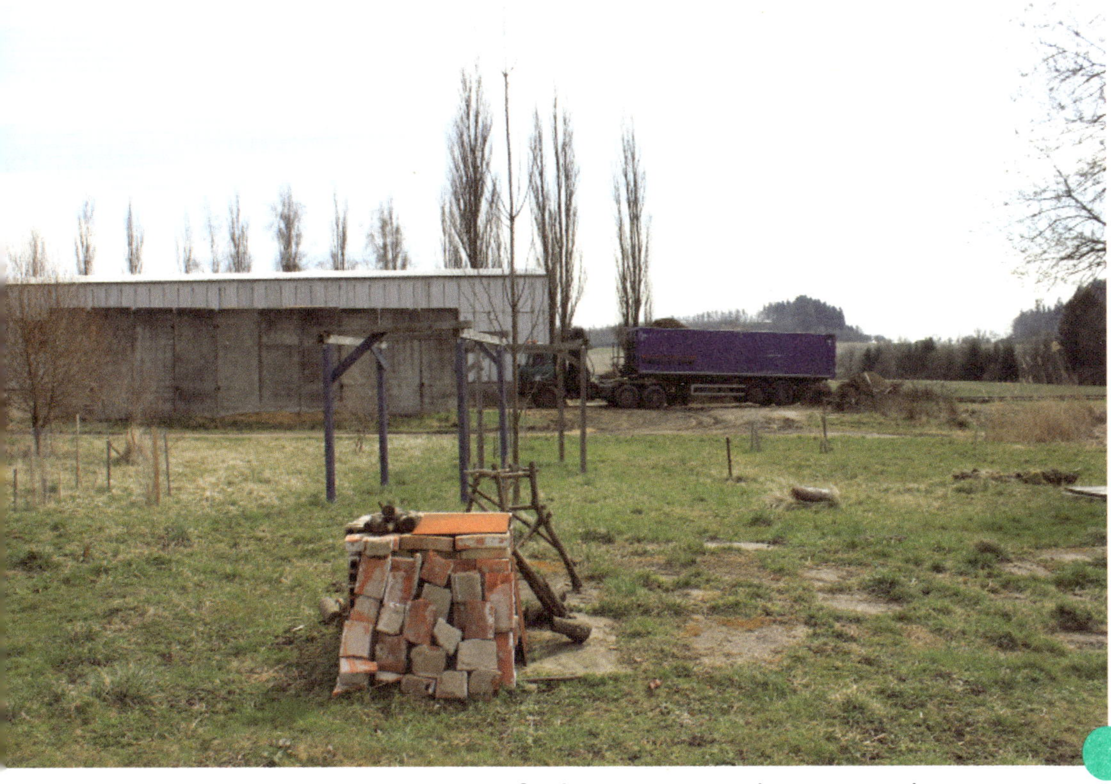

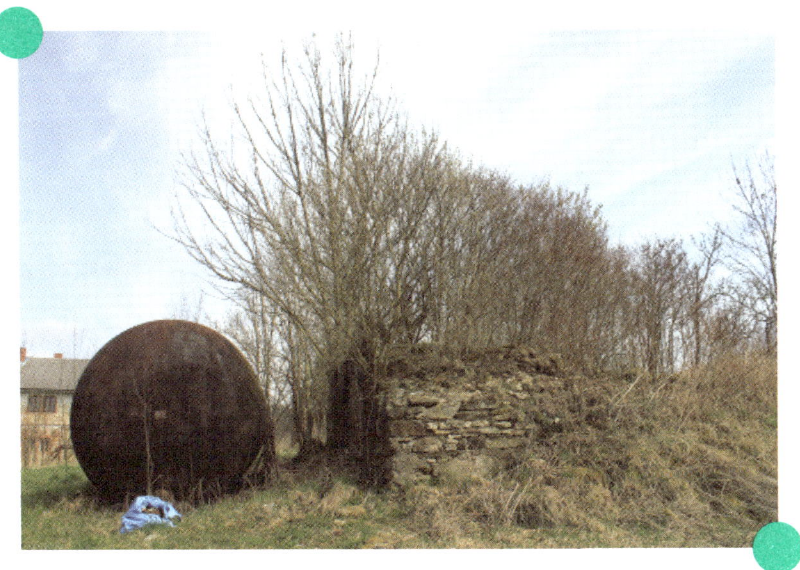

■ 16. The notion of the experimental

■ 17. The notion of the ecological

3. instruments, labs and other concepts

123 the, 90 and, 78 a, 74 of, 48 to, 39 is, 38 in, 30 as, 27 for, 24 it, 21 that, 20 with, 20 media, 20 an, 16 are, 15 this, 15 on, 15 be, 15 art, 14 but, 14 all, 13 can, 12 not, 11 we, 11 artists, 10 work, 10 or, 10 by, 9 today, 9 through, 9 from, 8 into, 8 instruments, 8 at, 7 there, 7 same, 7 programming, 7 other, 7 instrument, 7 computer, 7 also, 6 would, 6 these, 6 their, 6 technology, 6 new, 6 idea, 6 here, 6 has, 6 experimental, 6 different, 6 culture, 5 writing, 5 what, 5 was, 5 visual, 5 using, 5 still, 5 scientific, 5 science, 5 more, 5 making, 5 latour, 5 cultural, 5 concept, 5 arts, 5 artistic, 4 you, 4 years, 4 within, 4 well, 4 video, 4 time, 4 they, 4 so, 4 open, 4 only, 4 notion, 4 material, 4 like, 4 lab, 4 have, 4 further, 4 fact, 4 environment, 4 between, 4 autonomy, 4 artist, 4 after, 4 about, 3 world, 3 works, 3 which, 3 were, 3 way, 3 use, 3 us, 3 tools, 3 tool, 3 together, 3 than, 3 source, 3 sounds, 3 sound, 3 social, 3 since, 3 should, 3 seems, 3 purpose, 3 processing, 3 point, 3 people, 3 out, 3 organisation, 3 ones, 3 one, 3 obvious, 3 network, 3 many, 3 least, 3 languages, 3 language, 3 its, 3 interesting, 3 images, 3 i, 3 he, 3 generating, 3 former, 3 even, 3 ecology, 3 digital, 3 design, 3 concepts, 3 action, 2 written, 2 worked, 2 whatever, 2 via, 2 too, 2 throughout, 2 third, 2 thermometer, 2 then, 2 technological, 2 technical, 2 special, 2 sole, 2 society, 2 skills, 2 single, 2 simply, 2 set, 2 sensor, 2 sense, 2 seen, 2 scientists, 2 related, 2 rather, 2 quite, 2 pure, 2 professional, 2 product, 2 practice, 2 possible, 2 possibilities, 2 policies, 2 part, 2 own, 2 over, 2 now, 2 networks, 2 networked, 2 music, 2 movements, 2 most, 2 methods, 2 medium, 2 max, 2 materials, 2 managers, 2 management, 2 light, 2 left, 2 last, 2 knowledge, 2 kittler, 2 kind, 2 just, 2 interests, 2 intended, 2 inscription, 2 initial, 2 industrial, 2 important, 2 impact, 2 if, 2 how, 2 his, 2 hand, 2 goes, 2 generation, 2 general, 2 gallery, 2 far, 2 ensemble, 2 easy, 2 dream, 2 done, 2 document, 2 diy, 2 discussion, 2 disciplinary, 2 differently, 2 describing, 2 data, 2 create, 2 controlled, 2 construction, 2 connected, 2 communication, 2 built, 2 building, 2 bringing, 2 briefly, 2 board, 2 been, 2 autonomous, 2 audiovisual, 2 audience, 2 aspects, 2 any, 2 am, 2 30.

WHAT IS ECOLOGICAL

0. introduction

123 the, 90 and, 78 a, 74 of, 48 to, 39 is, 38 in, 30 as, 27 for, 24 it, 21 that, 20 with, 20 media, 20 an, 16 are, 15 this, 15 on, 15 be, 15 art, 14 but, 14 all, 13 can, 12 not, 11 we, 11 artists, 10 work, 10 or, 10 by, 9 today, 9 through, 9 from, 8 into, 8 instruments, 8 at, 7 there, 7 same, 7 programming, 7 other, 7 instrument, 7 computer, 7 also, 6 would, 6 these, 6 their, 6 technology, 6 new, 6 idea, 6 here, 6 has, 6 experimental, 6 different, 6 culture, 5 writing, 5 what, 5 was, 5 visual, 5 using, 5 still, 5 scientific, 5 science, 5 more, 5 making, 5 latour, 5 cultural, 5 concept, 5 arts, 5 artistic, 4 you, 4 years, 4 within, 4 well, 4 video, 4 time, 4 they, 4 so, 4 open, 4 only, 4 notion, 4 material, 4 like, 4 lab, 4 have, 4 further, 4 fact, 4 environment, 4 between, 4 autonomy, 4 artist, 4 after, 4 about, 3 world, 3 works, 3 which, 3 were, 3 way, 3 use, 3 us, 3 tools, 3 tool, 3 together, 3 than, 3 source, 3 sounds, 3 sound, 3 social, 3 since, 3 should, 3 seems, 3 purpose, 3 processing, 3 point, 3 people, 3 out, 3 organisation, 3 ones, 3 one, 3 obvious, 3 network, 3 many, 3 least, 3 languages, 3 language, 3 its, 3 interesting, 3 images, 3 he, 3 generating, 3 former, 3 even, 3 ecology, 3 digital, 3 design, 3 concepts, 3 action, 2 written, 2 worked, 2 whatever, 2 via, 2 too, 2 throughout, 2 third, 2 thermometer, 2 then, 2 technological, 2 technical, 2 special, 2 sole, 2 society, 2 skills, 2 single, 2 simply, 2 set, 2 sensor, 2 sense, 2 seen, 2 scientists, 2 related, 2 rather, 2 quite, 2 pure, 2 professional, 2 product, 2 practice, 2 possible, 2 possibilities, 2 policies, 2 part, 2 own, 2 over, 2 now, 2 networks, 2 networked, 2 music, 2 movements, 2 most, 2 methods, 2 medium, 2 max, 2 materials, 2 managers, 2 management, 2 light, 2 left, 2 last, 2 knowledge, 2 kittler, 2 kind, 2 just, 2 interests, 2 intended, 2 inscription, 2 initial, 2 industrial, 2 important, 2 impact, 2 if, 2 how, 2 his, 2 hand, 2 goes, 2 generation, 2 general, 2 gallery, 2 far, 2 ensemble, 2 easy, 2 dream, 2 done, 2 document, 2 diy, 2 discussion, 2 disciplinary, 2 differently, 2 describing, 2 data, 2 create, 2 controlled, 2 construction, 2 connected, 2 communication, 2 built, 2 building, 2 bringing, 2 briefly, 2 board, 2 been, 2 autonomous, 2 audiovisual, 2 audience, 2 aspects, 2 any, 2 am, 2 30.

Part 1. a book review

193 the, 102 of, 86 and, 72 is, 61 a, 53 in, 46 to, 39 ecology, 38 are, 28 it, 26 with, 25 this, 25 that, 23 an, 22 for, 20 ecological, 19 we, 18 by, 18 as, 17 on, 17 entities, 16 science, 16 be, 15 not, 15 but, 14 or, 12 has, 11 from, 10 philosophy, 10 more, 10 can, 9 work, 9 they, 9 parts, 8 within, 8 there, 8 how, 8 have, 8 at, 8 also, 8 again, 8 about, 8 3, 7 what, 7 was, 7 very, 7 nature, 7 knowledge, 7 community, 7 5, 7 2, 7 1, 6 will, 6 which, 6 way, 6 theory, 6 their, 6 stability, 6 selection, 6 rationalism, 6 part, 6 one, 6 natural, 6 important, 6 empiricism, 6 ecologists, 6 diversity, 6 different, 6 context, 6 approach, 6 all, 5 today, 5 than, 5 texts, 5 reader, 5 rather, 5 process, 5 our, 5 mentioned, 5 issues, 5 into, 5 first, 5 evolution, 5 entity, 5 discussion, 5 debates, 5 concepts, 5 coming, 5 between, 5 being, 5 been, 5 back, 5 anthology, 5 4, 4 where, 4 variety, 4 together, 4 through, 4 though, 4 them, 4 studies, 4 since, 4 seem, 4 richard, 4 point, 4 philosophical, 4 out, 4 no, 4 new, 4 much, 4 metaphysical, 4 may, 4 many, 4 living, 4 like, 4 its, 4 included, 4 human, 4 holism, 4 historical, 4 his, 4 get, 4 fundamental, 4

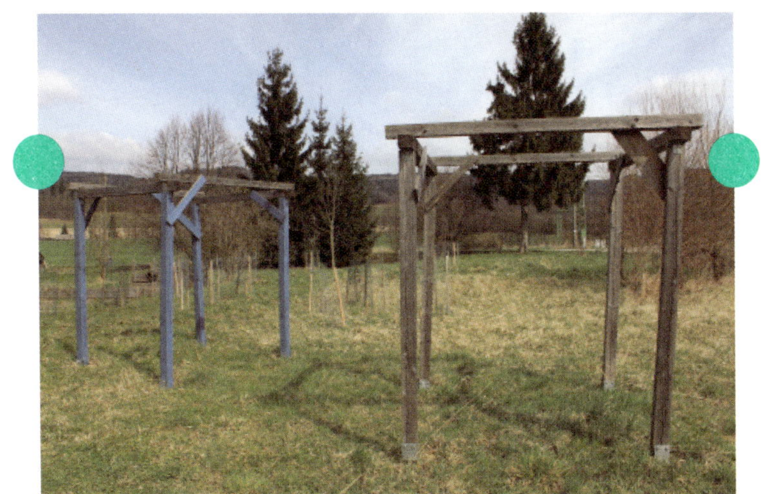

▓ 18. http://alotof.org/w/Article:A_alotof _experimental and http://alotof.org/w/ Article:B_alotof_ecological [1]

environment, 4 darwin, 4 contemporary, 4 book, 4 becoming, 3 worldview, 3 whole, 3 were, 3 used, 3 understand, 3 trying, 3 topics, 3 time, 3 these, 3 terms, 3 still, 3 species, 3 so, 3 smaller, 3 simply, 3 scientific, 3 relations, 3 reductionalism, 3 realism, 3 question, 3 processes, 3 problem, 3 possible, 3 p2, 3 p, 3 origin, 3 organisms, 3 ones, 3 notion, 3 niche, 3 most, 3 malthus, 3 major, 3 made, 3 long, 3 lets, 3 less, 3 larger, 3 kind, 3 keller, 3 itself, 3 interaction, 3 inductive, 3 golley, 3 going, 3 go, 3 genetics, 3 following, 3 few, 3 ferré, 3 explanation, 3 explaining, 3 explained, 3 editors, 3 early, 3 does, 3 dialectical, 3 definitions, 3 concept, 3 communities, 3 central, 3 both, 3 biotic, 3 biosphere, 3 authors, 3 any, 3 already, 3 above, 3 6, 3 2000, 2 would, 2 world, 2 who, 2 viewpoints, 2 variation, 2 valid, 2 up, 2 ultimate, 2 throughout, 2 thomas, 2 themselves, 2 theme, 2 text, 2 term, 2 systems, 2 synthesis, 2 subversive, 2 statement, 2 start, 2 stake, 2 stable, 2 some, 2 simple, 2 shorter, 2 settled, 2 set, 2 sense, 2 sciences, 2 scheme, 2 saying, 2 same, 2 robert, 2 relating, 2 related, 2 rejecting, 2 really, 2 purpose, 2 publication, 2 provides, 2 problematic, 2 principles, 2 practice, 2 position, 2 population, 2 political, 2 plato, 2 per, 2 other, 2 organism, 2 ontologies, 2 only, 2 old, 2 ok, 2 observation, 2 now, 2 nonscientific, 2 nonhuman, 2 need, 2 naturalism, 2 must, 2 methods, 2 methodologies, 2 means, 2 meanings, 2 maybe, 2 materialism, 2 make, 2 main, 2 lewontin, 2 leading, 2 laws, 2 latter, 2 landscape, 2 karl, 2 introduced, 2 internal, 2 interesting, 2 informs, 2 if, 2 humans, 2 historically, 2 high, 2 hierarchy, 2 here, 2 henry, 2 hard, 2 haeckel, 2 given, 2 generating, 2 further, 2

frederick, 2 found, 2 formal, 2 focus, 2 fine, 2 find, 2 fact, 2 evolutionary, 2 ever, 2 ethics, 2 essential, 2 element, 2 ecosystem, 2 easily, 2 each, 2 due, 2 difference, 2 describing, 2 define, 2 deeper, 2 debate, 2 dealing, 2 daniel, 2 danger, 2 currently, 2 critique, 2 critically, 2 core, 2 contribution, 2 connections, 2 concerned, 2 complexity, 2 complex, 2 common, 2 comes, 2 closer, 2 clear, 2 characteristics, 2 chaos, 2 case, 2 cannot, 2 broader, 2 bringing, 2 boundaries, 2 biophysical, 2 beyond, 2 better, 2 because, 2 based, 2 area, 2 apparently, 2 answered, 2 another, 2 among, 2 aggregate, 2 adaptation, 2 actually, 2 action, 2 2011.

Conclusion

30 the, 18 to, 18 and, 14 of, 13 ecology, 10 is, 9 in, 6 that, 6 a, 5 are, 4 from, 3 works, 3 work, 3 we, 3 there, 3 processes, 3 have, 3 etc, 3 certainly, 3 as, 3 any, 3 after, 2 with, 2 what, 2 understand, 2 time, 2 this, 2 thinking, 2 they, 2 systems, 2 sources, 2 so, 2 reading, 2 reader, 2 provided, 2 part, 2 over, 2 other, 2 one, 2 on, 2 nature, 2 media, 2 many, 2 made, 2 knowledge, 2 keller, 2 it, 2 introduction, 2 humans, 2 human, 2 how, 2 history, 2 has, 2 ethics, 2 each, 2 can, 2 by, 2 an, 2 again, 2 about.

added Last Minute

6 in, 5 the, 4 of, 3 a, 2 this, 2 published, 2 nature, 2 is, 2 how, 2 for, 2 economy, 2 came, 2 by, 2 and.

▬

1   word frequency counter written in Python by the author as part of the ALOTOF Media Writing Workshops.

The Sound Beehive Experiment

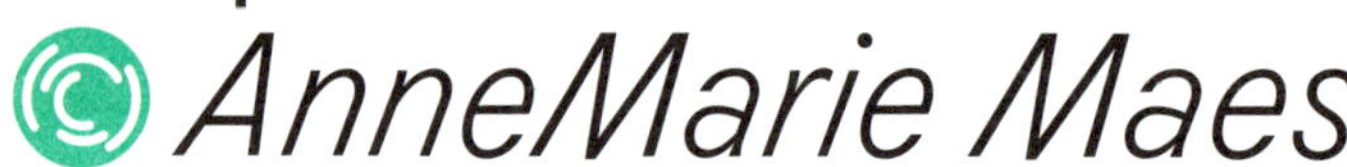

AnneMarie Maes

The Sound Beehive Experiment monitors the development of a bee colony on the basis of the sounds it generates. For this purpose, we developed a beehive that is equipped with sensors, microphones and cameras. We made sure that this equipment is not hindering the bees in their daily action. The Sound Beehive is installed in our field laboratory on a rooftop in the Brussels city centre.

The following description of the Sound Beehive Experiment is based on the field notes that I made between early April 2014 and early April 2015. I am a media artist collaborating with computer scientists and engineers to develop art-science projects. Interested in showing the hidden structures in nature, I am using innovative technological methods to probe the living world. My preoccupations with bees come from a fascination with these amazing insects. Bees exhibit very original solutions on the level of communication and of collective decision-making. They are an endless source of visually stunning images and sounds and their remarkable collective behaviour provides inspiration and metaphors for the functioning of human society.

An Ethological Approach

Honeybees are bio-indicators. They provide a constant stream of information on the environment in which they forage, via their daily activity, and via the pollen and nectar they harvest. Diseases like colony collapse disorder and environmental problems such as the use of pesticides can be analysed in a different way by monitoring the colonies with audio and video tools, and by analysing their daily activity over several years. In nearly all industrialised nations, bee colonies are now threatened. There are many causes — among them pesticides and parasites — but the compromised state of the foraging areas for bees is just as worrisome. By using bees as bio-indicators and by translating the information into artworks, I make citizens aware of the increasingly negative effects of our lifestyle and methods of industrial production.

We study the bees as a super-organism. To study them in their natural environment, we have built a customized 'sound device'. Microphones inside the beehive enable us to continuously monitor the colony's buzz. Together with outside and inside video monitoring it forms a non-intrusive scanning device for controlling the colony's health and development. We also installed a network of temperature sensors spread throughout the beehive.

Aside from the biological study of the collective behaviour of the bees, the goal of the research is to make artworks, making use of the data collected from observing them. The annotated video and audio data are uploaded to our open source video database at pandora.okno.be. All corresponding sensor data from the weather station, as well as the temperature and humidity data measured inside the beehive, are made public on opensensordata.net.

Communication Systems

The bee colony operates through different communication systems such as pheromones and body language. Pheromones are chemical messengers released by the queen and by individual bees that strongly define the activity and behaviour of the colony. With our sound device, we look for information on specific situations such as alarm situations, stress situations, or on the amounts of brood in the nest. Bees are very sensitive to vibrations on the wax comb during the so-called waggle dance, one of their major means of communication inside the beehive. With the waggle dance, a successful forager bee communicates to the other worker bees in the beehive the exact distance and direction from the nest to the foraging field she has discovered. As the bees dance, they emit low-frequency sounds that play a critical role in bee communication. An accelerometer installed in the beehive measures the vibrations of the wax comb along three axes, inlcuding: audio, video and sensor toolboxes.

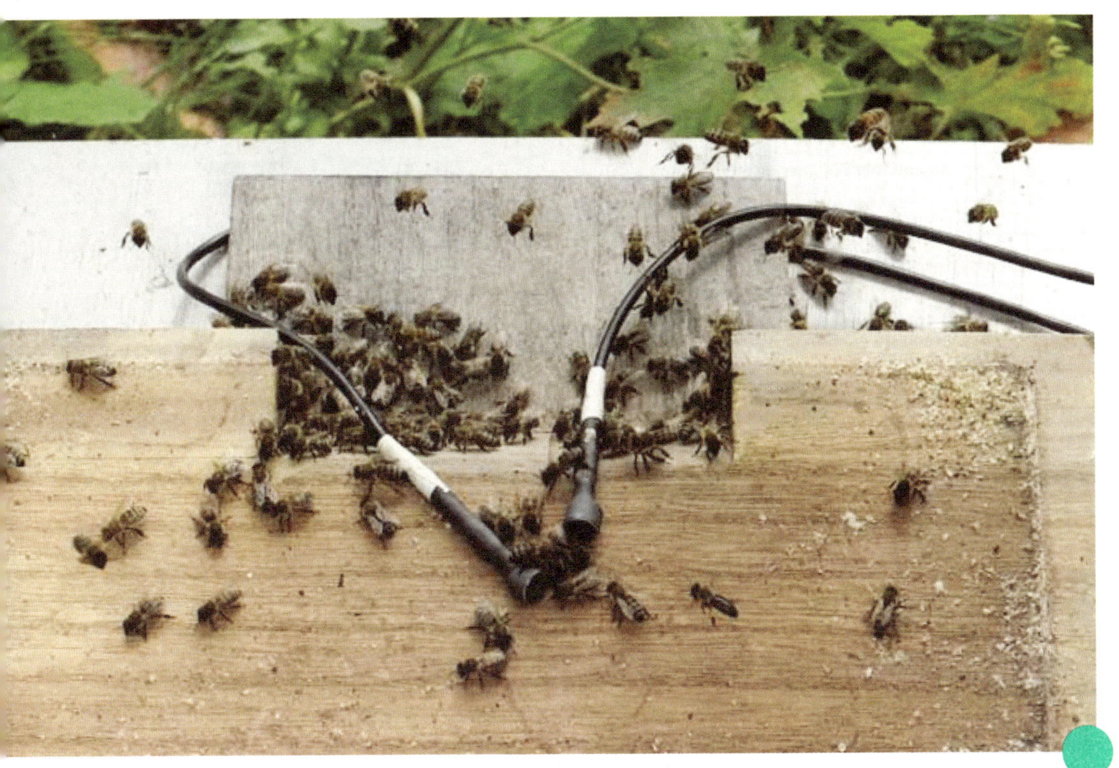

✖ 19. Two *electret microphones* at the bottom of the (open) beehive

Our custom-built audio, video and sensor device is based on the model of a Warré beehive, a sustainable beehive originally designed by Abbé Warré around 1920. It is a beehive in which the colony develops at its own pace moving slowly down into a new brooding box the moment they want to expand. This is contrary to commercial models of beehives that force the bees to build more combs by adding more so-called supers on top of the nest. We started to customize our Warré beehive by putting four electret microphones in the four corners of the top cover. Four Piezo contact microphones were attached with thin metal wires to the frames numbered 1, 3, 5 and 7 of the brood box. All microphones are connected to pre-amps stored in the rooftop. They are powered by a battery that is located a few meters away from the hive to avoid the creation of electro-magnetic fields.

For recording the video images, we use Raspberry Pi computers. The Raspberry Pi is an ultra-low-cost, small Linux computer. The Raspberry can easily be integrated in complex installations and is equipped with a series of USB and Ethernet connections to function in a network of devices. We integrated two small high-resolution cameras in our setup. One camera is mounted at the outside of the beehive and frames a top shot of the landing platform. A second infrared camera with infrared LED lights is mounted at the side of the beehive. It records the activity inside the brooding box. An analysis of the images will give us information on the relation of the bees to the environment. We can count the bees in order to determine the in/out flux and detect homing problems related to pesticide contamination. The images also give us information about the pollen supply and the development of the colony related to the activity level of forager bees, fanning bees, dead bees and lazy bees on the landing platform.

Beginning in the middle of August, 2014, we added a real time audio/video streaming set up. We connected two more microphones at the entrance of the hive to record the taking off of the forager bees, and to record the ventilation processes of the guard bees. All outside activity is filmed from sun-up to sunset.

Bee Activity Related to the Environment
A bee colony is very responsive to the biotopes of which it is a part. The production of honey is dependent on the flowers we grow, the plants we like, and the garbage or pollution we produce. The colony is also very sensitive to environmental variables such as outside temperature, rainfall and humidity, the wind and hours of sunshine. We therefore compare

the behaviour of the bees and the development of the colony with the data from the weather station. In our rooftop field lab, we have installed a Libellium agriculture kit, including several environmental sensing devices, e.g., an air temperature sensor, an air humidity sensor, a soil temperature sensor and a solar radiation sensor, among others. We can determine the degree of air pollution by analysing the number of dust particles on dead honeybees. We also observe the hours of solar activity related to nectar flow of the flowers and the visits by the bees. Nectar secretion increases as pollinators visit the flower. Soil composition might also be important for the nectar flow of the flowers. We set up a database of the pollen contained in the honey of our urban bee colonies and we try to determine the pollen source. By studying the pollen in a sample of honey, it is possible to collect evidence of the geographical location and genus of the plants that the honeybees visited. As such, we can start to trace green corridors through the city, helping the bees to extend their foraging fields.

Processing the Data: From Point To Line To Cloud, Developing the Art Work

Beginning in January 2015, we started analysing the recorded files. We first worked with the frequency and the amplitude of the sound files. We analysed the files in terms of their brightness, loudness and noise level. For the analysis of the video files, we made use of motion detection via the frame difference method. The analysis of the sound files is a complex matter. We therefore use techniques of Artificial Intelligence (AI) in collaboration with the Brussels Free University. We have recorded large amounts of data in order to investigate whether we can detect patterns that help us to both monitor the environment as well as the bee colony's health. The challenge is that there is a large amount of real-world noisy data in which the patterns may not be stable over time, as bee behaviour changes with the seasons. All together these data give us plenty of parameters to combine and to play with, to create models and to compare different moments in time and thus to study the behaviour of the colony relative to timeline/season and environmental parameters.

A video shows a graphical rendering of AI analysis of colony behaviour combining real audio data with measurements of the microclimate inside the hive: temperature, CO2 and humidity, using machine learning to detect patterns in the data. Another video shows 365 days of activity inside a real observation beehive, played back at high speed. The images were recorded with an infrared camera inside the hive and processed using pattern recognition, AI and computer graphics algorithms. These images offer the stunning visual experience of a bee colony in action.

To create an immersive sound installation — The Scaffolded Sound Beehive — we analysed the sound files recorded in the hive. We processed the recordings using sophisticated pattern recognition algorithms and artificial intelligence analysis software, and edited the sound files from several months down into a 15-minute sound piece by adding swirling electronic sound clusters to sonify the ebb and flow of swarm activity in the hive. For the composition, different ideas around swarm formation were investigated. The increase and decrease of the activity in the hive became a guiding principle for the transformation of the recordings.

Natural phenomena were used as musical tools and in retrospect, musical tools were used as an artistic rendition or analysis of natural phenomena. The Scaffolded Sound Beehive was printed at fablab BrusselXL using open source digital fabrication and is mounted on scaffolds that are 2.5 m high. Visitors can put their head into the top and experience an auditory artistic interpretation of hive activity, making this an interactive immersive installation. It will be shown at the Institute of Evolutionary Biology (IBE) in Barcelona (May-June 2015), and will later travel to the exhibition AI and Art for the international conference of Artificial Intelligence in Buenos Aires, Argentina (July 2015).

AnneMarie Maes

AnneMarie Maes works on the interwoven threads of multi-media installations, ecological issues, and social and anthropological projects. Her current work focuses on the ongoing Bee Monitoring project which sets up laboratories for bee colonies and urban gardening. She is a founding member of the organizations So-oN and OKNO and holds masters in fine art and cultural studies.

The Brussels Urban Bee Lab — BUBL

BUBL is an independent international collective of artists, scientists, beekeepers, technicians and creative people. It uses artistic, scientific and technological research to tackle challenges related to sustainability and the monitoring and survival of city honeybees. An extensive rooftop garden in the centre of Brussels hosts the headquarters of the BUBL laboratory. It houses several experimental beehives and instrumentation equipment. From this laboratory, data are continually being broadcast via streaming technology. The installations developed by BUBL explore highly experimental technologies, such as microbial fuel cells, digital and organic fabrication using OpenStructures, bio-mimicry, spatialised sonification, web-based continuous data streaming, data mining based on Artificial Intelligence, organic electronics, solar energy for powering low-energy computing, etc. Our lab collaborates with several universities and a network of artistic research centres throughout Europe.

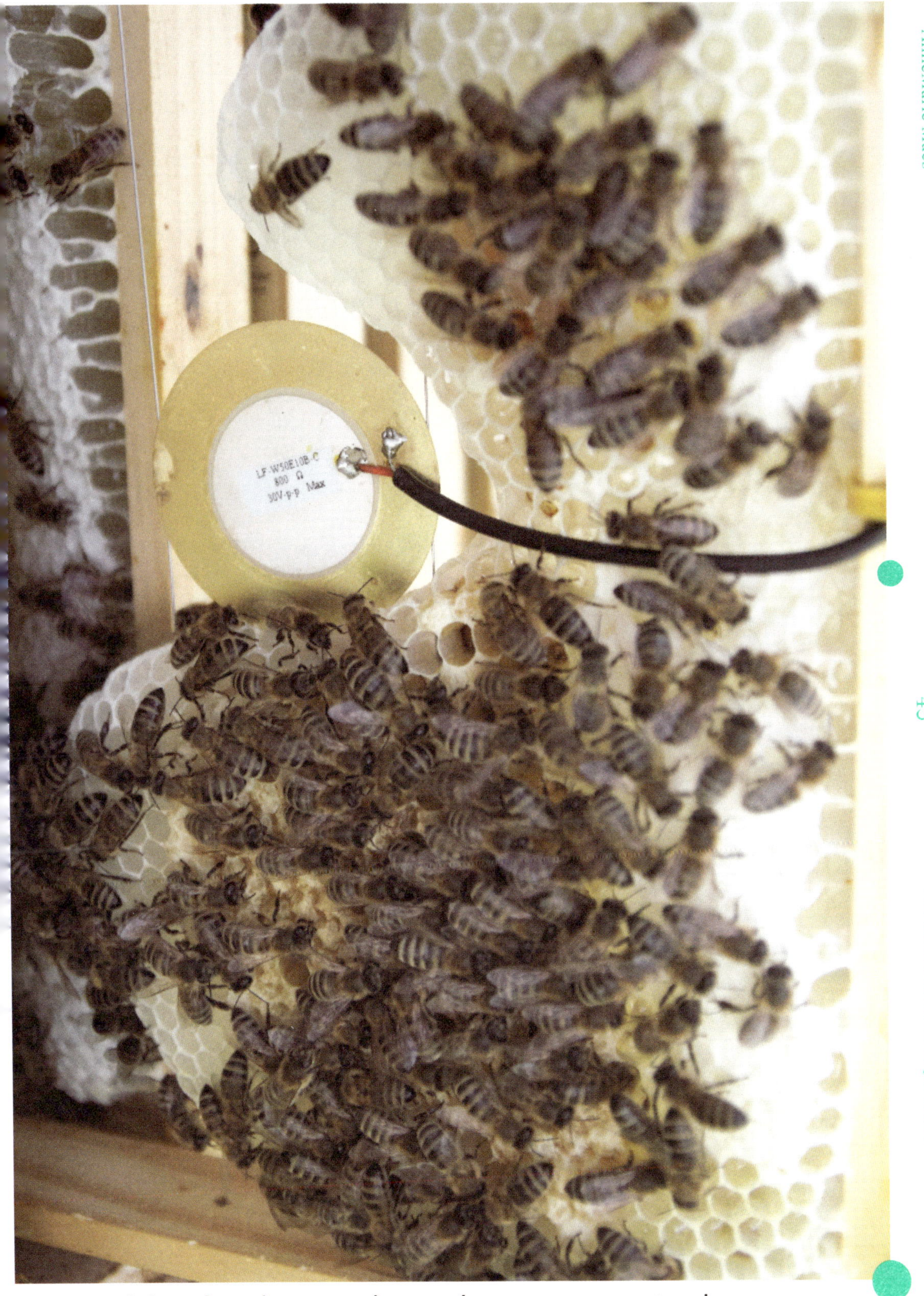

20. A *piezo microphone* mounted on a frame – the bees build wax around it

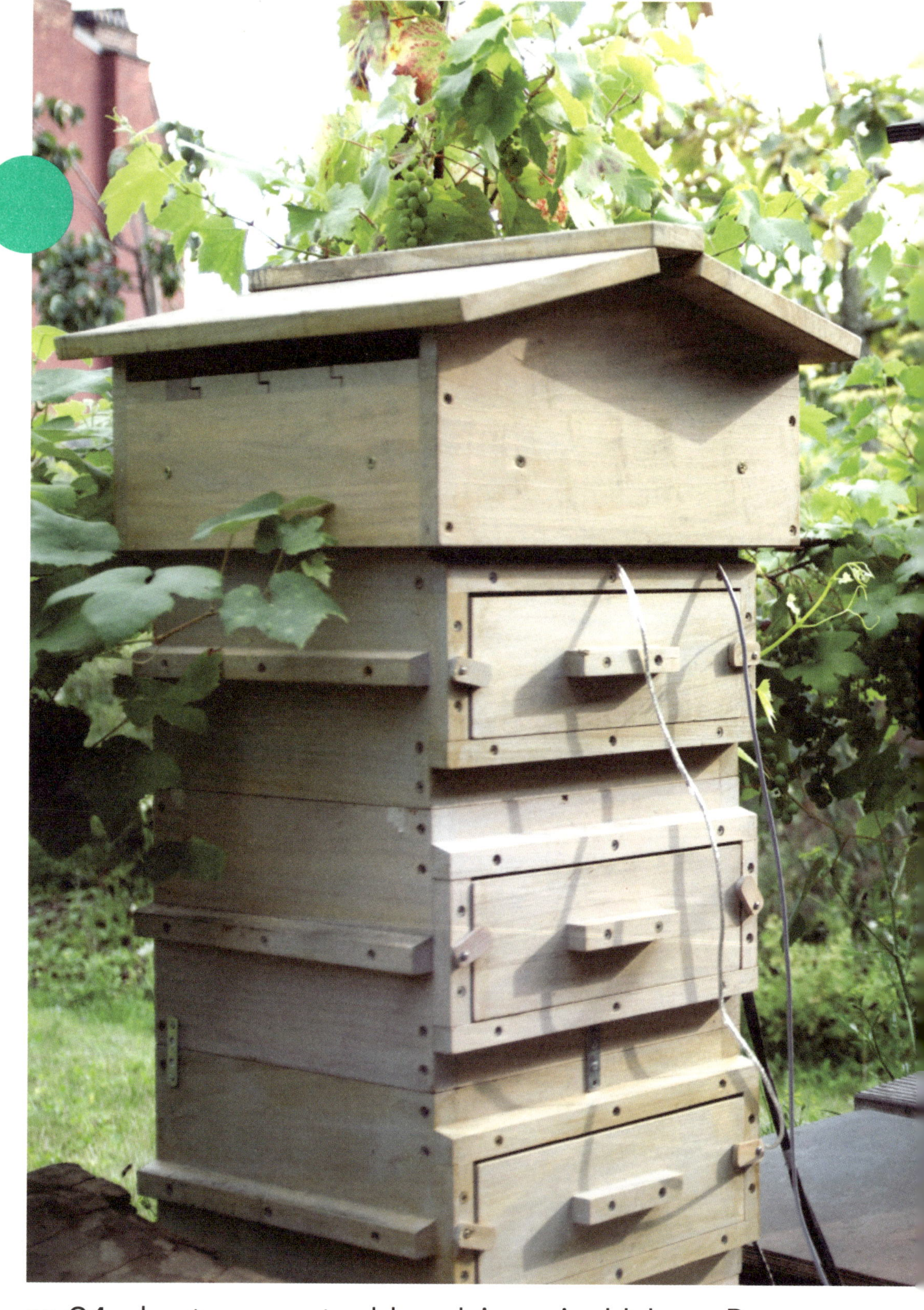

✖ 21. Instrumented beehives in Urban Bee Laboratory, left: *The Sound Beehive*

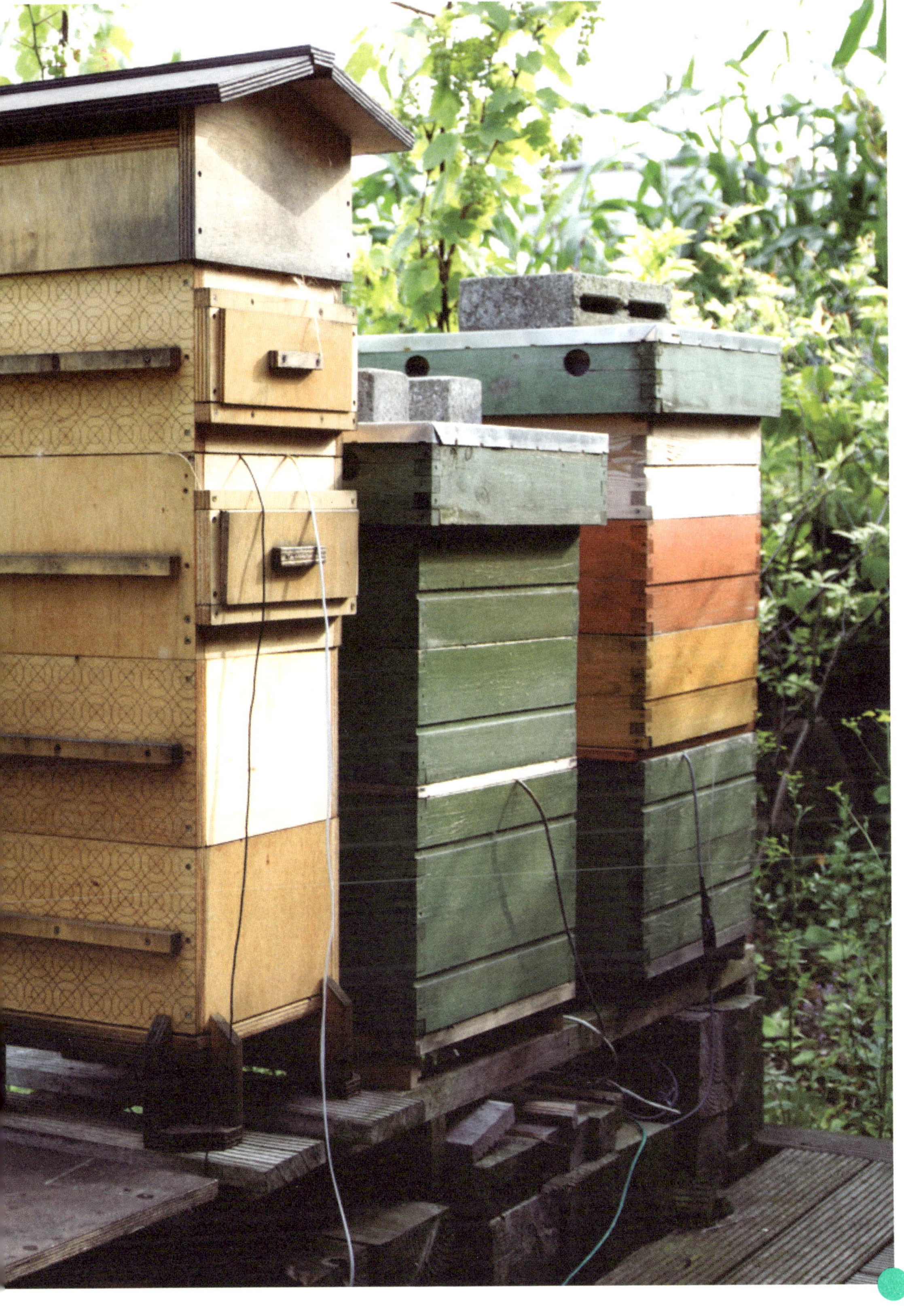

II.

Fieldnotes from an Urban Beekeeper
AnneMarie Maes

I am a media artist and beekeeper. Since 2009, I have studied the tight interaction between city honeybees and urban ecosystems. Urban bee populations function and evolve in accordance with the human activities developing around them. The honey that an urban colony produces differs depending on the flowers we plant and the garbage and pollution we produce.

My preoccupations with bees come partly from a fascination with these amazing insects: The way their bodies look and function, they way they organize their complex societies, and the way they explore their environment. But I have another motivation. In many industrialised nations, bee colonies are now threatened. There are many causes — among them pesticides and parasites — but the compromised state of the foraging areas for bees is just as worrisome. So I work also towards an improvement of the environment of bees with the creation of urban gardens and guerilla planting. Moreover, because bees reflect the health of their surrounding ecosystem and the cumulative effects of different pollutants, I use them as bio-indicators to make citizens aware of the increasingly negative effects of our lifestyle and methods of industrial production.

For many years now, I have been creating experimental setups using sustainable beehives that have been augmented with sensors and sensory processing algorithms to analyse the state of the colony, the quality of pollen and propolis and the behavior of the bees. These 'Intelligent Beehives' are progressively linked in a Europe-wide network and the data is being made available online.

More specifically, I have set out several urban test fields in the Brussels Canal Zone. This area features diverse activities: from community gardening and urban agriculture to accidental nature, interspersed between industrial buildings, office zones and living areas. My test sites are connected by the flight routes and foraging activities of the bees. They create a green corridor in the city. My Bee Laboratory should be seen as an open framework. It is a long-term project on the edge of art, science and technology.

Guerilla Beehives

I want to populate cities with a network of intelligent 'guerilla beehives'. These beehives should offer shelter to bee colonies 'in the wild' — rather than force bees into artificial apiaries. The bee colony should be able to thrive without the help of a beekeeper. Guerilla beehives are intended for pollination and thus preservation and remediation of biodiversity.

I imagine a world where biological fabrication replaces traditional manufacturing and thus new sustainable beehives can be generated simply by growing them. The design of such beehives will be inspired by art forms from nature and so I am searching the scientific literature to find the requirements for an ideal honeybee nest and create physical prototypes using smart and organic materials. A guerilla beehive is intended to function completely independently. I equip them with biodegradable sensors that make distant, non-intrusive monitoring possible. The hives therefore do not need to be opened and bees are not disturbed in order to monitor the colony. The audio and visual data is aggregated, processed and shared in real time over the internet. Moreover, I believe that solar energy, honey batteries or microbial fuel cells can power the sensors, and I am collaborating with scientists to make this possible. The whole system is set up as a fully organic project: cradle-to-grave. If the bees decide to leave the hive in search of another home, the hive (with its integrated electronics) will biodegrade and compost completely.

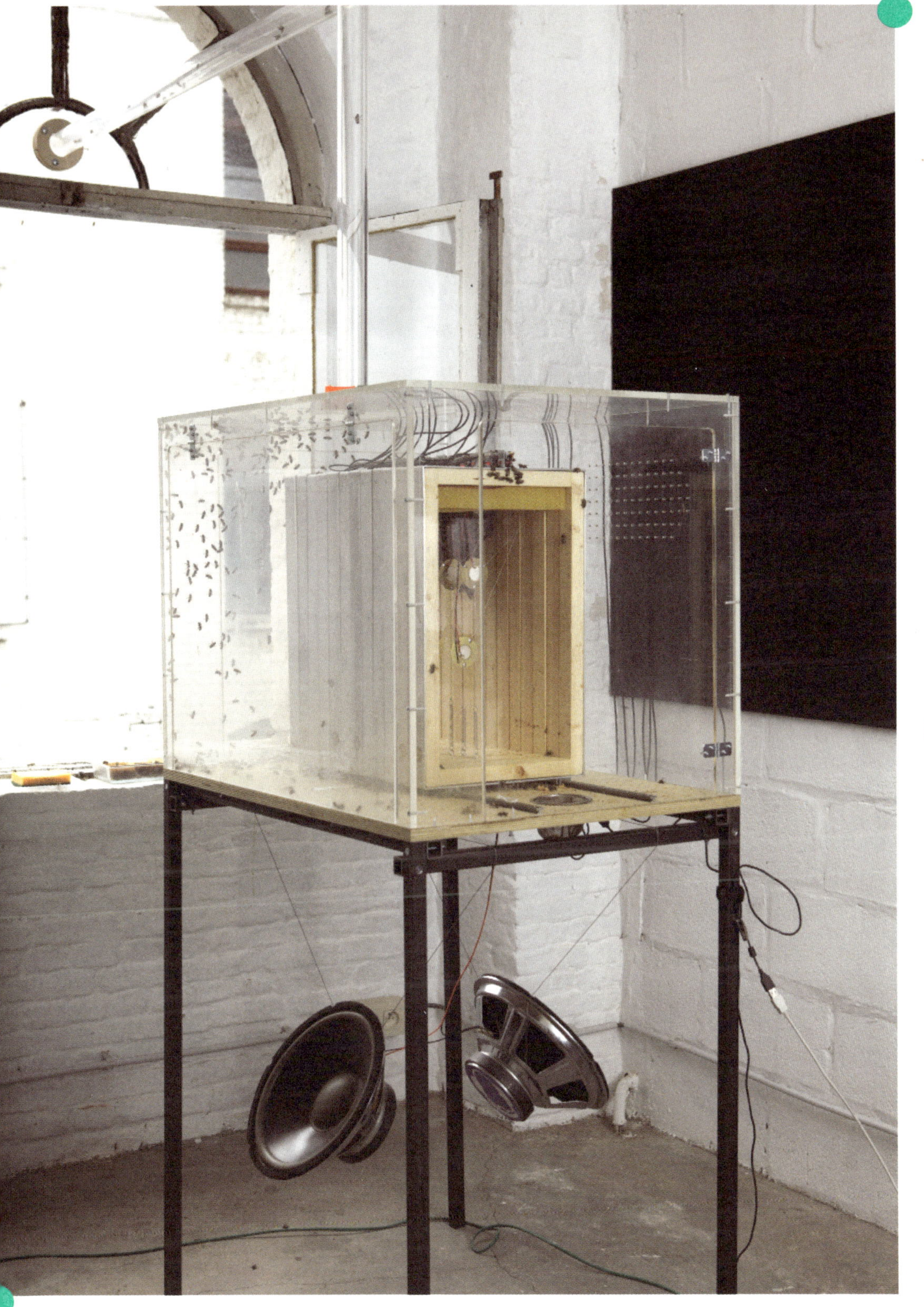

22. The Transparent Beehive audio-renders in realtime the development of the colony

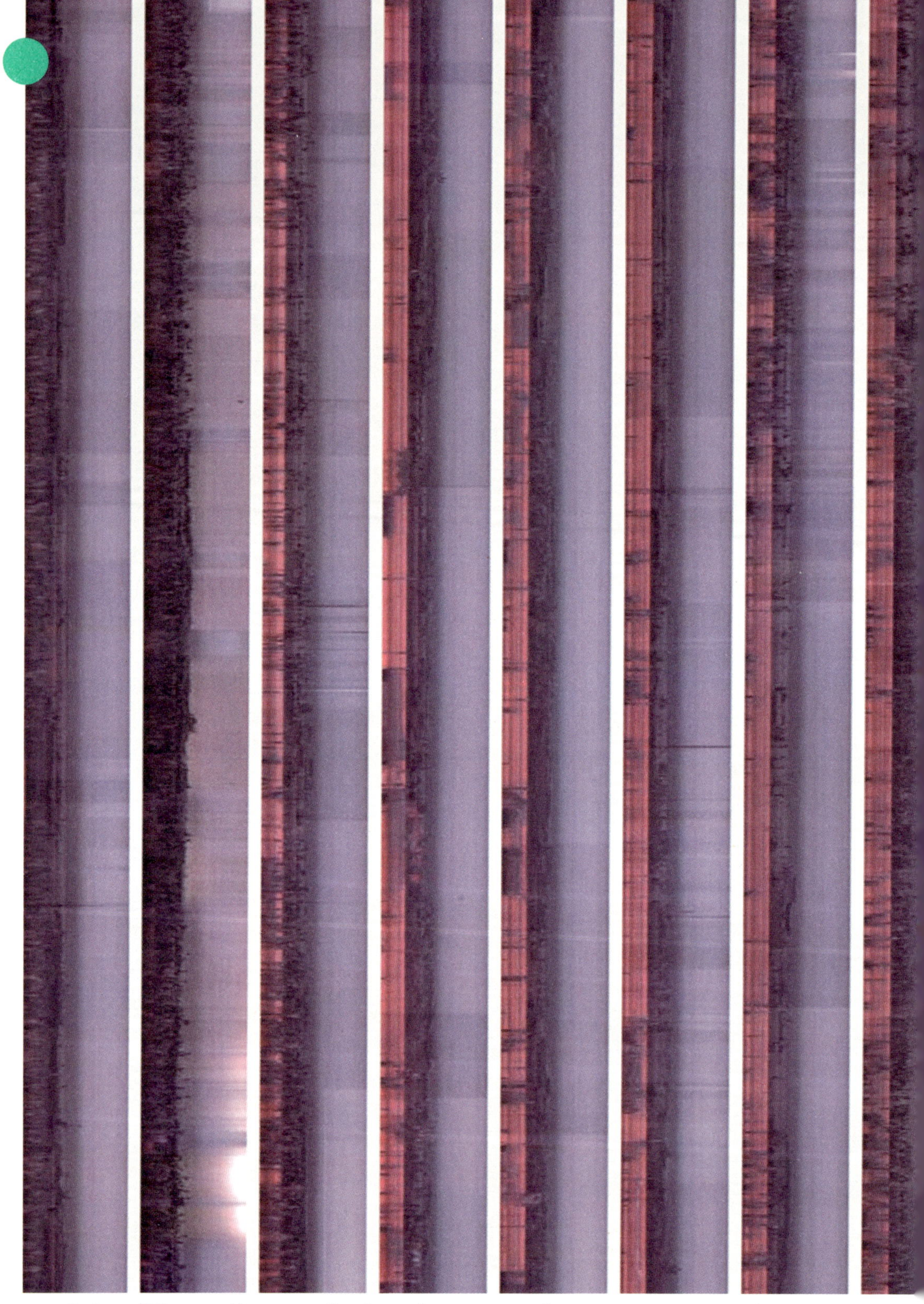

23. Timeline of the bee colony monitored inside the beehive

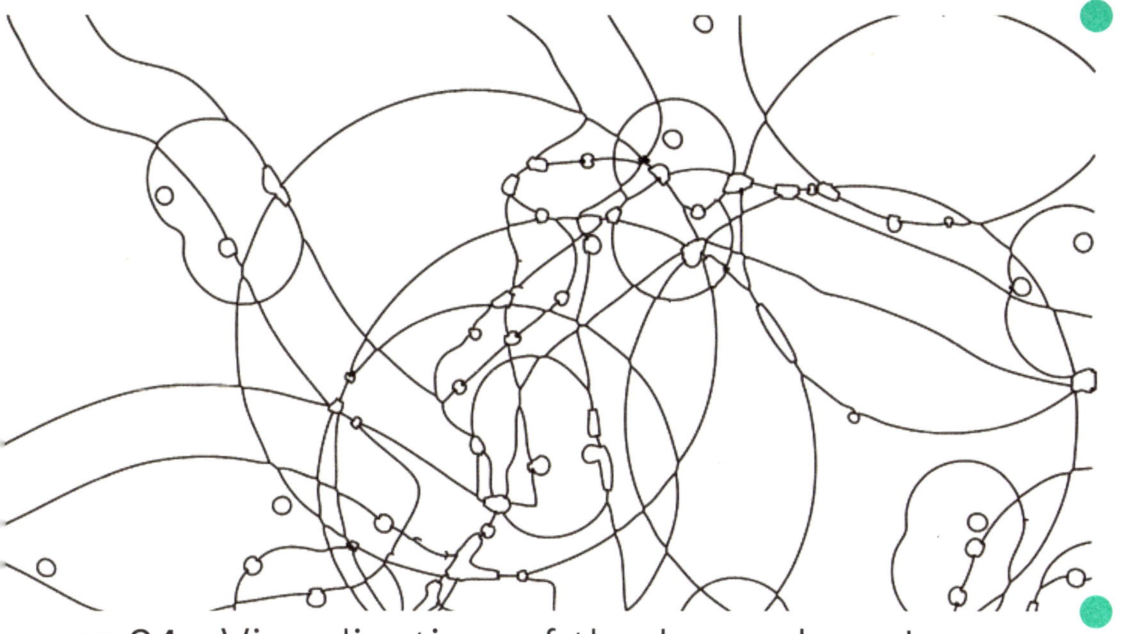

✖ 24. Visualisation of the honeybees' flightroutes over the city

The Urban Farm

Bees are a means for exploring how humans interact with and understand nature. As an urban ecologist, I study the link of the honeybees to the environment. The bees' overlapping foraging areas create ecological corridors throughout the city. By hacking rooftops and transforming them into urban gardens, I am experimenting with new forms of sculpting the public space. This generates a form of site-specific art intended to provoke change. Ecological corridors in urban environments are a new medium of social sculpture, a Gesamtkunstwerk that relies on the creative participation of many. The Urban Farm, Brussels' first rooftop farm, is one of my open air laboratories. It is built on a set of connected rooftops in the historical center of Brussels on the same spot where, in medieval times, vegetable and fish markets were set up, among houses and cloister gardens. The farm, built on top of a big parking lot, is a place where artists and urban gardeners develop new strategies for sustainable living in the city. An artistic attitude, green technology and the philosophy of permaculture present new opportunities to contribute to sustainable living.

Bee Monitoring

How can we study the differences between a biological corridor and the rest of the city? The honeybee colonies forage in a radius of 3 kilometers around their beehive. They fly on their own airborne roads back and forth from their collecting jobs and bring a sense of rural to the urban environment. I analyse the pollen that the bees bring back from their foraging trips, and compare it with existing scientific databases. With this information I can determine and map the melliferous plants in the green corridors and monitor the evolution of plant diversity. Complex systems analysis and machine learning techniques then detect patterns to predict ongoing social and biological processes.

The Transparent Beehive is one of the observatories to study how a bee colony evolves. Contact microphones are embedded in the hive and its comb frames, and bee activities are recorded on 12 mono audio channels. The final — slow art — output creates 3D sound-scan of life in the hive. It is complemented with additional measurement of internal temperature and humidity and external measurements of climate, soil and vegetation. Storing the data over a twelve-month period provides very detailed observations and it allows us to discover and follow long term trends in the complex relations between the colony and its environment.

—

P2P Food Lab

From 3 to 8 March 2014 we meet for an OKNO OpenGreens workshop at the Self Sufficient labs of Valldaura, Barcelona. The focus of the workshop is the P2P Food Lab project: the making of the P2P greenhouses and sensorboxes. At the beginning of spring it is the right time to spread the greenhouses in the network where they will be used as an incentive for starting garden communities. The aim is to motivate people to strenghten sustainable living by growing their own food and by sharing knowledge, produce and labour with other community members. The P2P Food Project is part of a bigger whole, a resilient way of living.

Other related topics will be discussed during the workshop. We'll learn about bees, discover the fantastic domain of Valldaura with age-old orchards and vegetable gardens, make music for plants, work on the OpenGreensWild app for mobile phones, connect different environmental sensors to raspberry pi's/arduino's/smart citizen and olimex boards, talk about creativity and reappropriated islands, be creative with data, share seeds to grow our own food, and much much more ...
→ *http://alotof.org/w/AlotofOpenGreens*

P2P Food Lab is a collaborative project to help you produce and share food, in your local neighbourhood. The philosophy behind P2P Food Labs can be summarised in the following four points:

From seed to composter
Get involved with every aspect of the life cycle of your food. For example, P2P Food Lab helps you get started growing your own vegetables. For that reason we developed a Starter Kit to make growing vegetables easy and fun. We also help you exchange food with neighbours or help you set up composting.

Bringing the peer-to-peer spirit to food
P2P Food Lab is there to help CITIZENS to organise food production COLLABORATIVELY. Peer-to-peer means that we blur the distinction between food producers and food consumers. Be a food prosumer! It also means that you plan food at a community level, together with neighbours, on a voluntary basis.

Technology & tools
P2P Food Lab proposes new tools to help you in the local food production chain. We designed a first version of a small greenhouse together with advanced equipment to measure plant growth. We also provide tools to share your experiences or to ask for help online.

Commons
Over time, these exchanges will create a very useful source of know-how about gardening, by and for gardeners. And because we believe in Free Software and Open Hardware, we will make all of our tools freely accessible so that you can improve upon them. Build your greenhouse, your food I/O box, your community garden or your composter using our instructables. Happy Hacking!

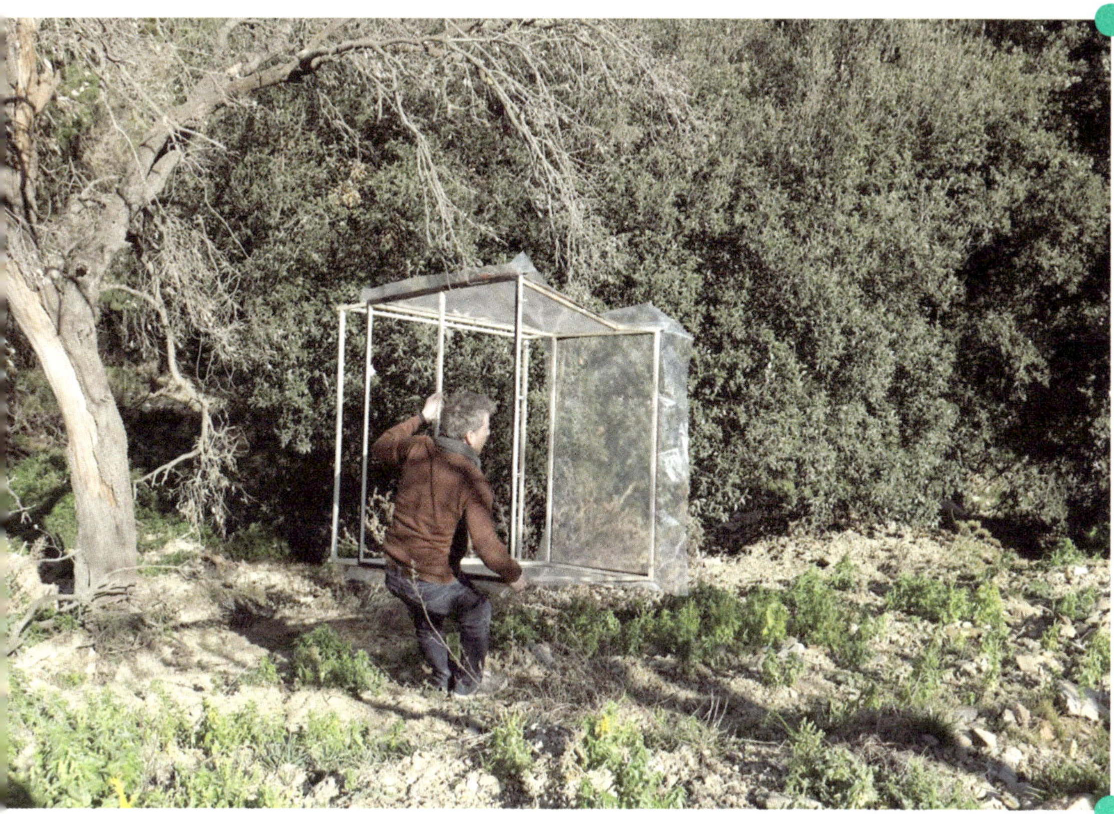

⬩ 25. Struggling

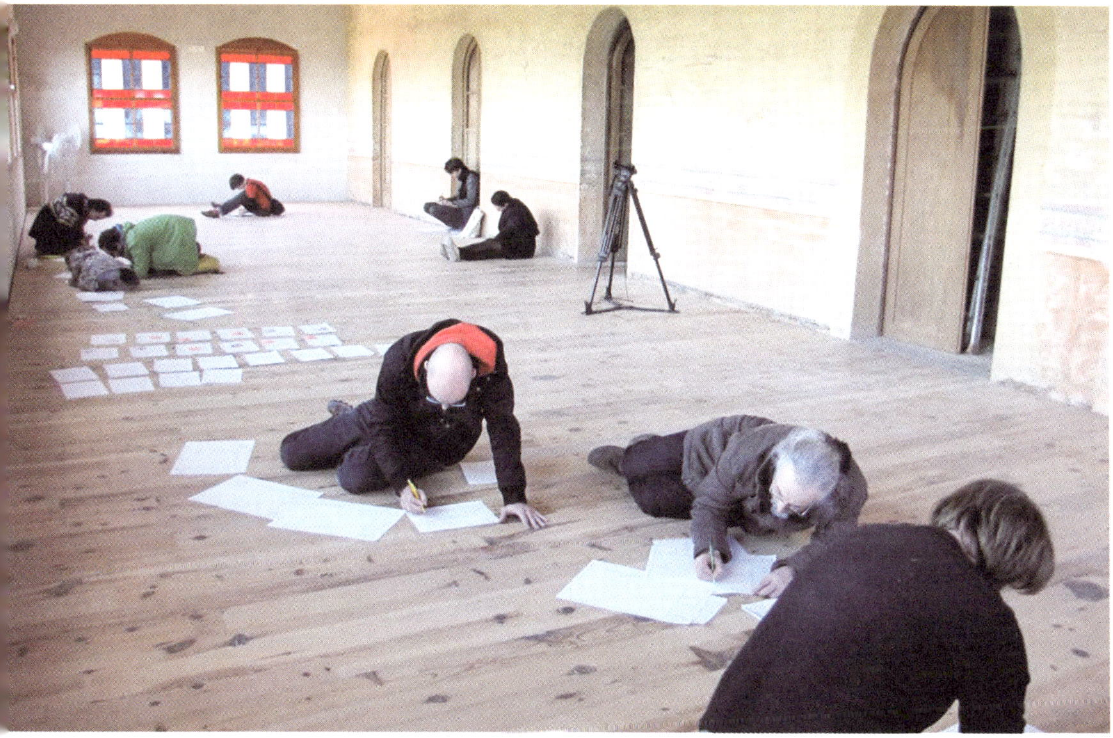

⬩ 26. Designing

Corrosion:
a sound lecture
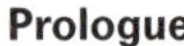 *Franziska Windisch*

Prologue
You don't know how you came to be here;
you just hear a sound
you've heard it for a long time
it' s the waves
you're somewhere at sea.

Above a glaring sun, your mind is blank.

You wear a white laboratory coat
long hair and no shoes.

In the left pocket of your coat you feel a cool glass:
it's a lens, a magnifying lens.

You look into the pocket on the other side:
there's a rectangular piece of aluminium
some cables in different colours
and a pocket radio.

These things seem familiar to you
but you can't recall if you've ever used them
before.

Again, the sound of the waves
your feet move down
towards the water
and where the waves hit the sand
lies something
round and shiny
in the shallow water.

You come closer:
it's a disc of metal,
slightly red, turning to copper
a small hole in its centre.

You move your hands towards it
and hold the metal high
in front of your eyes
to look at the horizon through the hole.

Only from up close do you notice the fine,
circular lines
engraved into the surface.
Is it writing?

A quiet sense arises,
that in an unknown manner
the disc and its traces are associated with you.

If you were able to decode its marks
find out where it came from
an idea could emerge
translucent and sharp
like the lens in your pocket

Part One
The woman lays the disc on the ground
seawater drips from her fingers onto the metal
and with the lens she bundles the sunlight inside
a drop
until the water starts to boil
and slowly the sun's rays transform the water
into steam -
she listens.

. . .

Finally, all the water is gone.
On the metal remains a tiny, solid cube.

I am SALT
when dry, I form a crystal
and light rays that touch my surface
are reflected in white.

The woman says:
I found a round piece of metal here on the shore
tell me SALT
what do you know about it.

SALT answers:
I can have an idea about a thing
only to the extent that the idea
is already embodied in myself.
This is what I can say about the disc:
it exists in space
it can move and it can rest.

She rotates the disc slowly in her hands:
I guess this applies to all physical things.
And as for the engraved circles?
The disc was probably moved
when they were scratched into the surface
or something was moved upon it.
But what do they mean?
Is there a way to read them?

SALT keeps silent.

She connects the salt crystal to two cables.
and the cables again to the radio.
She turns the radio on: but it remains silent
there's no signal.

Part Two

The water in the air, in the sea and in the
land speaks:
I am in myself and I am in you
I rise up and I flow down
I dissolve

The woman thinks:
Let's find out then
what we can hear in dissolution
and submerges the grain of salt in water.

As she moves it in circles over the plate
the loudspeakers of the radio start to vibrate
and the continuous drawing
becomes a continuous sound.

. . .

Everything that has been affected by something
enters a state of transformation
and everything in transformation
is sensitive.

Who is speaking there? She asks

It is us.
You can call us DISSOLUTION.

The woman says:
I found this round plate here on the shore
Tell me Dissolution
what do you know about it?

Dissolution answers·
we can have an idea about a thing

only to the extent that the idea
is already present in ourselves.
About the disc we can say:
It exists in space
it can move and it can rest
it is a sensitive body.

She asks:
what do you mean by sensitive?

Sensitive is what reacts
sensitivity just equals the strength of the reaction.

She repeats:
When something enters a state of transformation
it becomes sensitive, which means it reacts.
Couldn't we also read the reaction as a signal?

But salt already dissolved completely into water:
dissolution is over.

Part Three

She looks at the disc and notices a slight change:
the surface is not as shiny any more
it's turned darker, uneven, with stains and spots.

The change you see is due to us, she hears
call us CORROSION.
Do you know what happens when a material
burns?
A substance gives away electrons when it
combines with oxygen.
This is happening in front of you, right now.
A reaction between copper, salt, water and air.
When burned fast the surface turns dark,
when burned slow into blue-green.

The woman says:
Tell me CORROSION,
what do you know about the copper disc and
its marks.
These lines, aren't they signals?

CORROSION answers:
We can have an idea about a thing
only to the extent that the idea
is already present in ourselves.
About the disc we can say:
it exists in space
it can move and it can rest
it is a sensitive body
it has a specific duration.

She asks:
What do you mean by duration?

CORROSION answers:
Everything that is marked by a beginning,
has an end:
The material. It is finite, as it decomposes by time.

The writing. It is finite, as it disappears the more
corrosion proceeds
The process of corrosion itself. It is finite,
as it can continue only as long
as the material is able to release electrons.

By stroking lightly with her fingers over the
corroded surface she says:
From now on I will not be able to read the lines
any more
even if I had the key to do so.

And she adds:
Maybe it is like this: each thing has its own speed
and time
and whatever we want to understand
should be met it in its specific speed and time
As anything written that enters the world remains
moving
until it diminishes into non-existence.

Part Four

Where the waves roll ashore
she sticks the two metal shapes into the sand
one foot distance between them
the copper disc and the aluminium plate.

Through the seawater ions migrate from one
pole to the other
from copper to aluminium.
She connects each of the metals to a wire
and the wires again to the radio
she turns the radio on and listens for a long time
to the steady flow of electrons.

. . .

Later she asks:
Can you tell me, what this copper disc here is
about?

It answers:
We can have an idea about a thing
only to the extent in that the idea
is already embodied in ourselves.
About the disc we can say:
it exists in space
it can move and it can rest
it is a sensitive body
it has a specific duration
and it consists of actual and potential experience.

Experience? She asks

Well, this is just a word.
Within anything you can find sensitivity
and within anything can you find intensity
those two qualities give rise to one another
to create what you could call experience.

You see, over the course of time
copper and aluminium were equally transformed
only the direction of change differs:
copper releases electrons
aluminium receives electrons.

We are a BATTERY
and as a battery we sound
we have a specific capacity of experience
that unfolds between two poles and in time.

As a BATTERY we sound.

And what is the meaning of this sound? She asks

BATTERY says:
what I speak, is what I forget,
what I forget, is what is written down in me
what is written down in me, is what I will
remember
what I will remember, is what I speak.

Epilogue

We all wear shoes here
and we are not at the sea
but sitting on chairs
in a room with white walls.

But certainly those four things happened in
the last twenty minutes:
water evaporated
salt dissolved
copper corroded
and an electric current was generated between
two metals in salt water.

And certainly the elements we heard about
water, salt and copper
circulate in our bodies
now and tomorrow
until we die.

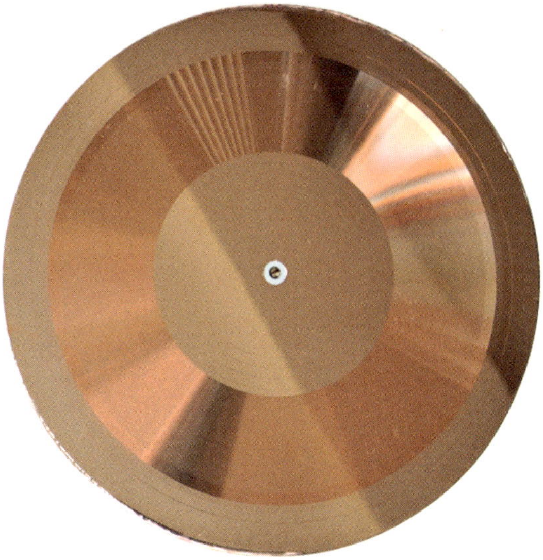

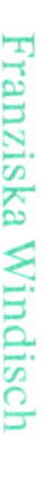

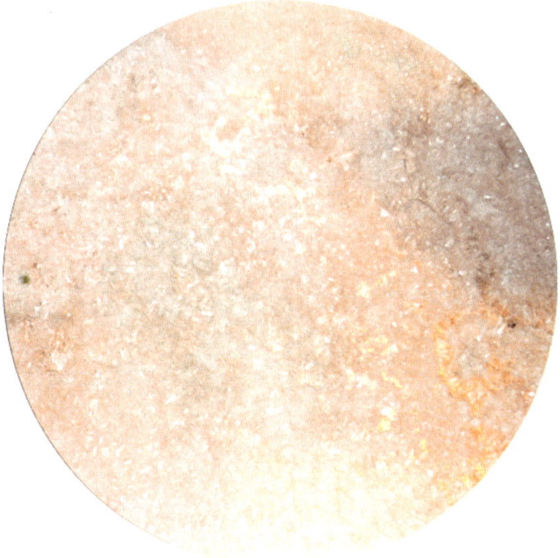

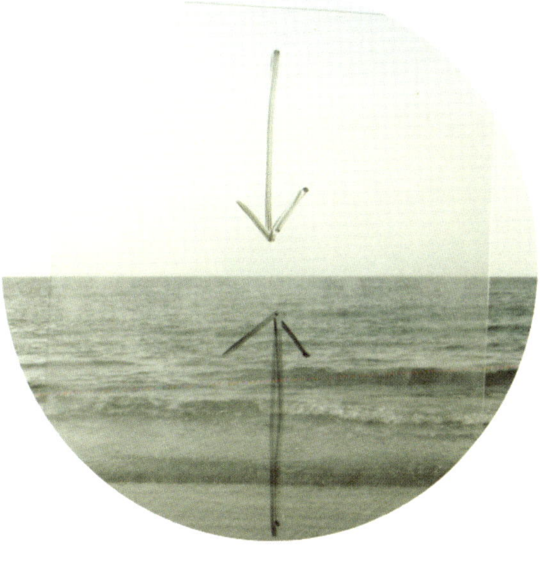

Corrosion

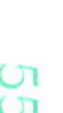

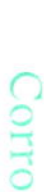

⣿ 27. The Disc, The Salt, The Glass

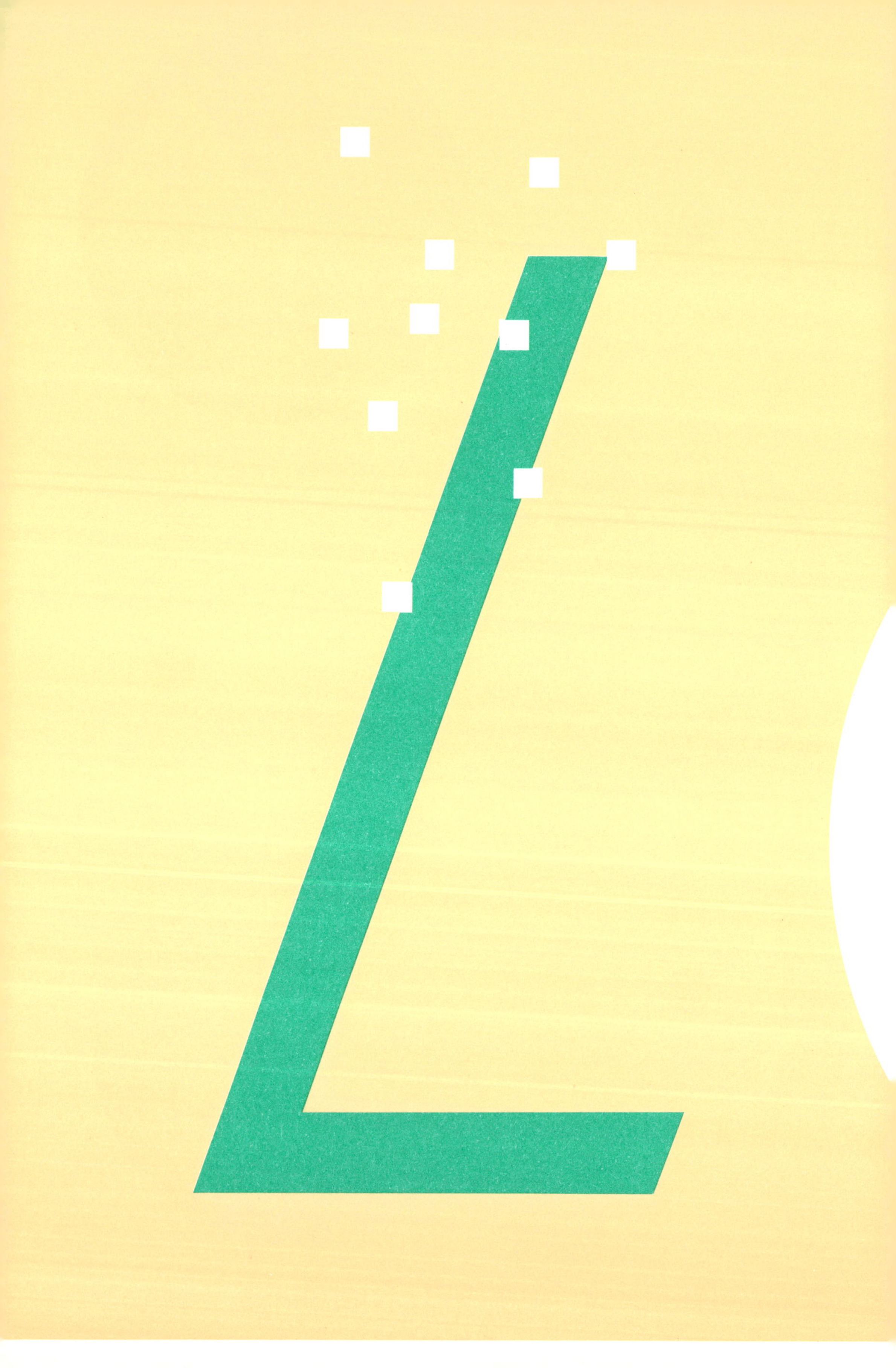

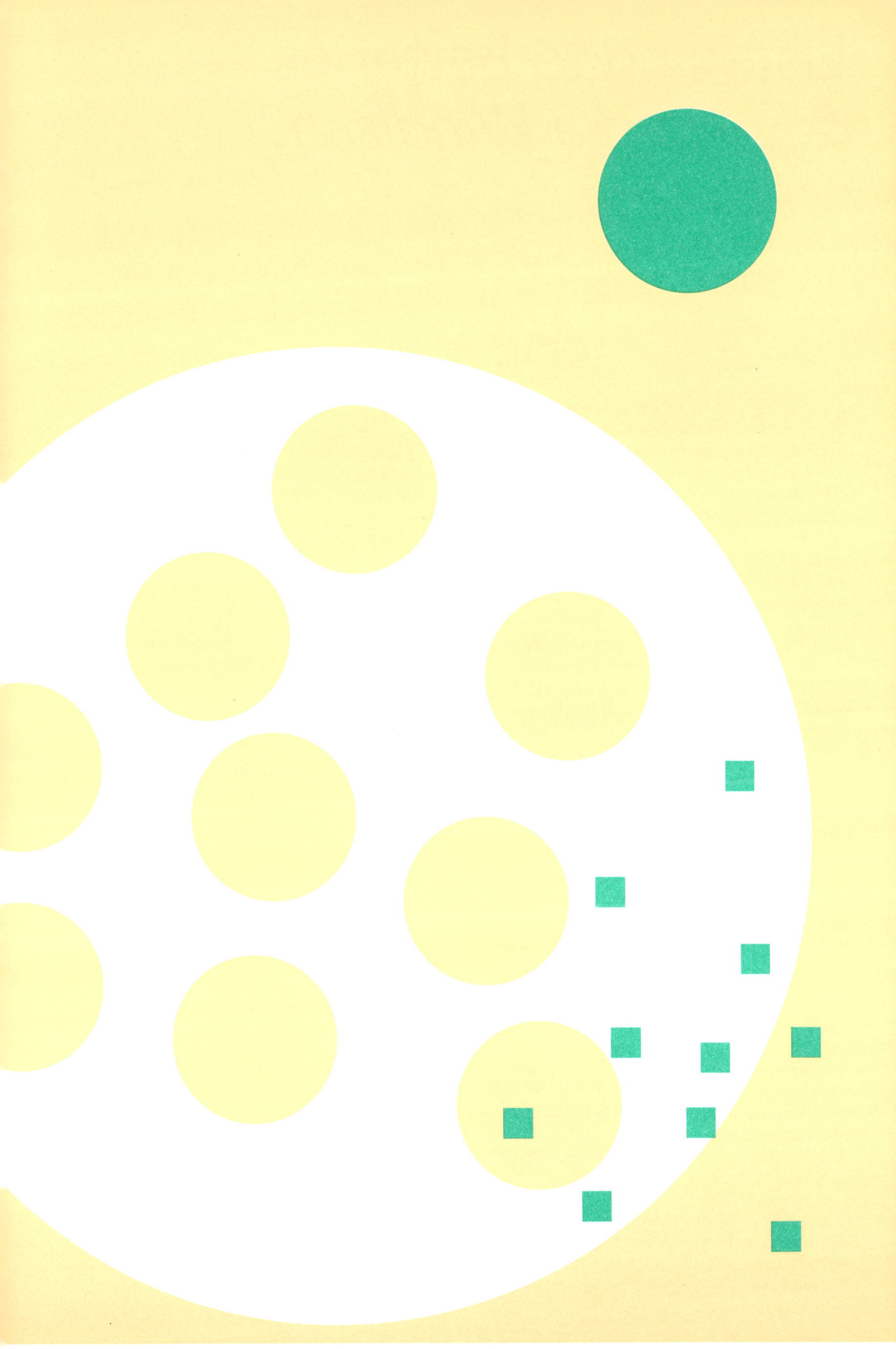

Listening to Batteries
Franziska Windisch

The two-year long ALOTOF program started around the time my daughter was born. It was an event that drastically changed my working practice but, at the same time, embraced the ideas behind ALOTOF much more than I would have thought: making art outside of the studio or gallery, working steadily in smaller time chunks, which in my case resulted in a quite slow, but profound, process and a strong emphasis on material, which was a result of spending less time in front of the computer.

I saw these two years as an experimental platform to test some questions for myself: How much technology do we really need as (media) artists? How much "art context" do we actually need in order to make art? What happens when we set no goal (as usually requested in project proposals)?

My starting point was: working with salt and water, to explore reversible exchange processes (as in batteries or osmotic systems).

In these two years I have been using my computer and other related technology a lot less in my artistic practice than ever before. It has made me realize that, in a world where we as a society, and as individuals, are highly dependent on technology, it might be a relevant exercise to think and rethink technological setups by minimizing the technological part, or going for possibilities without technology at all. Technology hasn't created simply machines and machine-processes (computation), it has also created concepts. These concepts shape how we perceive reality (think of terms like: interface, internet surveillance, real-time, connectivity, etc.) What happens if we unlink them from their technological context?

As an example: What is a sensor? What are the qualities and properties needed to categorize anything into a sensor? Is it possible to think of a sensor outside the framework of surveillance?

We could say the object would need sensitivity for a certain kind of power (pressure, heat, light, etc.), which means it reacts relatively to the intensity of the incoming force. If we think about it like this, we can see already many things naturally as sensors.

With this in mind, I have declared that salt is a sensor: The open ends of a cut wire carrying audio, attached to a salt crystal and plugged to an amplifier, acts as a sensor.

My aim was to not involve computation here, but to make the input force directly audible through the sensor itself. I wanted to avoid the individual esthetics that any model comes with, because an esthetic interpretation (assigning output parameters) would override the natural processes that are sonified. I wanted simply to stay as much as possible on a purely physical level.

When salt is dry nothing happens, as soon as a drop of water is added to the crystal, and it is moved over a surface, we can hear the sound of the movement: The salt crystal has been turned, to a certain extent, into a contact microphone.

I asked different people with backgrounds in physics about this phenomenon, and I was surprised to hear differing explanations. One of them said that salt eventually becomes sensitive because the structure of the crystal gets modified by the water and is thus sensitive to pressure (similar to a piezoelectric effect). Another said that the dissolution process eventually creates a quasi-chaotic state, similar to a state of phase transitions, which makes a substance highly sensitive to external influences. Yet another explanation was that a drop of salt water on a conducting surface creates an anodic/cathodic environment that enables the flow of electrons. By moving the drop of salt water, it produces a difference in potential, which increases according to velocity, and which in turn can be measured as voltage.

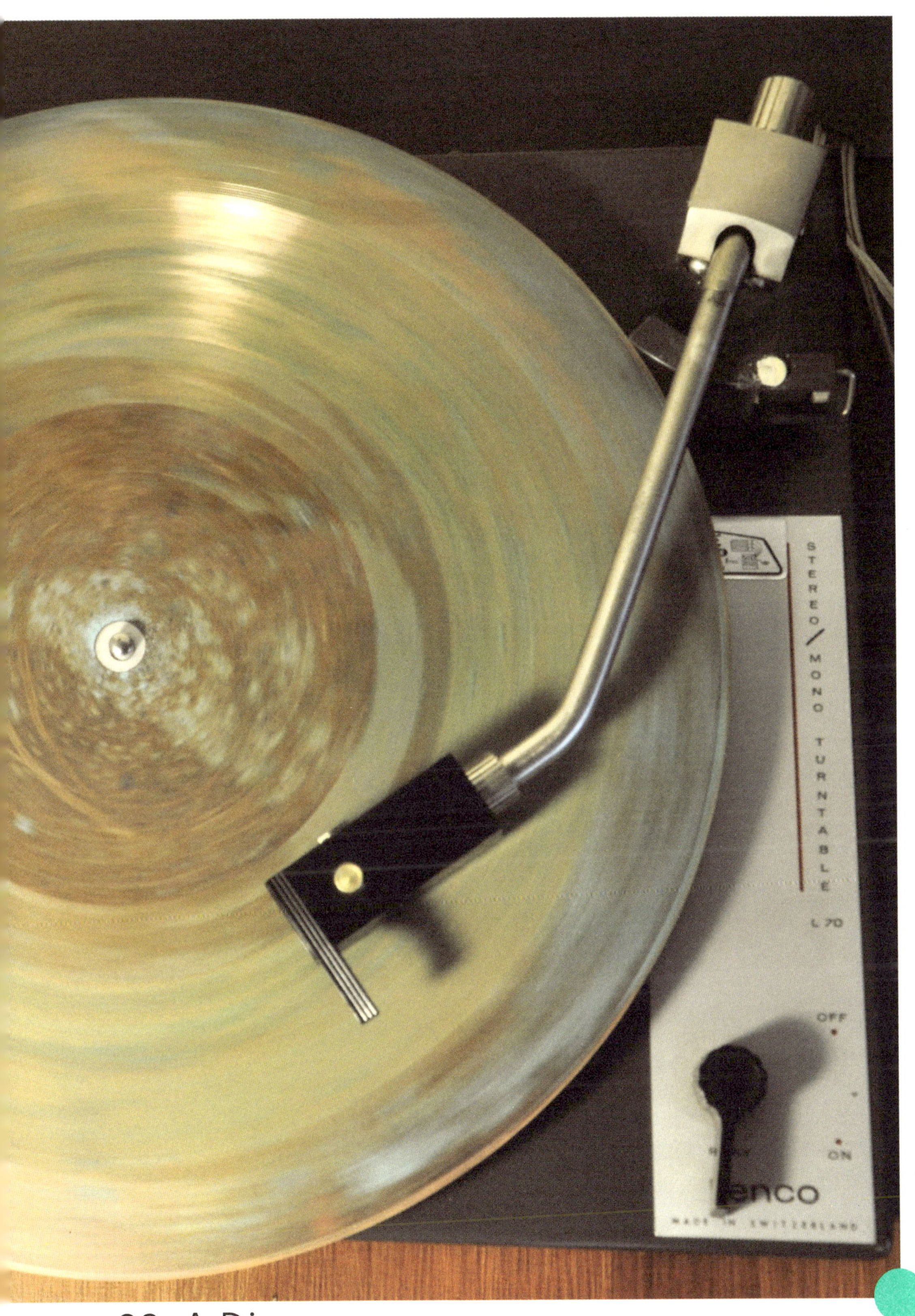

28. A Disc

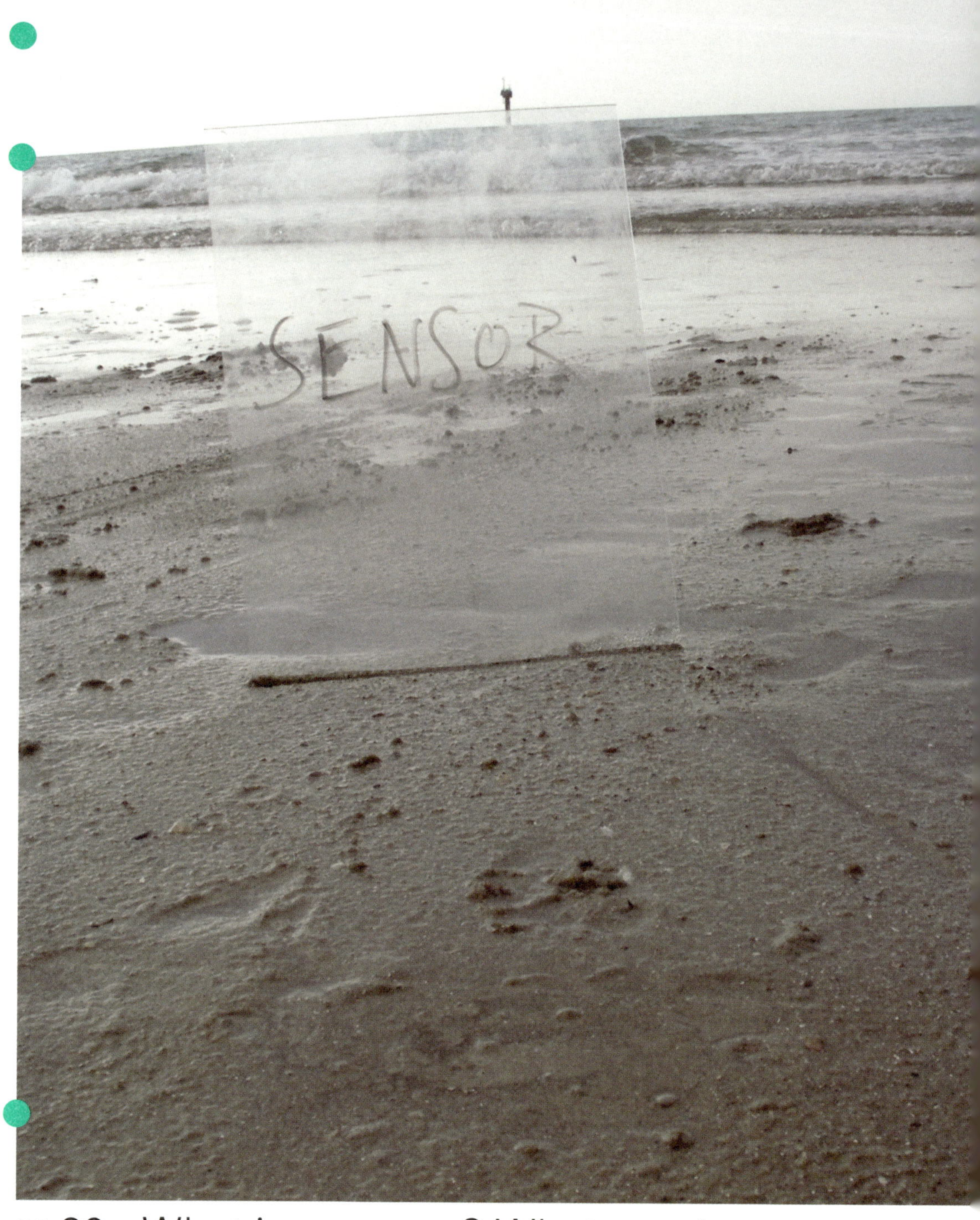

■ 29. What is a sensor? What are the qualities and properties needed to categorize anything into a sensor? Is it possible to think of a sensor outside the framework of surveillance?

Despite these possible explanations, as an artist, I am curious about the potential of a material. Each material inhibits a certain performativity that can be explored by experimentation. Every material is subject to change and is thus (re)active.

What happens when we ask more questions about a material, such as: What is a medium?

We could say a medium is an object that is able to record a signal. We might further say, that for recording we need a certain sensitivity for the signal or intensity to be recorded. (A hard disc is sensitive to electromagnetic waves, a piece of paper has softness to hold the imprints of writing or printing, a stone is not so hard that it cannot be marked by a chisel, and so on.) In that sense, we can say that any medium is already a sensor, a sensitive body. And it is this sensitivity that makes it non-permanent, which means it always has an inherent duration. Not only is the content itself defined by duration, but the medium is, too. And then, can we transfer this idea to a non-material level, too? For example: is text also a sensitive body? Is text non-permanent? Does text have duration? Then, what happens when we think about code, a score, a work of art, a concept?

But no matter which form of "medium" we look at, there is always a relationship between sensitivity and intensity. We can apply this in the context of chemistry, physics, art, and writing. When those qualities (sensitivity and intensity) act together, a transformation naturally occurs. The medium is not only a sensitive body, but also a constantly changing body. Can we be sure that it will be the same book when we read it again? The same record when we listen to it? The same image when looked at?

Medium = Battery?

The relationship between sensitivity and intensity as a system is demonstrated perfectly in the form of a battery. A battery contains two substances, usually metals, arranged as a cathode and an anode. Electrons migrate from one pole to the other and generate a electric current. The result is that both sides will be transformed: One side will be oxidized, and the other reduced. One side will become literally heavier than the other.

Using the same manner of direct amplification as before, I arranged batteries and metals in salt water and listened to the current. In the very low frequency band (under 50 Hz) I observed some irregularies on a spectrogram. Was this a phenomenon of corrosion?

A collection of notes emerged from various experiments. They were transformed into a text for a lecture on sound. In order to transfer this text back to a physical medium, I printed a spoken version onto a copper disc, like those used to make direct metal masters in vinyl production. Then the disc was oxidized by applying water and salt. Every two hours the disc was played back and recorded until the voice was barely audible and the copper disc had turned dark. Both pieces, the sound lecture and its corroded double, have been published as a vinyl edition under the title Corrosion.

"The (art)work has to be met at the level of production, of its becoming. It can be argued that production and productivity obey certain conditions. I see the real challenge [is] still in the transcendence of the circumstances and conditions, a transcendence of one's own fragility." [1]

Artistic practice always responds to time, space and resources. At the same time it is never exclusively dependent on them. Eventually, any circumstance can create the conditions for art making, but a change in conditions will not only change the artwork, but also the way we might think about artistic practice itself.

1   Steinwerg, Marcus Bataille Maschine, S.112, Merve Verlag Berlin, 2003

Island
Fabrice Gallis

Building lightweight structures allow the exploration of specific places such as islands, no man's lands, brownfields, suburbs, malls, etc... The principle is to conduct long term artistic research in places that were not meant for this purpose. These autonomous architectures, not so far from antarctic bases can create and experiment ways of producing on-site energies, but also facilities for guests or events for a public that has to be invented. These places can be considered as experimental platforms to welcome researchers from other laboratories.

The island is the archetype of an experimental place. As artists, we create autonomous objects that aim to exist in any context but when the projects become complex, the weight of the context always leads to crush project structures. We often figure the freedom zones that we create for a while as utopias. Utopias are useful as abstraction tools. AN ISLAND is an attempt to consider utopias as real spaces, a real island in which the context is modified for a limited space of time. One of these islands is located in Normandy, France, close to Cherbourg, (49°40'12"N – 1°35'01"W), its name is "L'île Pelée", an old military bunker not used anymore. The aim of this proposition is to organize the migration of an artistic laboratory (http://laboratoiredeshypotheses.info) developped in 2011 and 2012 in Rezé (44, France) to this island, the same way an antarctic base would settle. This specific place could welcome residencies in connection with the other research projects and shelter a resource center gathering diverse patterns of time invention. This project comes from a novel written in 1940 by Adolfo Bioy Casares, "Morel's Invention" in which a entire island is recorded in a machine, as a permanent and concrete dream. The autonomous machine draws its power from the tides, and so produces a discontinuated activity.

AN ISLAND tries to produce a situation in reality that could be directed by fictions. The fact that this island is subject to bad weather will force contributors to find technical solutions to hold on. That could be a perfect spot to test various propositions around the questions of time, energetic or symbolic autonomy and collaboration. For the moment this island is still a desert maintained by the army but some possibilities occur to conquer this piece of land, artistically.

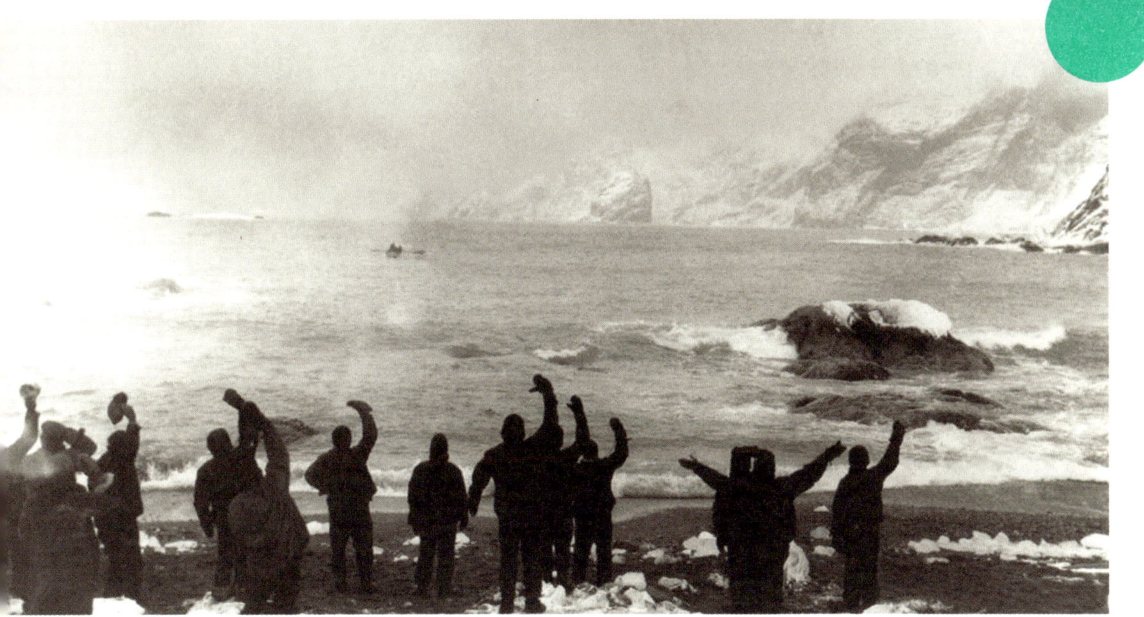

❖ 30. Survivors of the Shakleton "Endurance Expedition" (1914-17)

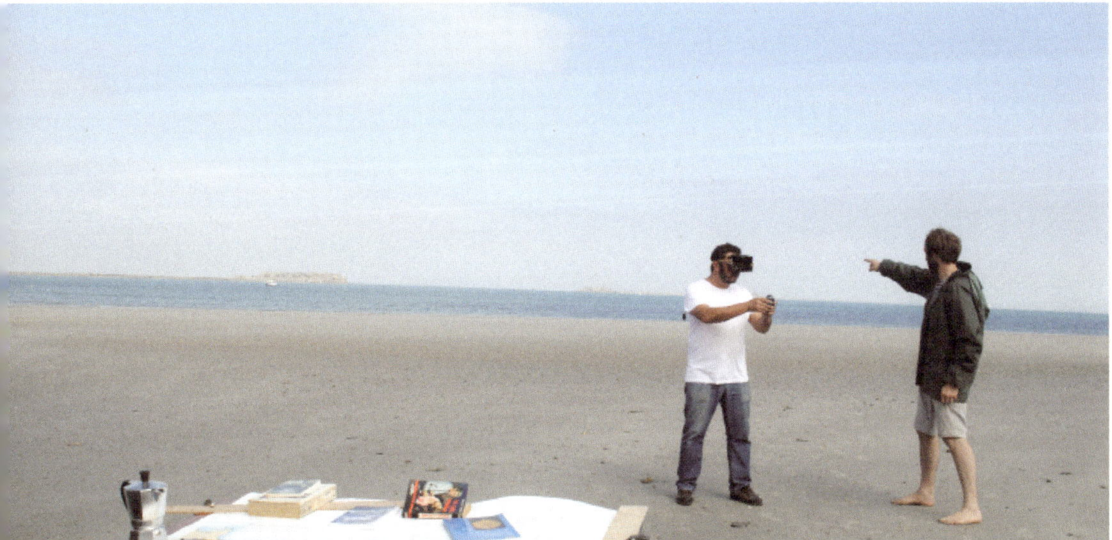

❖ 31. Island laboratory looking for another island.

Fetish
David De Buyser

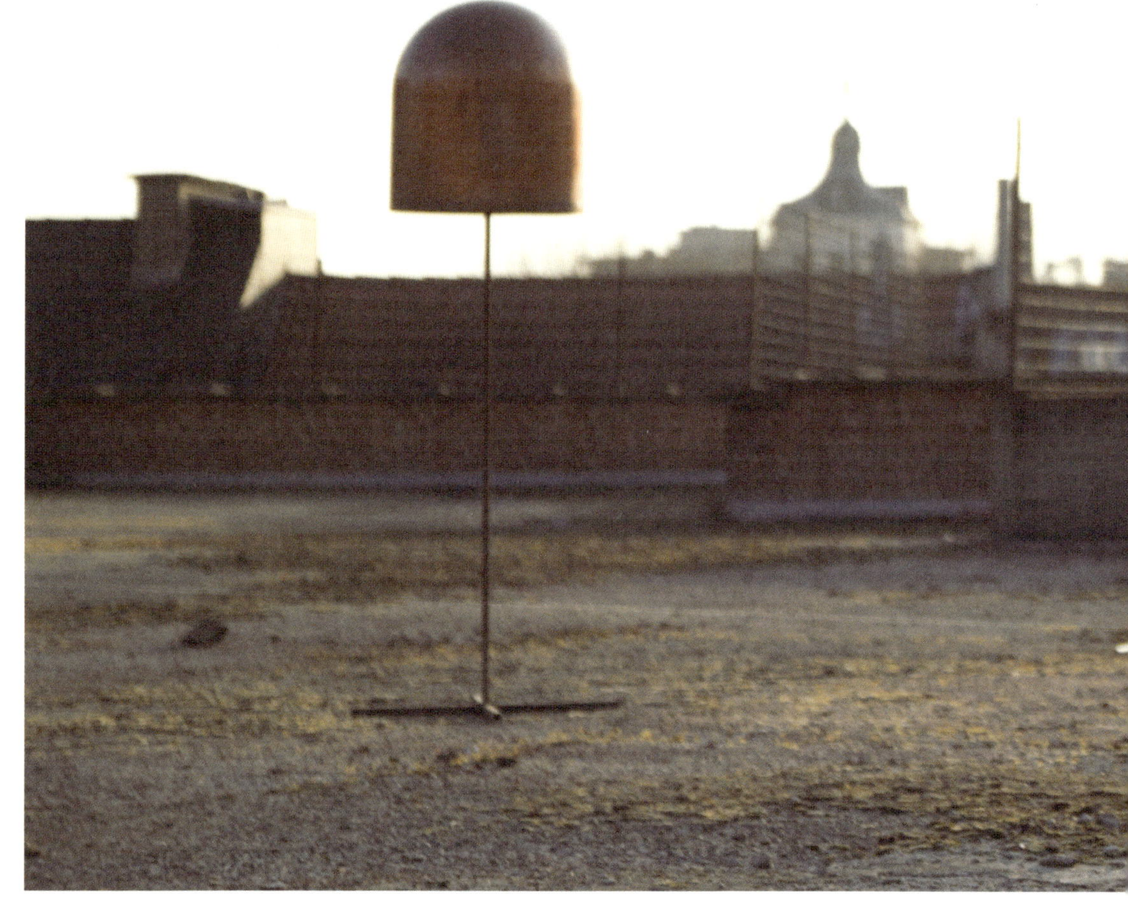

32. Fetish, *Sound Installation*, 2015, H: 175 cm, Ø: 45 cm, Steel, Copper, LDR, Arduino.

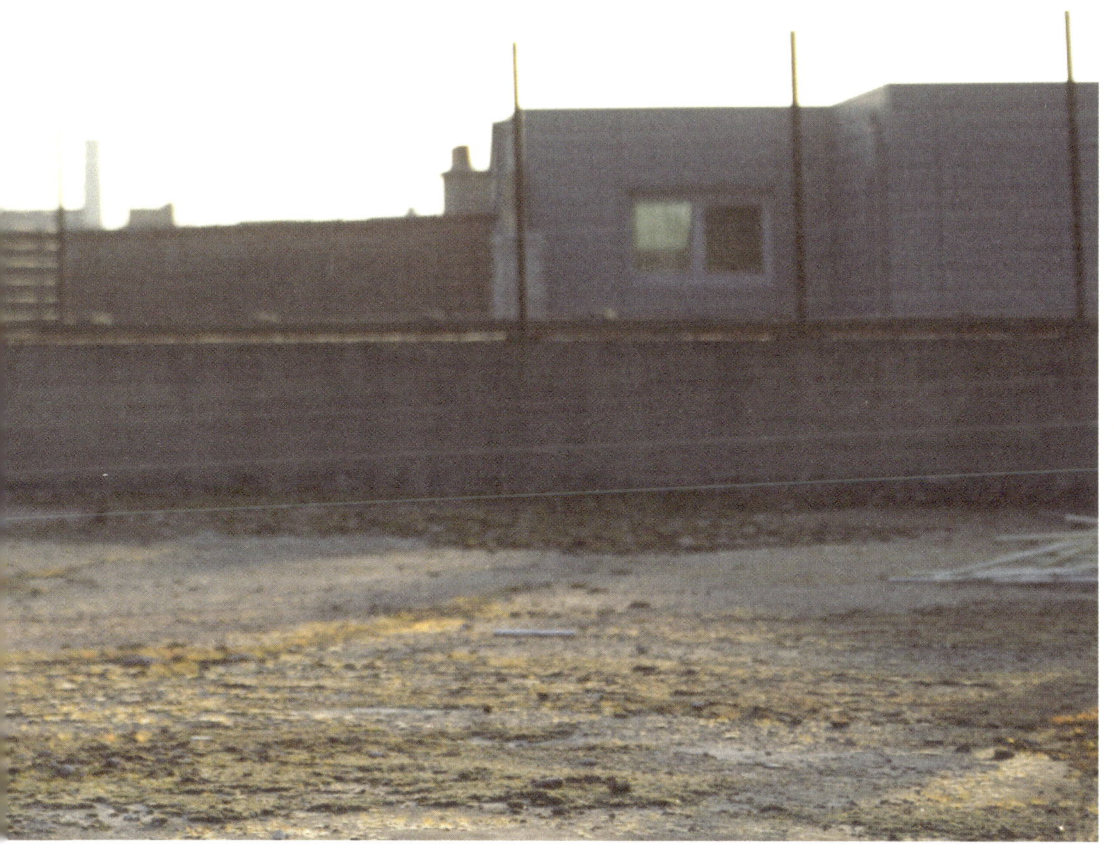

A fetish (derived from the French fétiche; which comes from the Portuguese feitlço; and this in turn from Latin facticius, "artificial" and facere, "to make") is an object believed to have supernatural powers, or in particular, a man-made object that has power over others.

II.

Aargh
Gert Aertsen

* Aargh ! sustained, ...
* AA : /a/
* A as a starting point
* A shape
* An object : A as an object
* Speech : as a mechanism
* Von Kempelen : Wolfgang, Mechanismus Der Menschlichen Sprache Nebst Beschreibung Seiner Sprechenden Maschine, 1791
* A is a vowel
* Ooo
* Ee : /e/
* U
* I : Finish, Japanese & Russian sizes
* Gunnar Fant: Acoustic Theory of Speech Production, 1970
* Talk : because that's what I thought I heard, people talking
* ALOTOF : a laboratory
* A Building
* High Rise : Why move out of the city, when you can go up to reach the open field
* The 9th floor
* In a field of concrete, bricks and buildings
* Open a window
* Shouts & screams : are the sounds from the city that reach you, up there
* Wind : has a stromg impact on it
* Drafts : when opposite windows are opened
* Whistles through cracks, cavities and fissures
* Cavities
* The Mouth : because the mouth is a cavity
* A as a Cavity
* A Resonator : blow across a bottle's top
* Godfried Willem Raes : for the many times I came across his work on the logos foundation
* Hermann von Helmholtz : apparatus for the synthesis of sound
* Hole : in the wall & floor.
* Wind as a potential source of energy
* Lungs blow
* An instrument
* Voice : the voice is an instrument

* Vox Humana
* An organ
* A reed replaces the vocal chords
* A generator
* Sound : a non sound
*
* Analog
* Persistence of now
* Time
* Throat
* larynx
* Moans & Murmurs as categorized by Luigi Russolo
* Mmmwwwaargh : or rather that's what it became

Aargh [1] is an exploration into the mechanics of speech. Inspired by the famous Wolfgang VonKempelen, Aargh explores the possibilities to create a site specific sound installation for the 11th floor of the Overtoon office building. This particular building stands high and free in the city center of Brussels. Wind has a strong impact on it. The offices are drafty spaces when you open them up on both sides. Can the energy created by the wind be used as a force or input to generate sound. Possibly something which remotely sounds like speech.

1   http://www.atkn.org/wiki/index.php/Aargh
2   copyright: Merel 't Hart

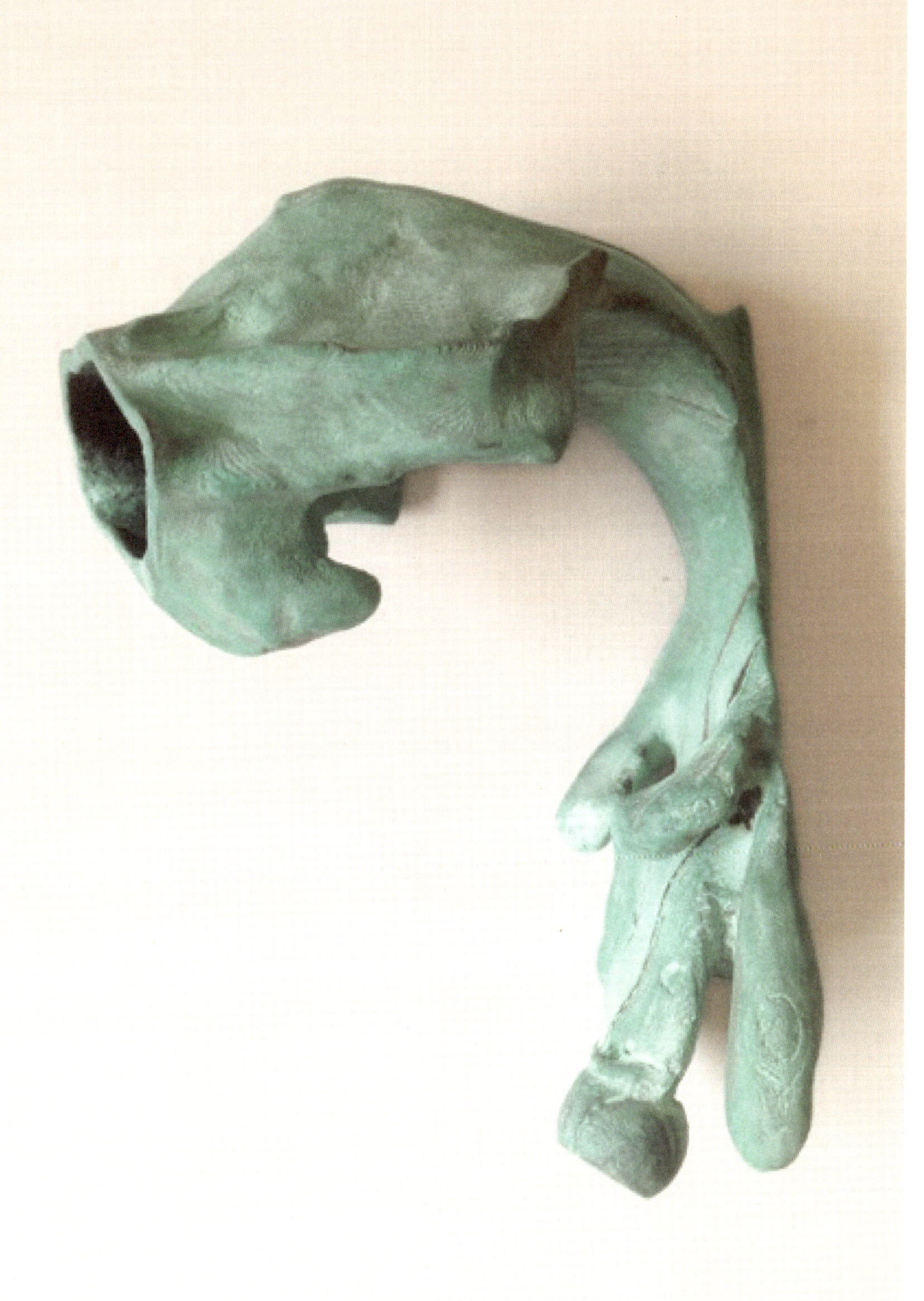

:: 33. Aargh, *A as an object*

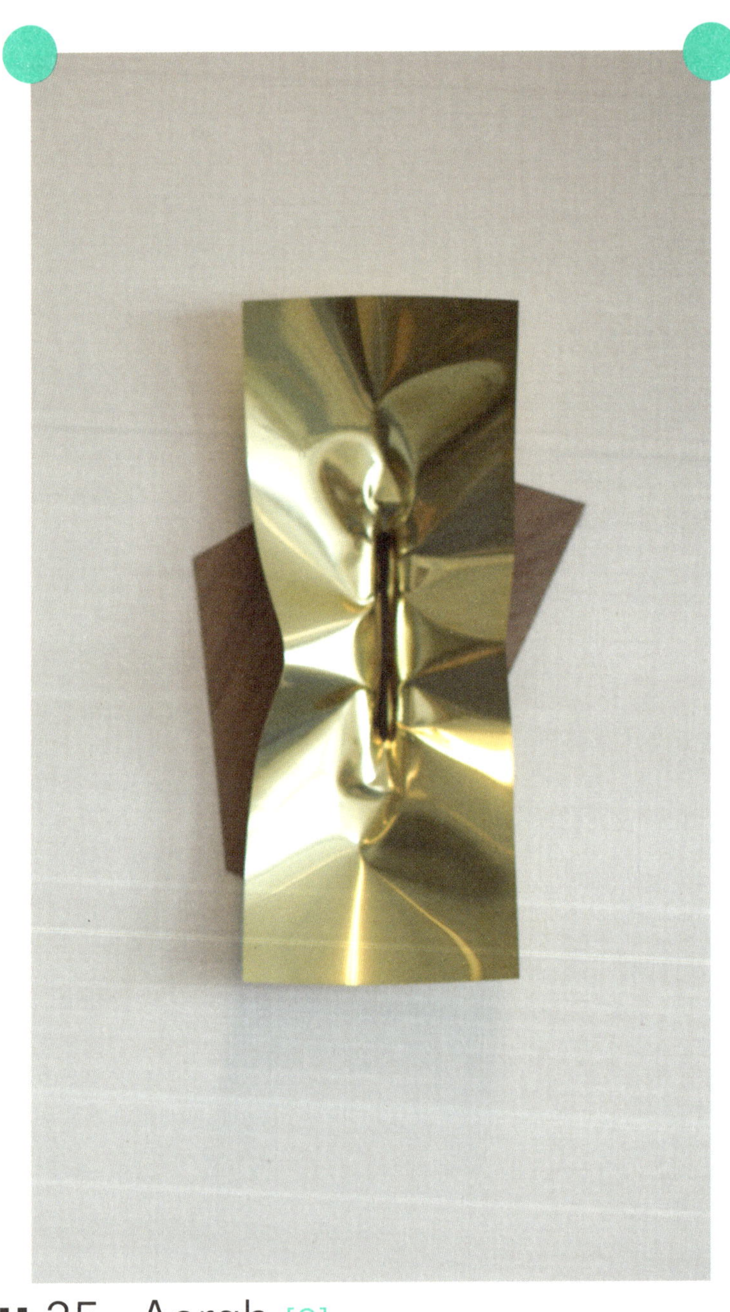

❌ 34. ❌ 35. Aargh [2]

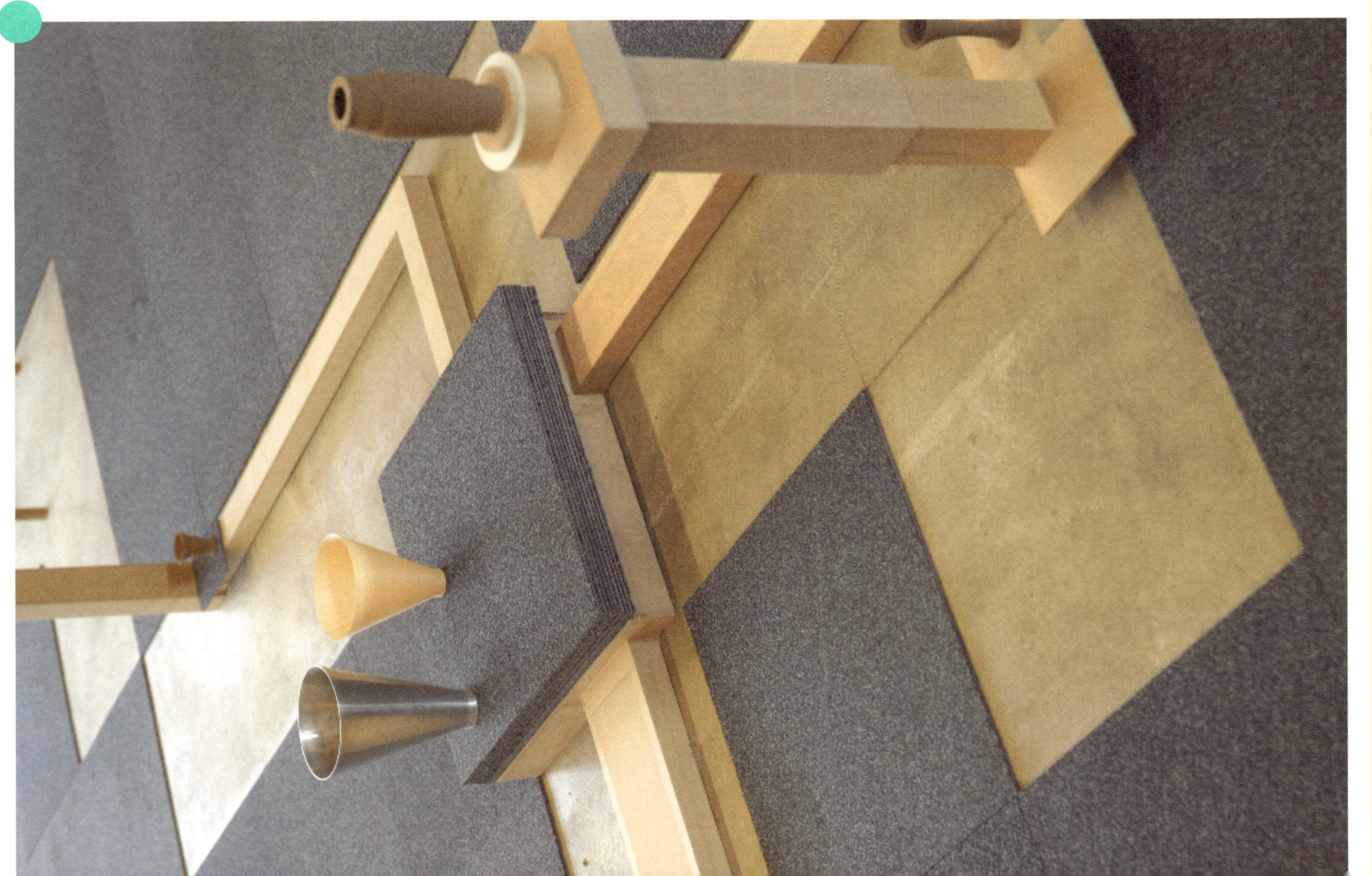

Aargh

II

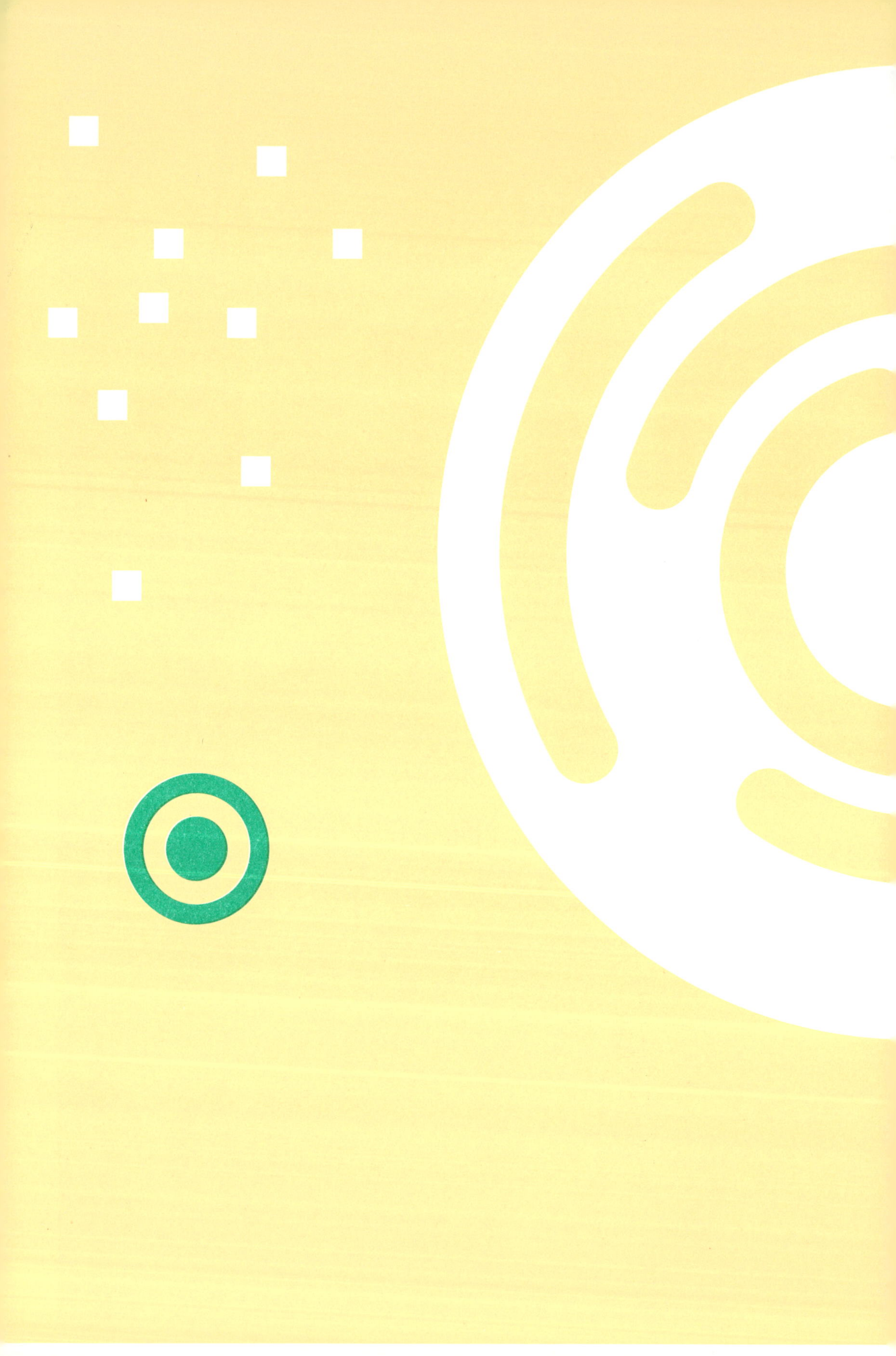

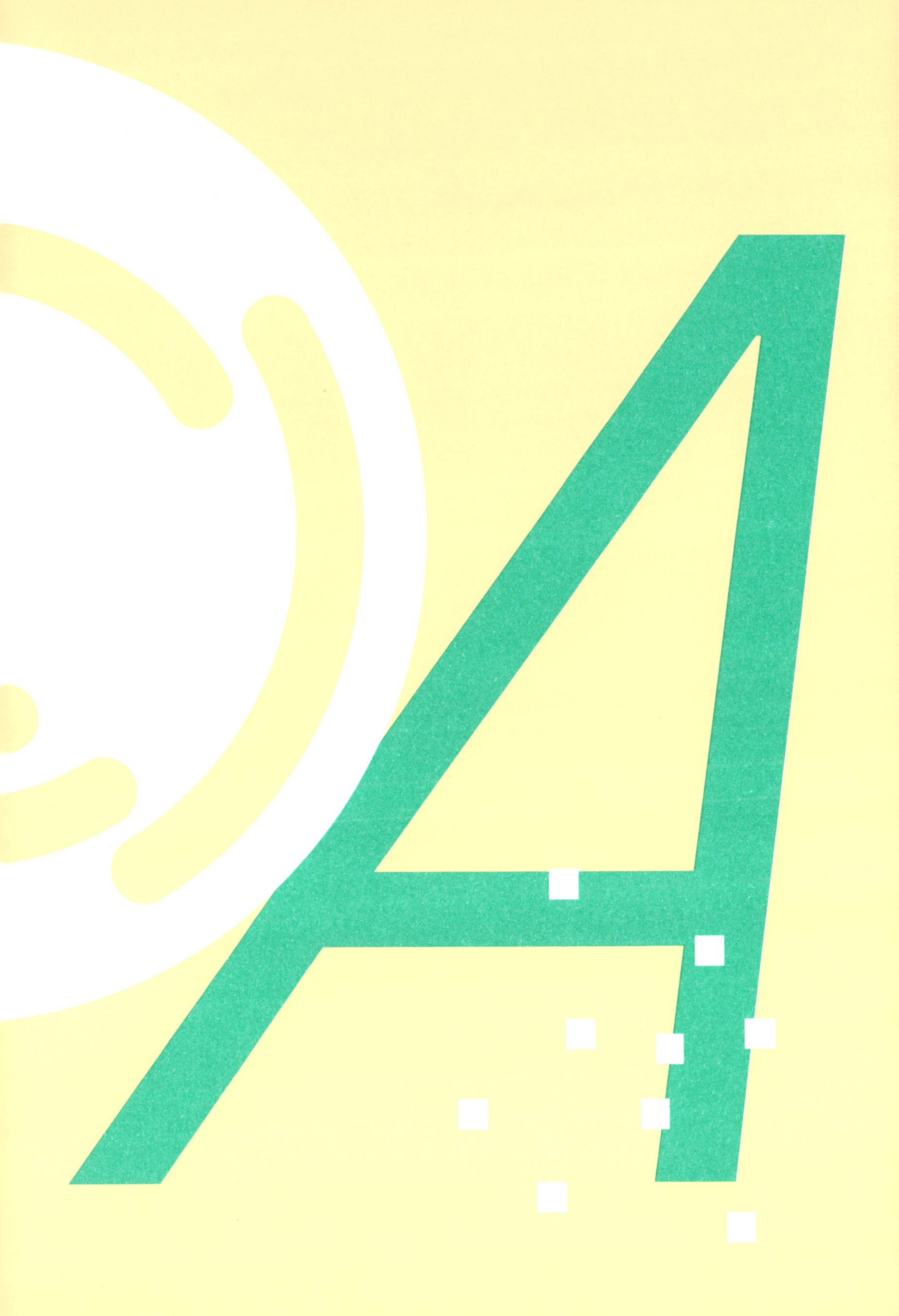

Velosynth
Luc Kerléo

During the summer of 2012, on the occasion of a workshop for the exchange of knowledge on self-built bikes, I laid the foundations of a project to build a streamlined horizontal tricycle. But in discovering the Alotof project, what could have remained a workshop adventure on the side has become an artistic project the meaning of which I am still trying to fathom. I am still amazed that I took up this creation. As I developed my artistic activity, I realized quickly enough that, in retrospect, I was more interested in understanding the ideas that had motivated my creations, while I felt much less comfortable predefining projects-to-be in a linear and controlled way. I play the oracle to see the direction my artistic activity goes, the point of this game being to develop a reflection on my own activity.

At the very beginning of my artistic career, I started with abstract painting, which quickly evolved into the creation of visual environments. I had connected my work with electronic sound experiment recordings to achieve sound environments, which I have been developing during the greater part of my career. The common point lies perhaps in an experience of everyday spaces, which is the experience that I am striving to put forward and convey to the public. I am interested in the spaces that we pass through every day — urban, peri-urban and road spaces especially — but in the sense of the sensory-motor experience that can come out of it.

It is through working on my sound environments, which hew closely to the idea of minimal sculpture, that I have taken an interest in the movements of the audience. How do we, as an audience, shift of our own initiative in the exhibition space around the sculptures and works of art in general? I find a similar movement at work in the urban space, through wandering there aimlessly. Building a machine that is able to transform the movements made in walking into a gliding on the straight surface of the streets, roads and other drivable surfaces has thus become particularly attractive. If the tangible space was to be visited in the manner of visiting an exhibition, why not then equip the human body with a movement transformer, giving it the fluidity of a car, all the while still maintaining contact with the direct sensory appeal of displacement. So this entails no motor, in order to sculpt the movement of the displacement, but wheels are needed.

You might think of a bike. But what would a vélo à regard be? The tricycle, or delivery tricycle, had

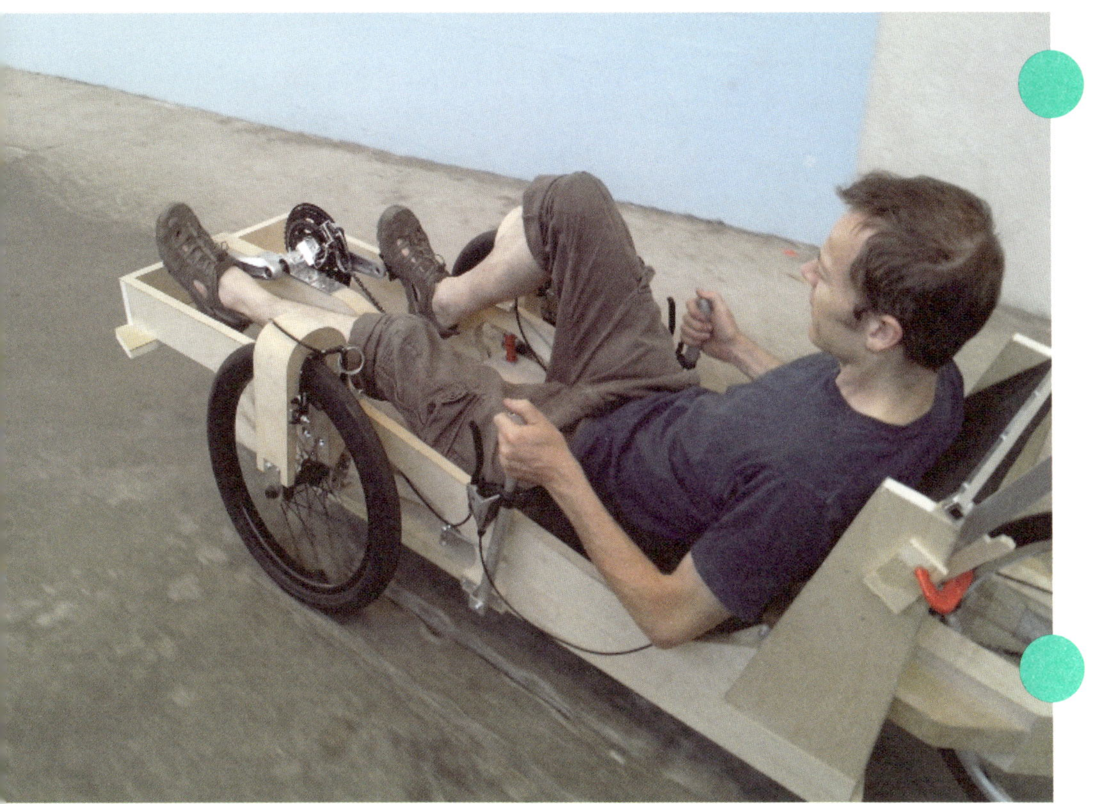

⠿ 36. Velosynth testdrive

already been appearing in my sketchbooks for some years, linked to ideas for video to shoot. It was an interesting trail to follow, in order to get certain camera movements in urban areas that I was planning to shoot. A vehicle based on three points spares its user from having to manage balance, hence freeing a part of his attention and his energy.

I had another very important picture in mind: that of a solid launched into space in weightlessness and endlessly following its course. However, on the surface of the Earth, what stands in the way of the object's course is friction, and notably — what interests me here — the friction of air molecules. And so my project, supported by aerodynamics, was made to adopt the position of driving in a deck-chair-like way, and streamlining its movement. And once these data were taken, my documentary research led me logically to an invention dating back to the 1980s: the bike-mobile, a human-powered vehicle, of which early versions were sold by manufacturers primarily based in Northern Europe.

But at the same time, I discovered the creations of self-builders, which encouraged me to build my vehicle myself. This was an exciting opportunity to experiment with reality bound to the laws of physics that apply to motion in space, by getting into the very manufacture of what was going to operate this change in movements. I worked as if preparing a work of art for exhibition, but with the difference being, that the location was, so to speak, movement. After all, this was for me the continuation of the introduction of sound into my work as a visual artist, along with everything that this invisible matter involves in movement in space and time.

The work is only presented to the audience as remnants, documents, a vehicle held in an exhibition — all the fragmentary forms, the artwork existing in its complete form only in the daily displacements of the vehicle. It is simply a question of the position of the audience, and is suggestive to them of a concrete mobility in its own space. It is rather a tool of regarding, rather than an object to regard. It is a project from a point of view, but a mobile one, a point of view on the move. One may think of kinetic art, but with the difference being that here, in the perspective of developing this artistic work, it is the audience who is set in motion. Its forms are the curves of the vehicle's trajectory.

—

Le déjeuner sur l'herbe

*Claire Astigarraga
& Dominique Leroy*

A Laboratory On The Open Fields

Art works

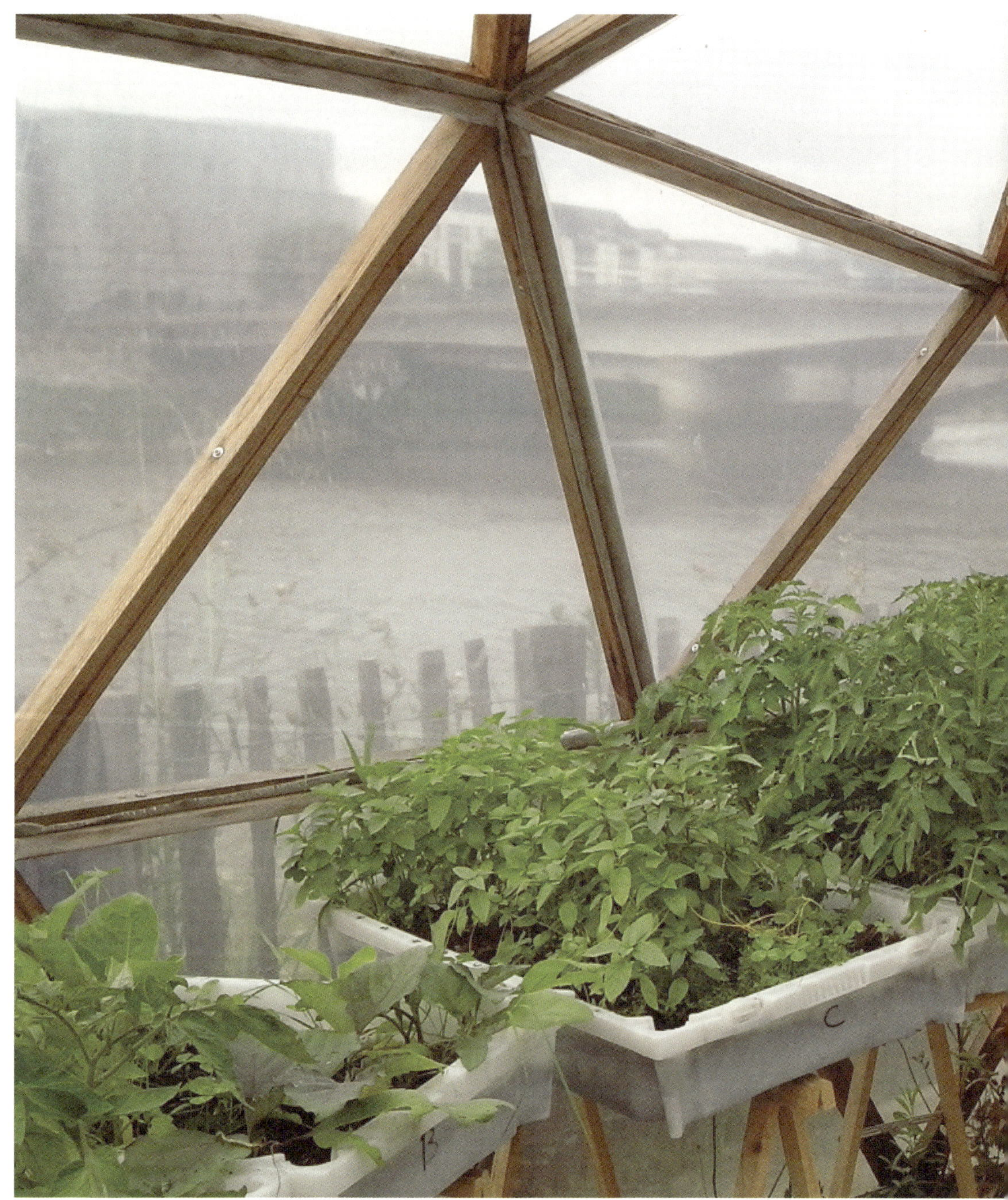

37. ECOS, Nantes

Le déjeuner sur l'herbe is an artistic action taking place in the Clos-Toreau area. Its goal is to co-direct and animate an ephemeral outdoor restaurant, as well as a cookbook, by cross-referencing culinary art, design, home improvement, gardening, photography, typography, editing, screen printing, etc.

Supported by the city of Nantes under the cultural proximity policy "l'Art en Partage", this project is a shared creation, developed not only with artists, but mostly with the inhabitants. ECOS is therefore joining with neighborhood associations and offers the inhabitants inventive and friendly activities to design their own picnic kit, their table and its scenography, with originality, by means of cardboard, cooking and screen printing workshops.

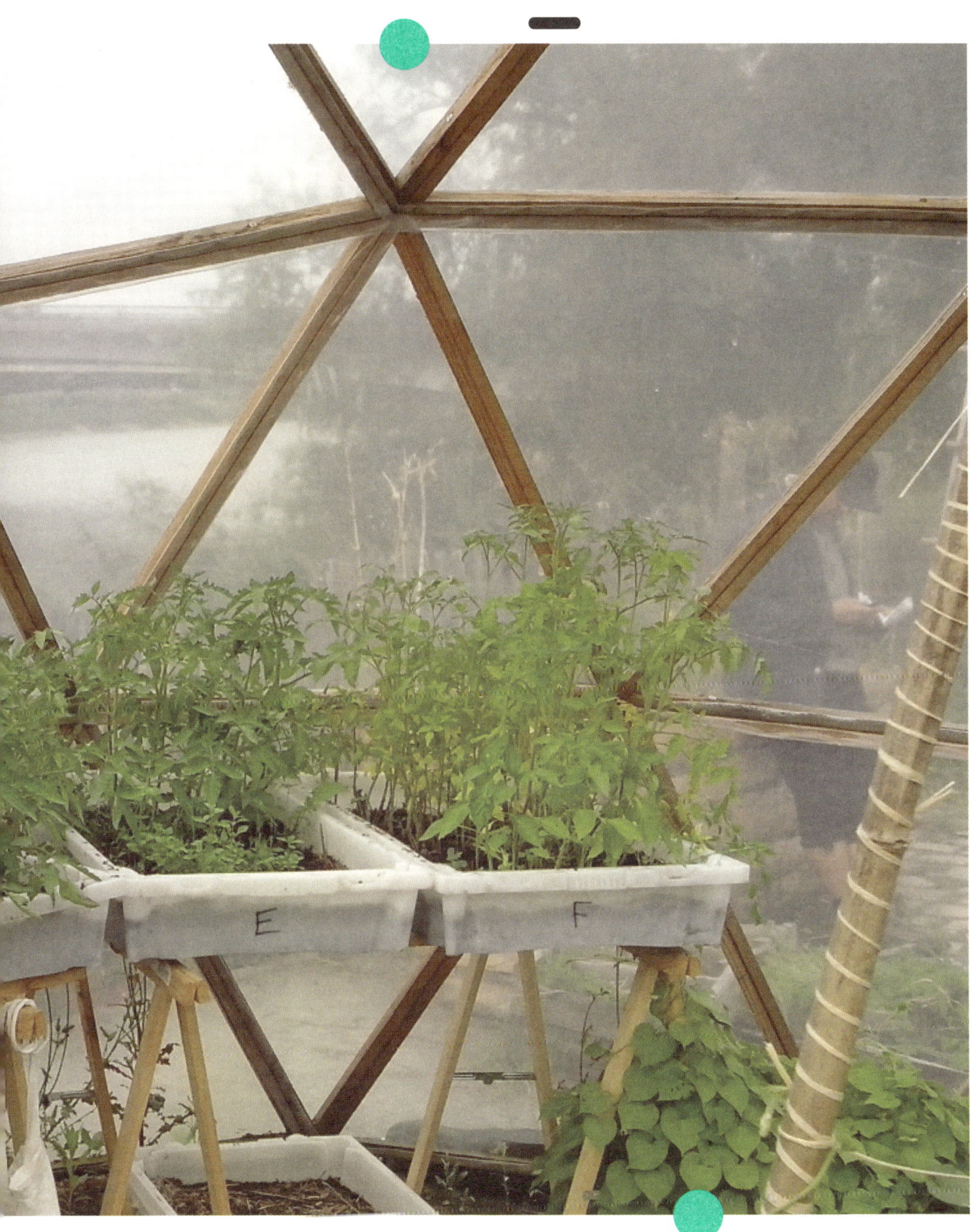

A Short Diary
Jan Kostolansky

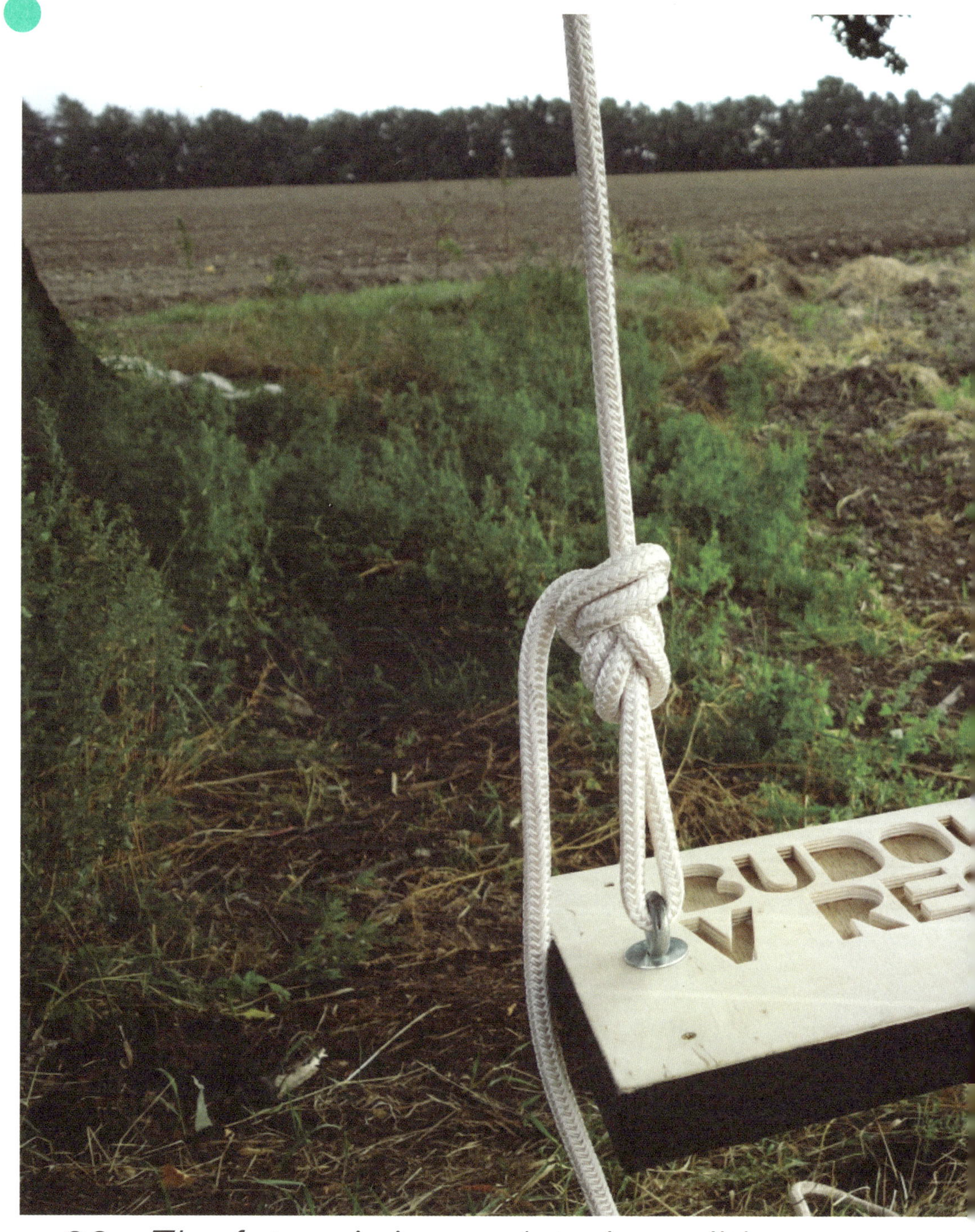

38. *The future is in regulated conditions*

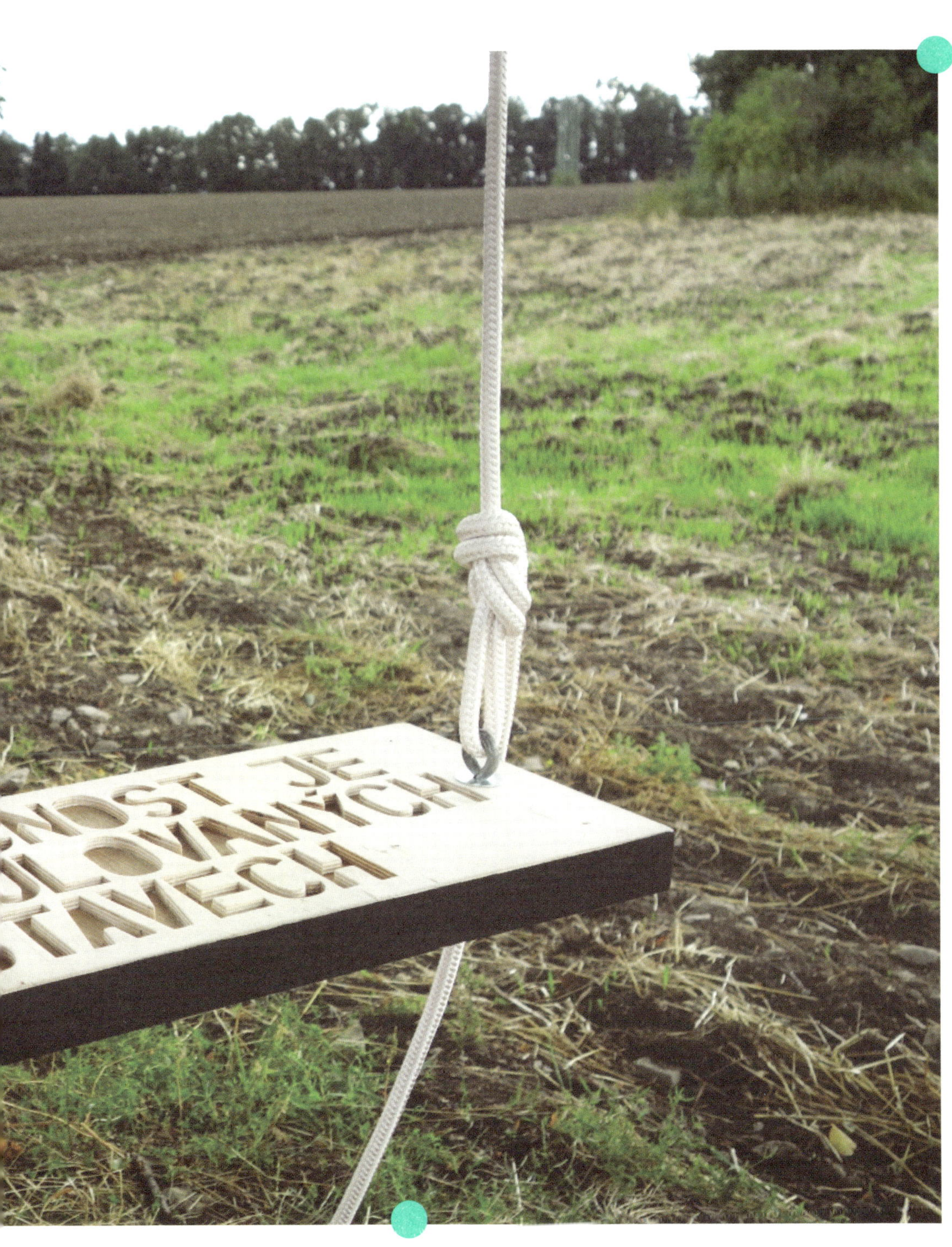
NOST JE
LOVANÝCH
TAVECH

August 2014. I'm travelling from Trenčín in Slovakia to Kravín in Hranice u Malče, located in the Vysočina region of the Czech Republic. I set out on my journey two days before the planned date of arrival. I travel by bicycle. I ritually cross the border at Starý Hrozenkov — ritually, that is, on a mental level. The culture of driving doesn't change, I still pedal through the easternmost, unrestrained block. Intensively, I try to feel the environment, especially in the context of hunting and all the related thematic areas it touches upon in this archaic style of life. Here, the architecture of hunting blinds (Czech/Slovak: posedy), one of observation and shooting, is different from Slovakia. Often, I see lightweight constructions that use the structure of trees, or simple A-form tent-like structures that resemble a portable step ladder, with space enough for one person, some with a small shelter. They seem to be quite uncomfortable compared to the massive Slovak watchtowers.

The first day: 174 km, excellent weather.

I look for budget lodging in the city called Černá Hora and its surroundings. A difficult task. A petit bourgeois and non-confrontational nationalism is at every corner. I lodge at a dadaist-communist dormitory, which at first sight seems improvised. It is damp and small. The janitor recommends that I keep my bike in the room. The second day, an almost identical story. I enjoy excellent scrambled eggs, together with the smile of an elderly waitress, on a plastic terrace on a busy street of an unknown town, in the middle of rush hour, as the working crowd hurries to their jobs, their morning faces still sullen and half-awake.

At the 105th kilometer, I reach Kravín. The service is excellent, the atmosphere wonderful, people friendly, the surroundings beautiful and desolate at the same time. I feel at home in this environment, despite the slight differences. In the following days, I explore the area on foot.

I create my first non-electrified, one-person interactive installation with a wide conceptual background, arbitrarily interpretable, with the working title "I hunt, because I like it". It is a material occupation of a real hunting blind. I enclose this "autonomous" space of primates who are avid hunters with cut-to-measure wooden blocks. The only way for the visitor inside the object to see the surroundings is to look through a peep hole in the front wall of the structure. The peep hole has the form of a carved interpolated textual idea, by which I denote the intentions of the large community of hunters.

Then I create my second non-electrified, one-person interactive installation with a wide conceptual background, arbitrarily interpretable, with the working title "The future consists of regulated numbers". It is a functional, publicly accessible wooden swing with a spatial carved textual record in its upper sitting layer. The swing is intended for a medium-slim adult. It is located on a strategically important and pleasant spot. It hangs from a height of approximately ten meters and is anchored on a huge branch of one of the two, evidently very old, landmark trees, which from a distance visually merge into one. The view from the swing is a panorama of the environment, a part of the Železné Hory (Iron Mountains). You can also see the local agricultural co-op, as well as Kravín. I strongly believe that this work will serve its purpose for a very long time.

My residency triptych culminated with a spontaneous object, which also could be described as a non-electrified, one-person interactive installation with a wide conceptual background, arbitrarily interpretable, with the working title "Civic surveillance". It is a wooden chair with a carved textual reference on the seat, with legs of different lengths. I intentionally "forget" this object in the forest road during the opening tour. Not interested in its destiny, I allow it be absorbed by the conditions.

I left the outdoor screening of the documentary movie "Hey to the Hunt", showing the world of the hunting community, after about five minutes, slightly pissed off, with elevated blood pressure and adrenalin. To my surprise I find a similarly afflicted group among the other participants of the screening inside Kravín who, like me, do not want to let their good evening mood be spoiled. Later I get to know that the movie was technically well made.

My residency ends up with a carnival party, during which I take advantage of the chance to be taken to the hotel in Chotěboř. It rains the following day. I travel home by train. The residency was physically very active for me. Traveling under on my own power, surveying the area, transferring from my night lodgings to Kravín and back, two walking trips to the town, installing the works, wine evenings. It was also very inspiring. I am glad I could participate.

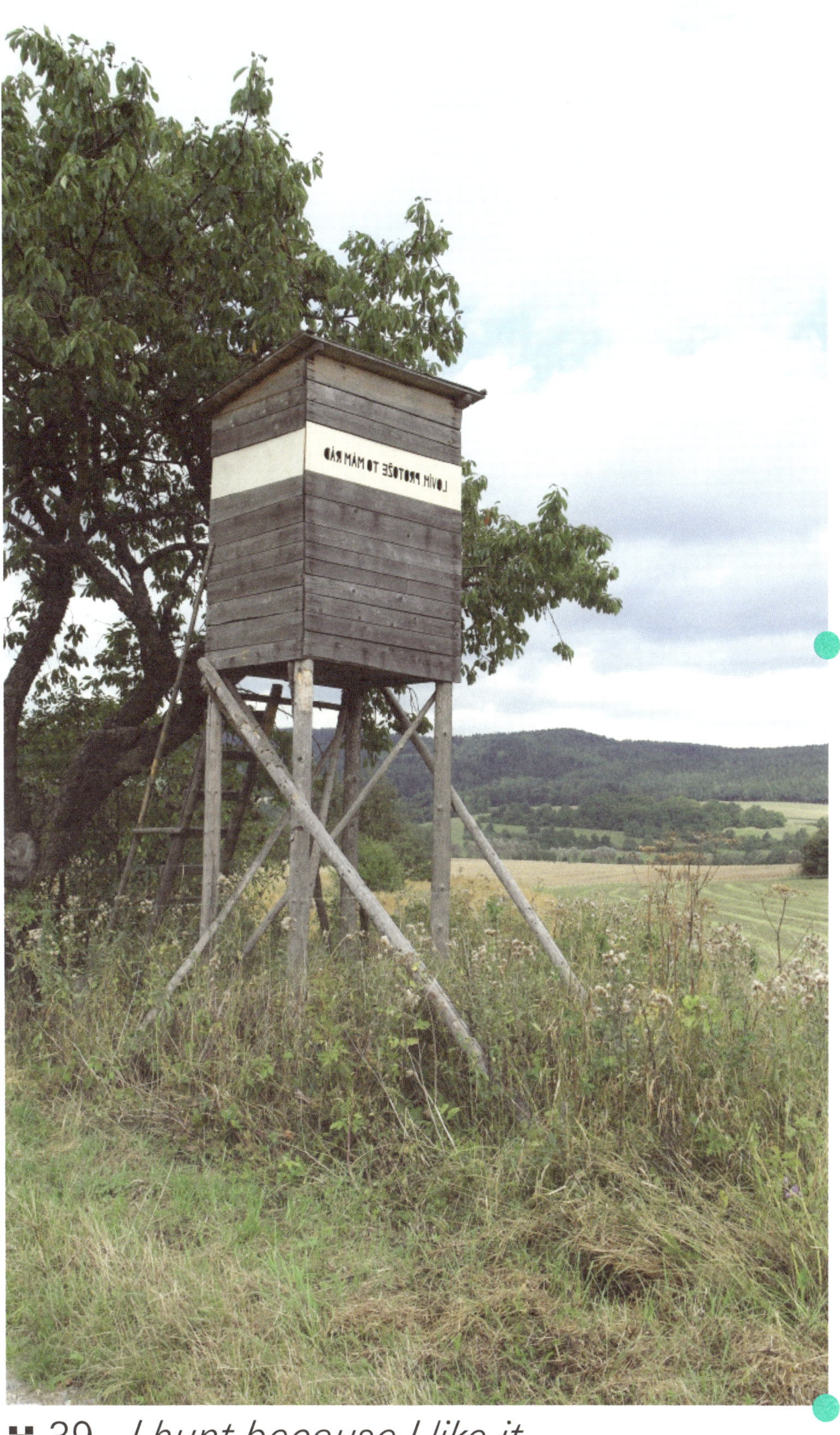

39. *I hunt because I like it*

Hunting Blinds
Martin Janíček

There were several layers present in my thinking about working with hunting blinds. Hunters – despite my total aversion for simplification and generalization – are a strange group of people with guns and an interest in shooting.

In the first phase, I had the idea of working with natural materials, I was thinking about camouflage, and recreating the current form of the hunting blind, and about creating a new form in the natural environment: Fusion? Contrast? Something about enclosure and separation, but also voyeurism, spying and snooping. But there has been already enough of that in our country. I also considered using stuffed animals and birds: Lures and snares. Later I realized the possibility of working with the sounds of animals, and eventually I remembered the phenomenon of animal calls, and the entire elaborated system of how to lure animals so that they – hoping to find a mate – come instead to death. The hunter hides, maliciously waiting, and shoots without restraint once the animal is within range.

I finally had it, once I realized that it would be best to combine both ideas and create a complete "UFO" that landed at the edge of the woods, producing sounds that certainly would not attract any animals. For the deformation of the sound I used a hundred-meter-long, red pipe for protecting electric cables, which I wrapped around the upper part of the hunting blind. I then connected four different animal callers and a vuvuzela to it. Entering visitors could whistle, howl and shriek, and the long pipe surely distorted everything beyond recognition.

I didn't have to wait long for reactions from the hunters' side. The very day before the opening tour, a hunter with his wife arrived in his Land Rover, astonished, asking what it represents, and what do we mean by saying that certainly no animals will come to it? When they found out that my French colleague Dominique Leroy at the neighboring hunting blind was "listening to grass", the hunter declared he doesn't want to understand it at all and then drove away. Other reactions came during the dismantling process. Another hunter came and asked, what does that mean? He explained that his hunting colleague, a bus driver, spotted it and was wondering, what is it that Franta has hung on his hunting blind? He said that it is not possible, it is like a rag for a bull.

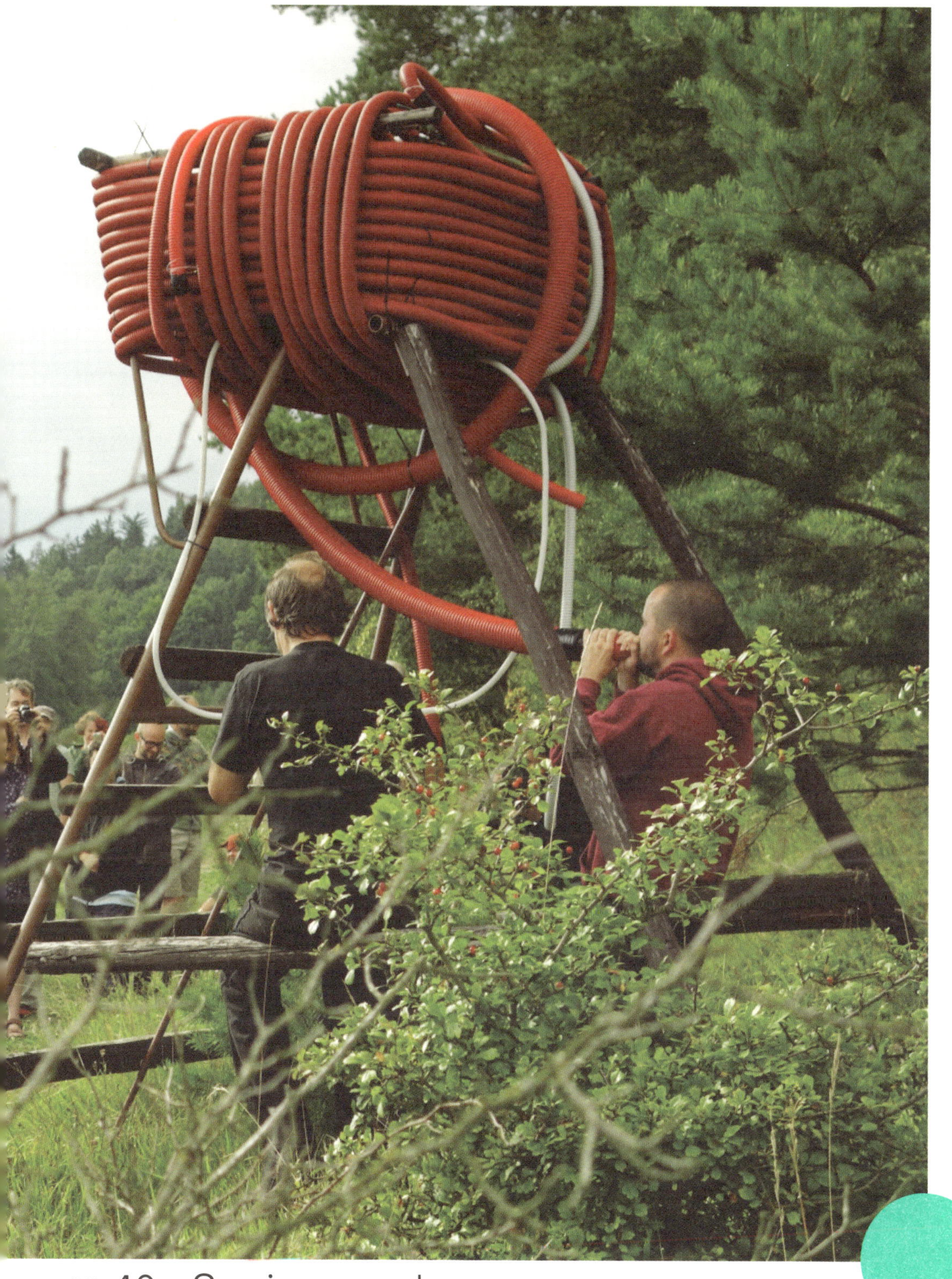

⚫ 40. Sonic posed

To See More
Jan Poupě

Kites are toys that make use of construction and architecture, inspired by the Bauhaus. At the same time, they foster a pure fascination with flying and the ability to build an object that can fly. The principle is simple, but the construction can be challenging. The seriousness and complexity of the building process arises after meeting certain requirements. For me, the central interest is carrying capacity, so that I can put a camera on the kite. This requirement necessitated more intricate constructions and new materials. The original concept began to produce the search for new forms and methods. A series of many variations emerges. There are many methods and approaches, but physical laws eliminate the false proposals. Kites are objects that are beautiful due to its functionality or — more precisely — function, which gives them their form. Here I could refer to Corbusiérs texts "Vers une architecture", in which he explains why airplanes and ships are beautiful but contemporary houses are not.

It fascinates me, and always surprises me a little as well, once the object takes flight. I admire the volume moving along in the air. The geometrical forms are in contrast with the landscape — they seem strange, but they are naturally connected to it. I didn't study at technical schools, I cannot calculate lift, but it makes me happy that this task cultivates my feeling for material; the ratio of weight, rigidity and utility of the individual components. Mostly, I start from existing structures and then make variations of them. This is my way of learning. I also try to apply those experiences and ideals in my other work.

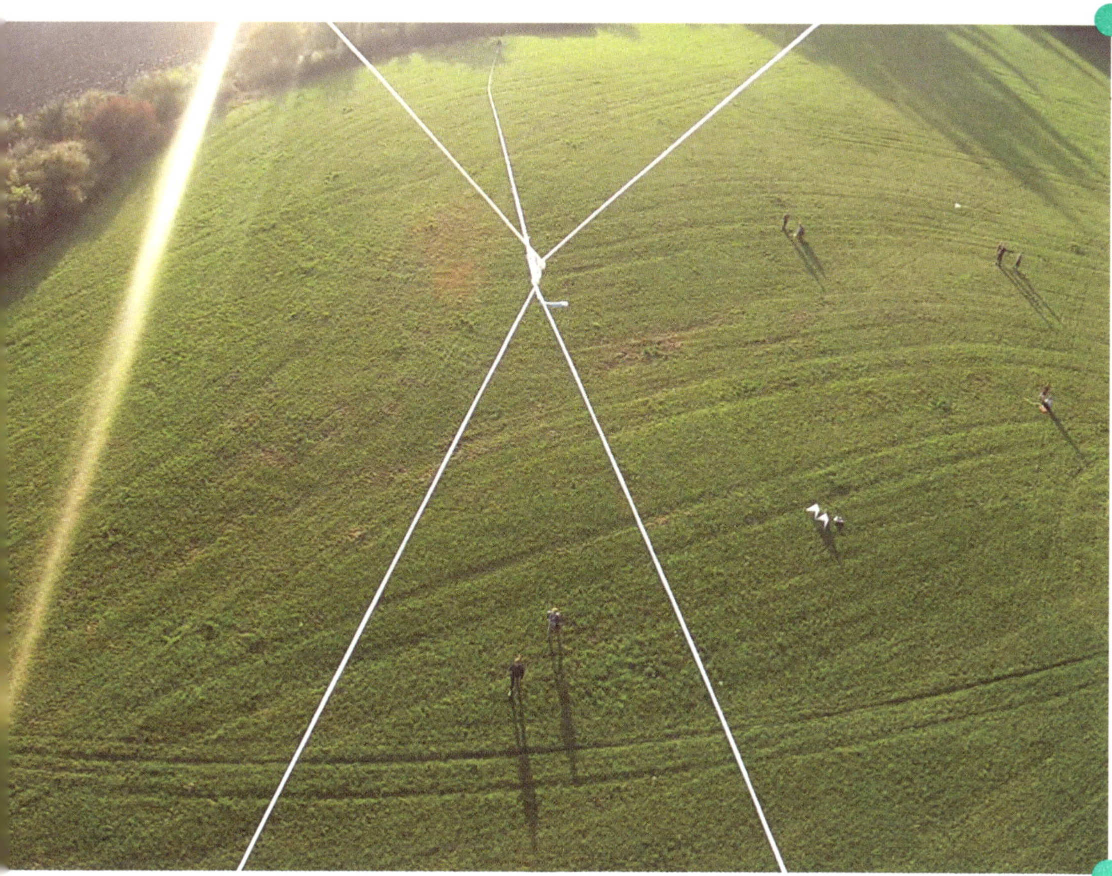

⌘ 41. Bell Kite, *the volume moving along in the air*

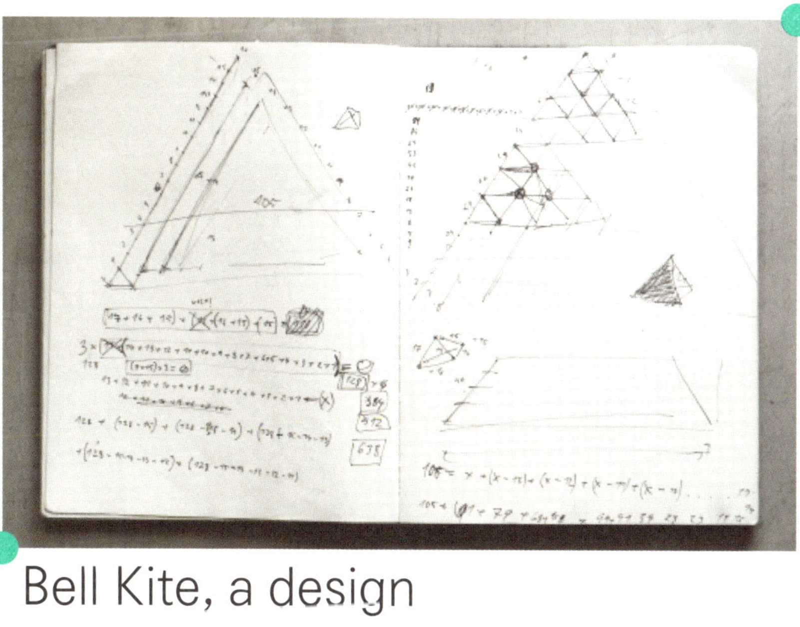

⌘ 42. Bell Kite, a design

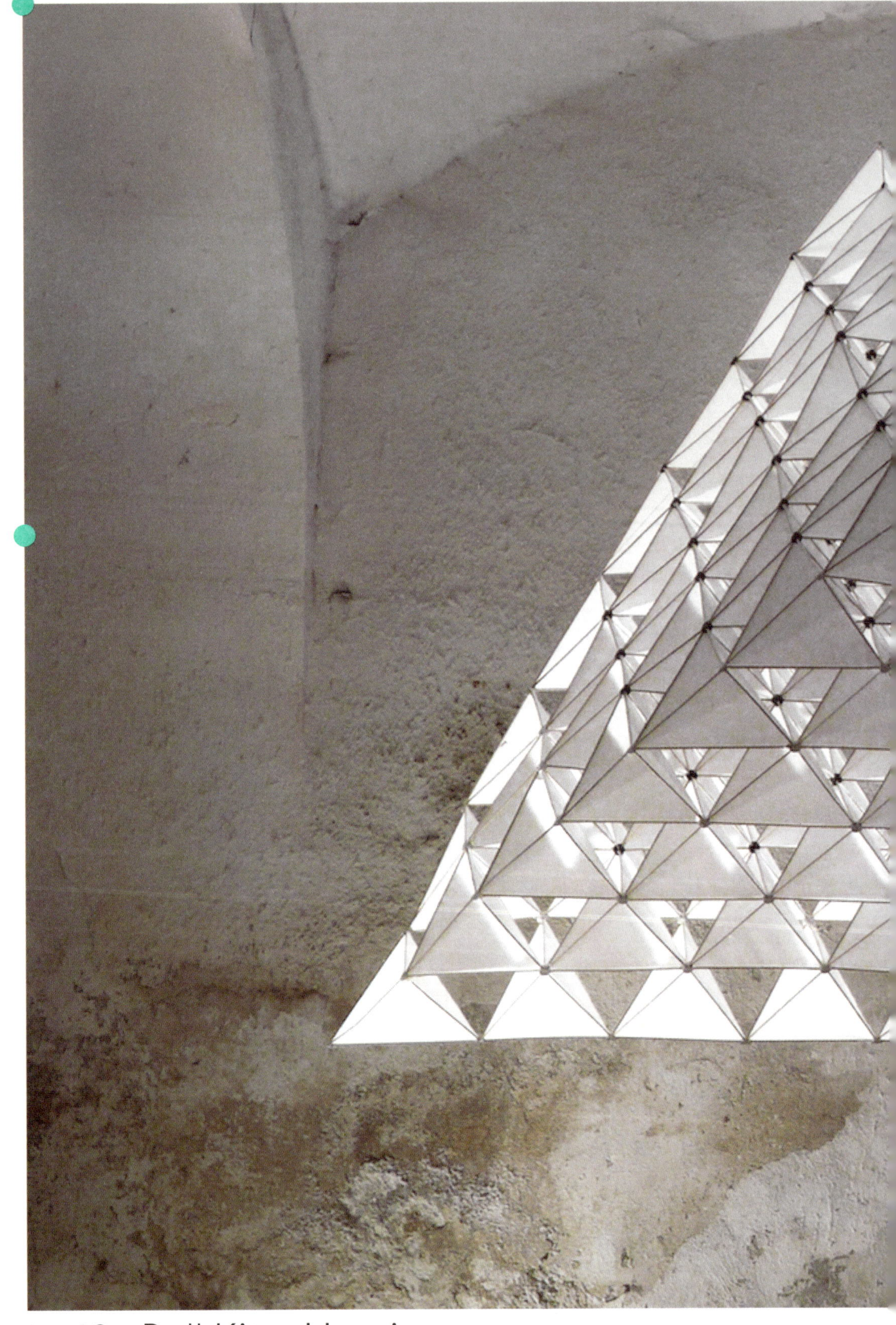

43. Bell Kite, Hranice

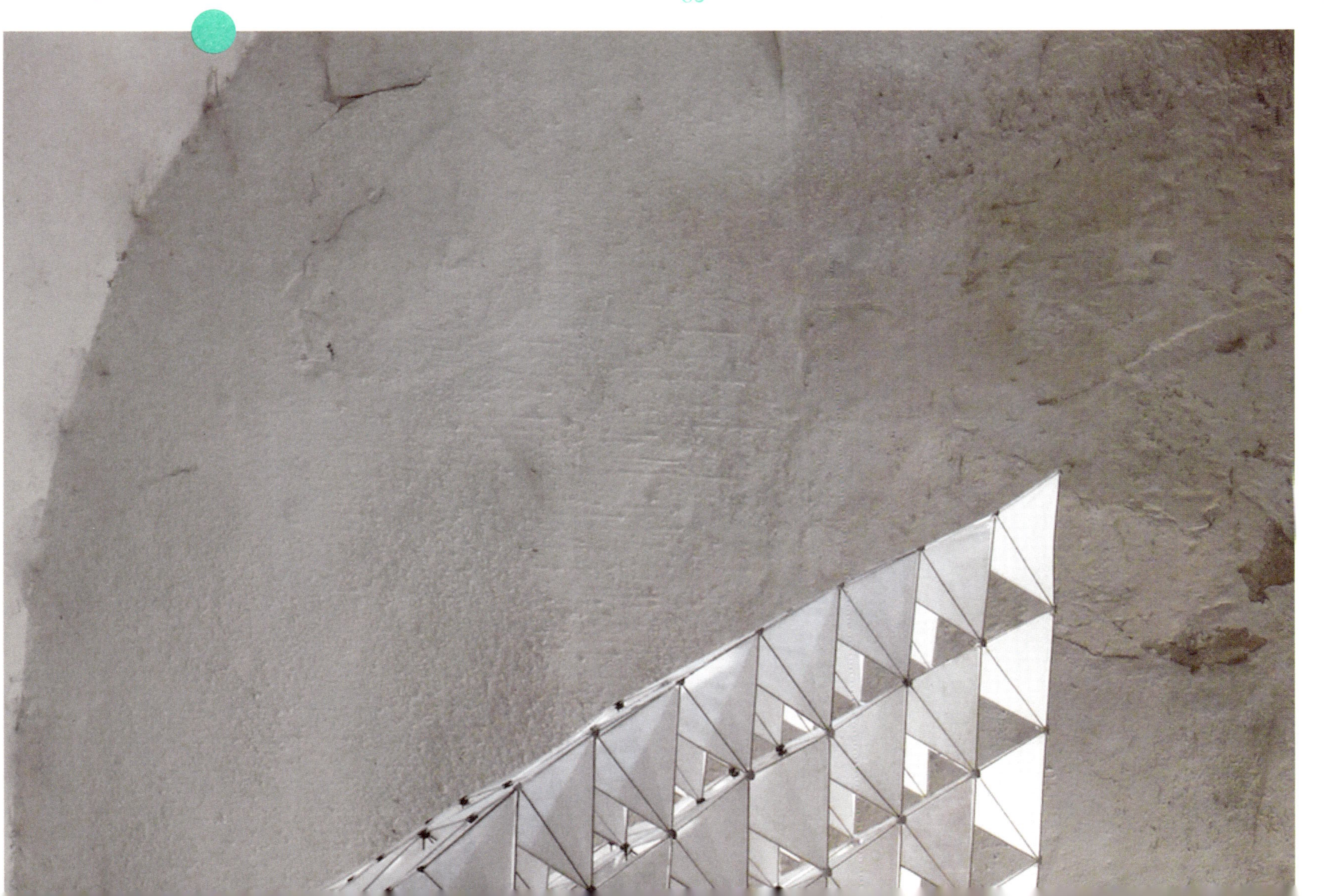

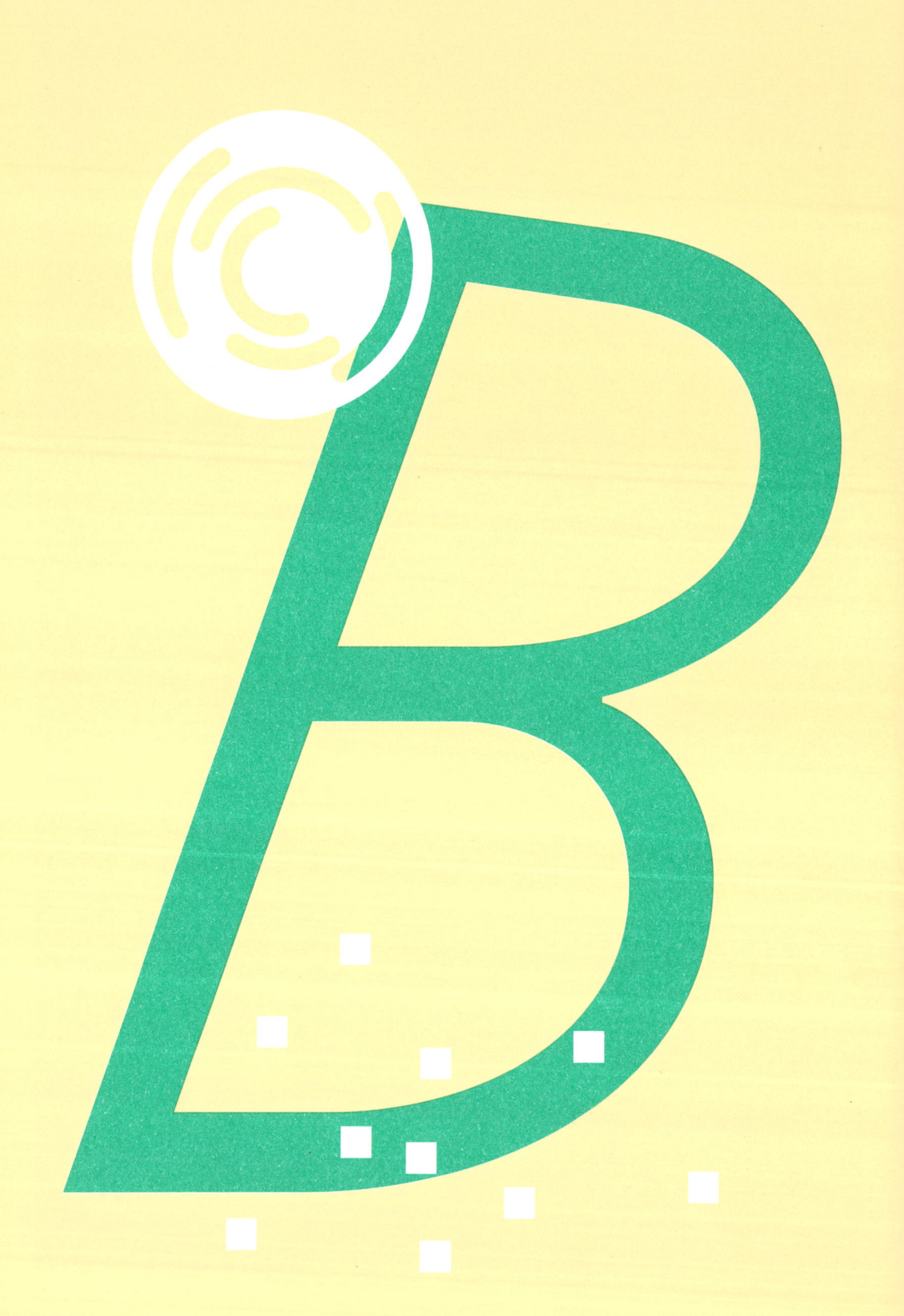

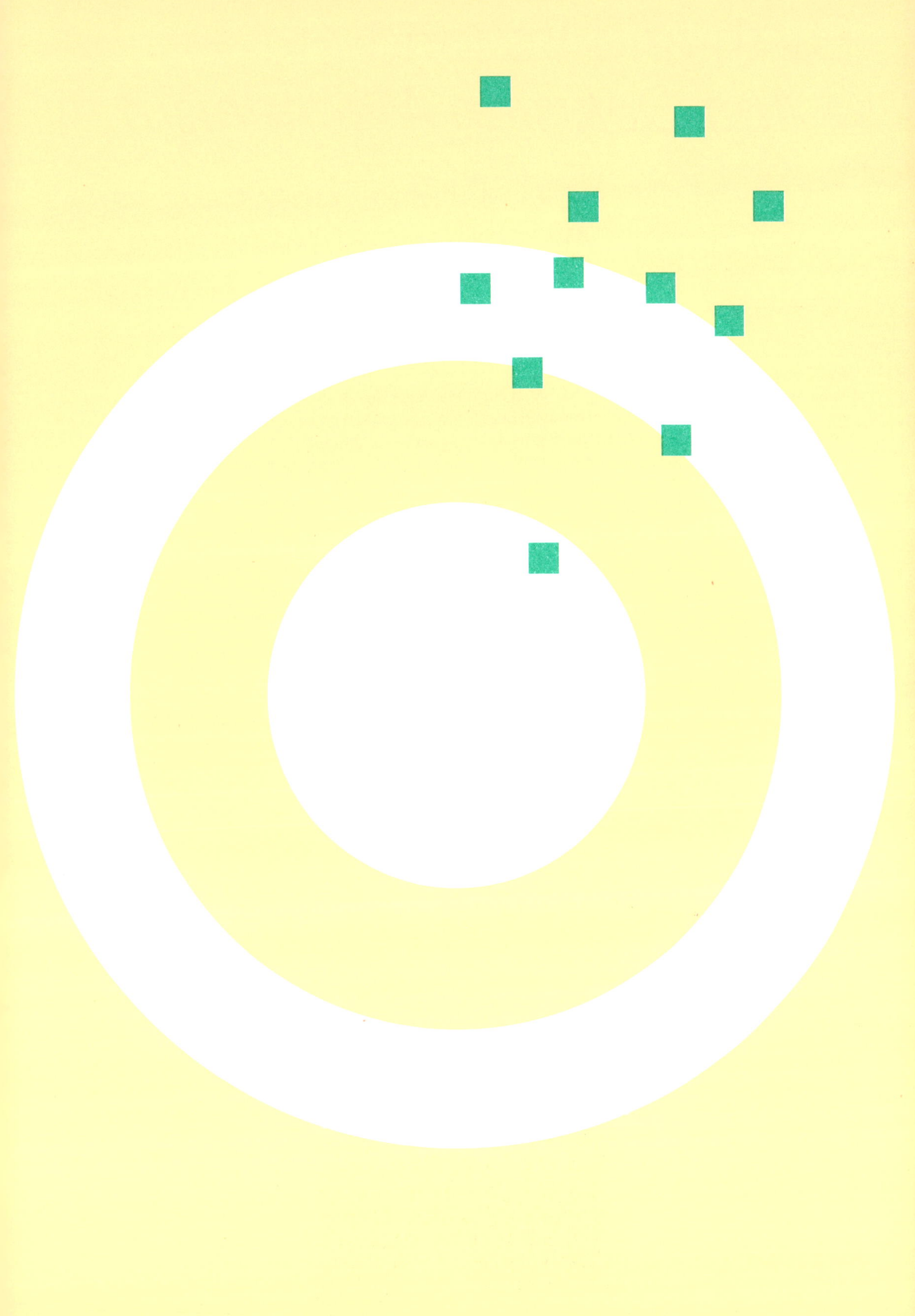

Earth and Beyond
Anti-Delusion Mechanism

It takes time to let ideas rise to the surface. It takes time to work together and imagine more than one thought was possible. And it takes time to let the imagined become real. And again more time to alter the real. We would like to move our activities with signals, sound and other time-based arts out of theatres and studios into the open air. We received a lot of inspiration —and we ask what form would it take to make possible an electronic artwork, disconnected from the electrical grid, and placed anywhere in a landscape? Can the electronic artwork enter into a life cycle with uncultivated surroundings? Can the unheard and the invisible enter our world through our devices?

For a long time, the earth has been known to carry electrical currents, so we decided to take up an investigation of this energy source, which we hoped could eventually serve to sustain installations. The telluric currents run from south to north, and stories about functional "earth batteries" go back almost two centuries. So we attempted to build such earth batteries. We placed metals in the ground in a variety of arrangements and measured their potential, but have yet to find potentials high enough to run small basic amplifiers and other things needed for an installation. But many possibilities are yet untested, and so the experiment will continue over the years as our knowledge and intuition grow together.

Although we have not achieved a successful method of drawing enough energy directly from the ground, at least the batteries which run our things are mostly charged with a Bedini wheel. (John Bedini is an American electrical engineer who has developed his own interpretation and implementation of Tesla technology [1]). Around this time, we stumbled upon some writings by Gerry Vassilatos from Borderland Sciences, in which he describes how, in the early 1990s, he was recording telluric signals onto magnetic tape and transposing the signals down in pitch by slowing down the tape [2].

We took this as an inspiration for our earth installations, using a small computer and sound card together with PureData to capture these signals and transpose the ultra-sonic signals down to audible frequencies, live. We also tinkered with copper figures hung high up in the trees under the sun, as proposed by the eccentric John Hutchison, in a search for electrical currents and signals. Then Bryan built 2 VLF (Very low frequency) receivers [3] and we drove to the coast to test them, since they are known to receive well near the sea.

Out, On and Under the Field

For the Posedy event at Kravín, Czech Republic, we spread our activities out in a few directions. We made six small speakers with amplifiers, which later turned out to be obvious references to the many posedy (hunting blinds) around Kravín, this being the theme of the event. The idea was to use two of them for VLF receivers, two units to transpose ultrasonic signals from the ground and two speakers for live amplified performance. One characteristic of this location is the presence of high tension power lines that cross nearby, which "bathe" the surroundings in 50hz waves, basically drowning out everything else. The reality was that the location offered no useable VLF signals, and so the signals from the ground became more central in the project. So an electro-mechanical "trap" was constructed, a reference to the use of traps by hunters, and therefore relating to the theme of posedy. This trap would warn or scare off potential hunting trophies from being captured or shot. We combined the installation with a performance of dance and music on and around one posed, using materials found in the field and a dead tree as musical instrument.

Succession

The project with Alotof has added a new path in our work. This year especially will be directed at refining and evaluating the sound installations that transpose the telluric signals. All instruments are

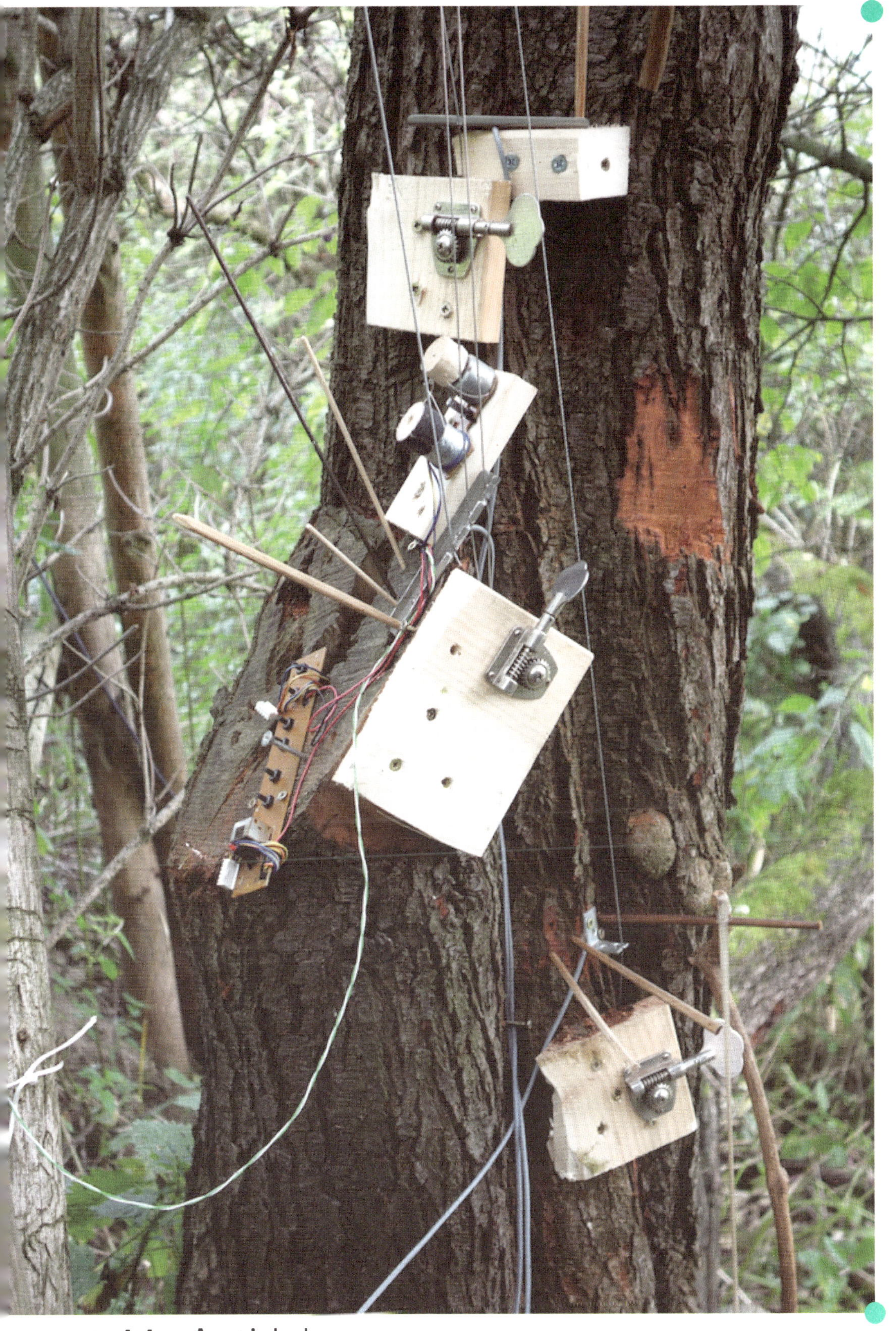

⊞ 44. Antidel

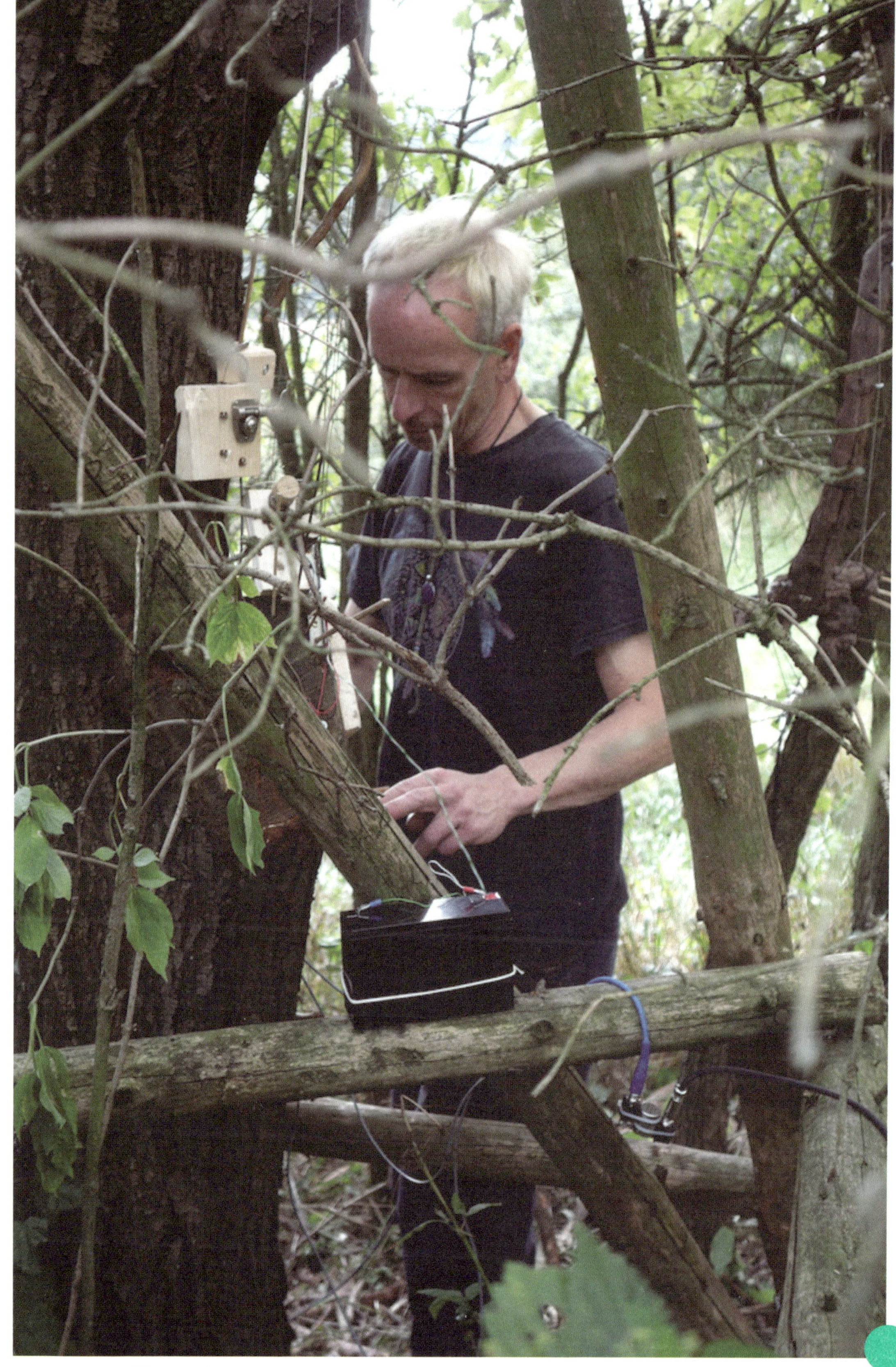

⦂ 45. Earth and Beyond

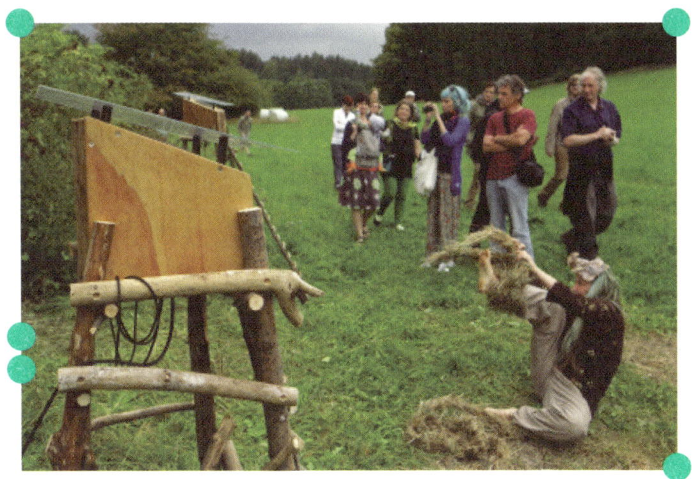

⚏ 46. Earth and Beyond

sources of noise — or sound, if you will — and to decipher exactly what comes from where is an extensive task when working with relatively small signals which are unknown, undocumented and further seem to change over time and from place to place. We have created a web page which is meant to document this process along the way. The page contains sound documents and analysis [4]. The telluric signals have shown themselves to be rather enigmatic. There are certainly frequency events carried in the earth, but it is still a matter of much investigation (recording and developing techniques) before one can even start to get a picture of what is derived from human activities and what comes from other sources, such as nature.

Yet another task is to make the earth installations mobile, and to adapt them to a semi-urban environment, perhaps by looking more for the man-made artifacts and accepting the elusiveness of nature within a city. Adapting to the environment is crucial to our success in bringing our ideas to life and further development. In addition to the installations, we strive to incorporate interaction, and current directions being considered are a brain control interface to interact with computer software, and integration of elements from the location(s) into the presentation.

———

1   http://johnbedini.net
2   https://borderlandsciences.org/journal/
    vol/48/n06/Vassilatos_Recording_
    Telluric_Signals.html

3   taken largely from the NASA
    project inspire: http://theinspireproject.
    org/default.asp?contentID=4
4   http://antidelusionmechanism.org/
    EarthPage.html

Fruit of Art
Andrej Poliak

Fruit of Art is an artistic interdisciplinary project by Periférne Centrá NGO, which is active in the field of contemporary art and culture in Central Slovakian village Dúbravica. Its idea naturally follows the activities of the NGO - bringing the emerging art into the Slovak village, and therefore culturally animate and develop the rural locations. Fruit of Art joins together the agricultural activities typical for the local environment with the artistic interventions. The primary aim is the work of artist in the space of gardens and orchards. Fruit of Art opens the theme of the status of the agrarian culture in the Slovak village. We consider the developmental stage of the agrarian activity, as well as art, a symbol of the cultural state of the given locality. That is why we understand the uncomplimentary state of the local fruit gardens and orchards as a signal, that culture here is in a difficult situation.

The project has a cyclical character and primarily it is tied to the vegetational period. It includes the activities by Periférne Centrá itself, as well as interventions by the invited artists.

In 2012 when we began to map the fruit trees in the village and its surroundings, an offer from Yo-yo came to participate in the international project Alotof - a laboratory on the open fields. In this context we worked out our contribution in such a way that it connected the two areas of our interest - cultivation and art. That is how the Fruit of Art concept emerged, as well as our first ideas about the possible connections between fine arts and the production of crops, and finding artists who are able to create such connections in their work.

In the Periférne Centrá team it is me, who actively grows fruits and vegetables, and that is why the conception of the project came naturally from me. I have been looking for and approaching artists who had participated in the project so far, and I myself have also tried to realise works in the garden.

Within the framework of my approach to this theme, I research the possibilities of applying the artistic strategies during cultivating crops and its variations applicable directly on spot - in this case on a field. My artistic interventions are focused on the cultivation of spaces of "wild" abandoned agrarian areas. Here I am interested in the manual work with substances like earth, plants, with its instability, working with living material. I consider the usefulness of art like this. Actually, I recast into the project my interest in gardening and growing crops and my professional interest in working and spending time in landscape. I see manual work in landscape as a counterpoint to currently widespread work with new media, motor-based or electronic tools, digital media, movements in virtual space. This kind of activity is on the other hand aimed at the contact with living material.

It is also obvious that such a cultivation work in agrarian environment necessitates a longer time interval to get some relevant results. Moreover it is work in contrast with the high speed of life, in opposite to except that it takes place in hidden places, at the borders of urban space, often in wild corners of landscape. Plants change its shape and size in a longer time period, so there is space and necessity to let the work ripe, grow. Which means that today I create only the rudiments of work, which changes with light, humidity, weather conditions, but also with the unplanned interventions by peope or animals. Such a work can gain, but also loose it's importance over longer time periods. The first attempts in interconnecting the work of artists with agrarian work were made by Periférne Centrá in 2013. For example a microevent "Dula" by painter Juliana Mrvová. In her painter´s work she lately makes drawing studies of plants, gardens or landscape, and also her contribution in our project was done painterly. She planted "kdoule" (quince) in the landscape by Dúbravica, which is the type of fruit that does not grow in the area. Her work she explained in a painterly way - she considered

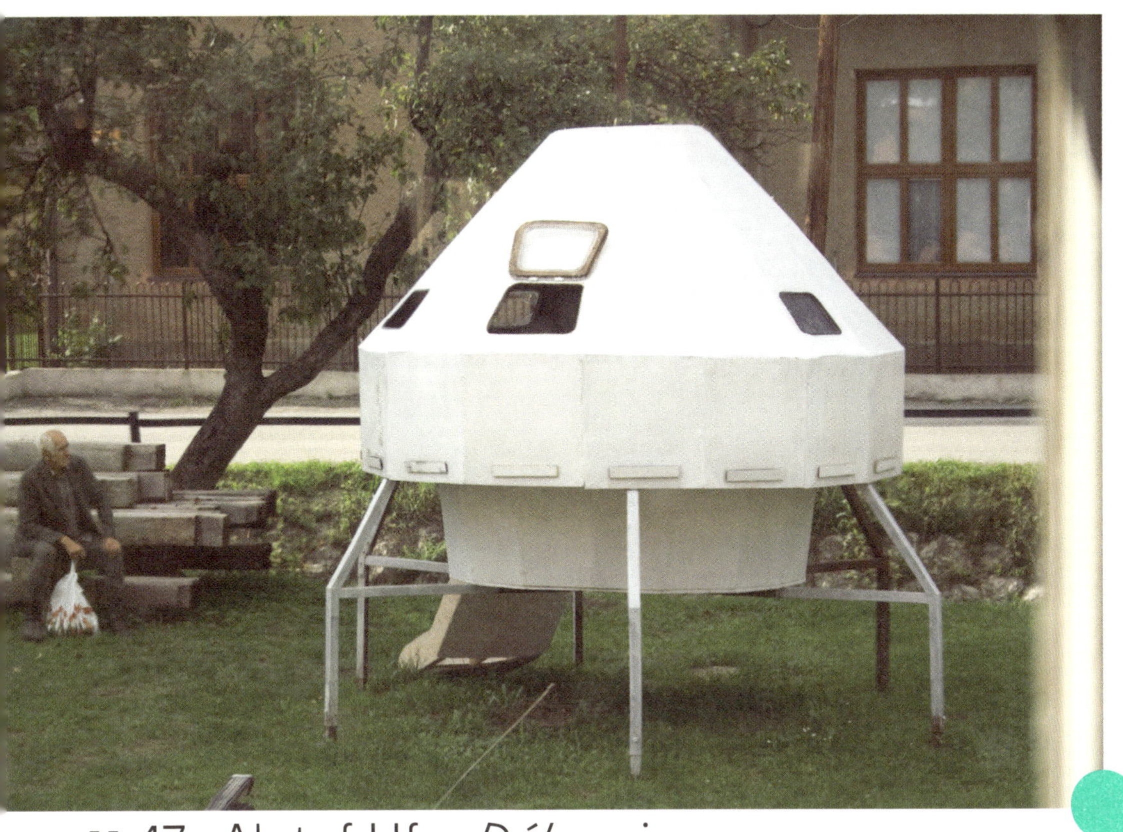

▚ 47. Alotof Ufo, *Dúbravica*

the colour of the plants or their shape on the background of the local environment as important aspects. In such a gentle way she attempted to improve the look and quality of the location. The act of growing quinces was later used by Juliana in her second intervention, realized in Dúbravica within our other project - a large format painting. Her painting on a large canvas installed in the exterior of the village depicted various hidden corners and events from the location, while the central motive of the painting is the real event of planting quinces together with helpers - local kids. While creating the artwork, she used pigments made from plants and berries common in Dúbravica gardens and in landscape.

In April 2013, the processual artwork Pestujma (Growme) was initiated in the park adjacent to Pôtoň theatre in Bátovce; additional work interventions took place in later periods of vegetation resting period. Andrej Poliak and Michaela Grznárová set up a small vegetable garden in the shape of the letters Pestujma. In the separate letters, various typical plants were planted. The proces of growth and transformation of the artwork was documented, so besides the temporary work of art growing for one summer also photographs were made which preserved the work.

In 2014 various other activities appeared in the program of Fruit of Art project. Its main focus was concentrated in spring when educational activities for public as well as creative work by artists were realized. At the beginning of April Oto Hudec started to build his object DBSP 01 (Dúbravica beekeeping space program), which - besides being a successful visual artwork - should serve as a functional beehouse as well as a small public library. He created this so called made-to-measure for Periférne Centrá. Our NGO have dedicated its time to beekeeping already for the third season. Because we would like to gradually increase the number of bee colonies, oto decided to help us and create a visual object as a beehouse. Unfortunatelly, due to the lack of experience, constructing outdoor objects, he quite failed, and the object needs to fine tune some important details to be really used as a beehouse. But it really serves as an interesting and appealing object already, located in the centre of the village it became an attraction especially for children but also visitors of the village. Oto Hudec subsequently elaborated his work by visual means and it was presented in various forms for example at his solo exhibition in Seoul, or at a collective exhibition in Bratislava.

A glance into new/digital technologies in connection to beekeeping was provided for us in Dúbravica by Guy Van Belle (Gívan Belá) - he presented his experiments with sensors installed in the beehives. These are located at various places inside the hives and measure temperature, count incoming and outcoming bees, and its data - apart from being practically used by beekeepers - also serve for art projects.

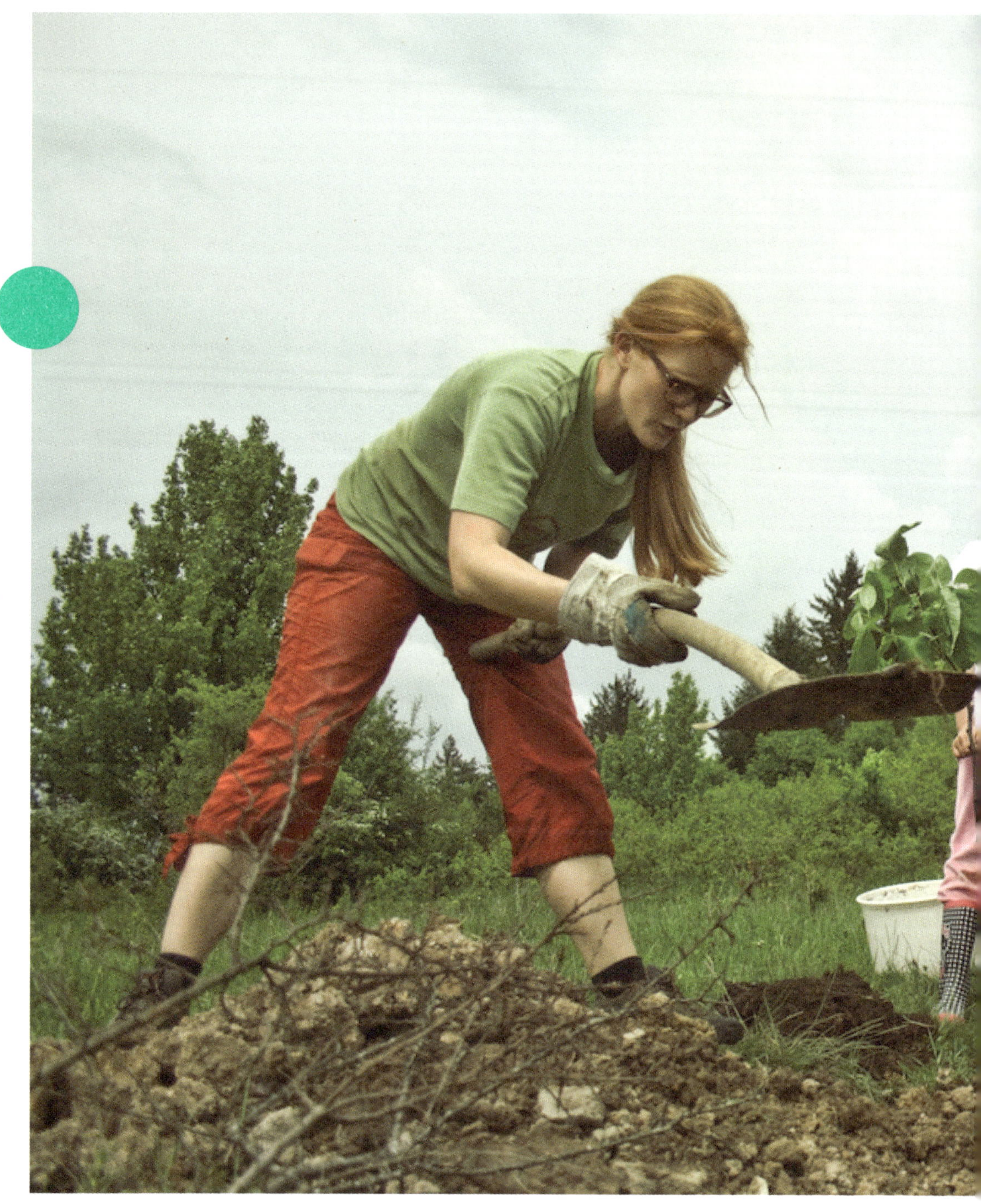

❖ 48. Juliana Mrvová and children planting an orchard

From the educational activities, which were not primarily artworks, we can mention fruit growing workshops led by fruiterers - Daniel Dioši, who showed above all the methods of clipping and shaping the trees, and artist and grower Martin Bendžela who taught the ways of entgrafting of fruit trees. Also Včelí kraj NGO presented its activities, for example experiential bee education for schools.

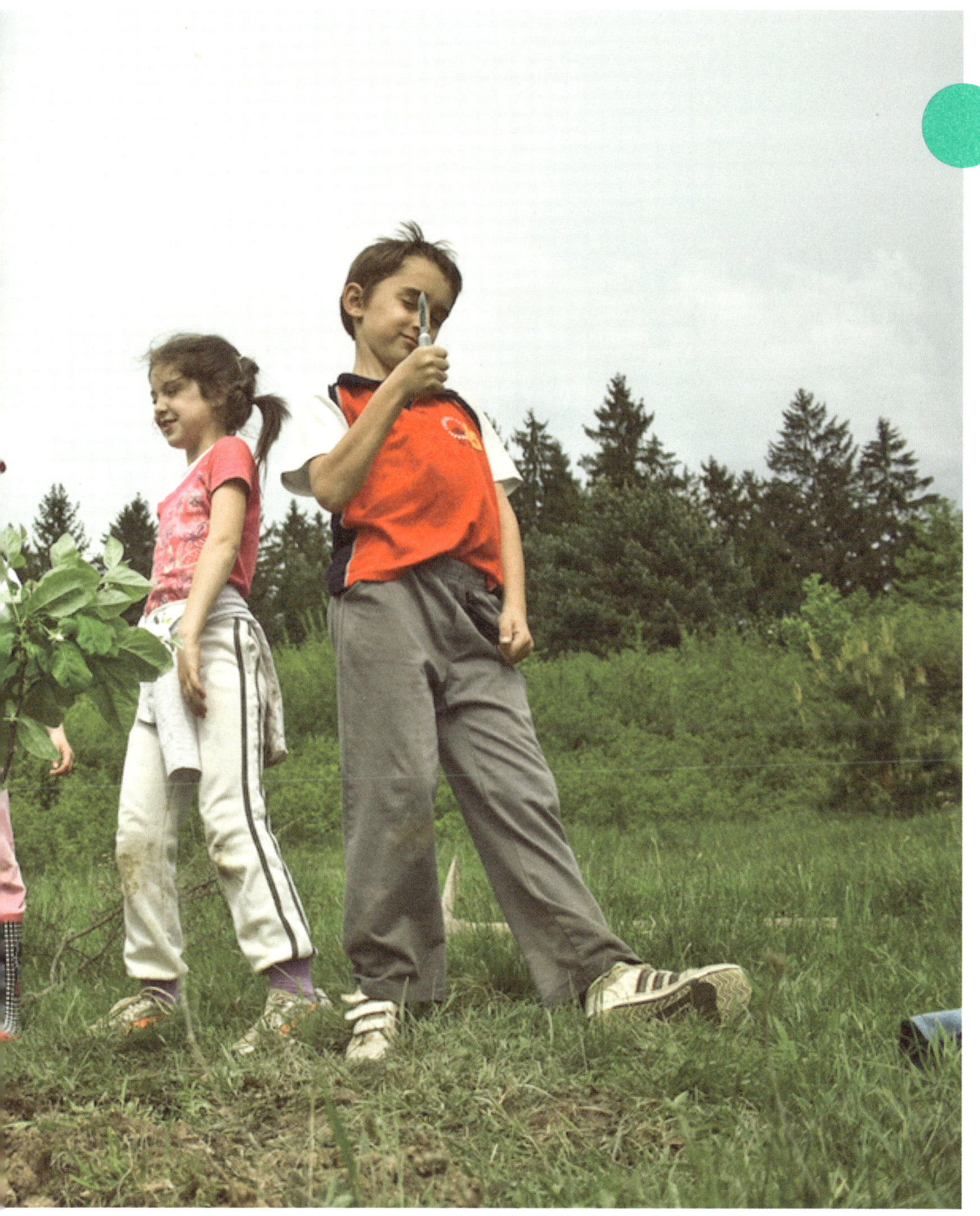

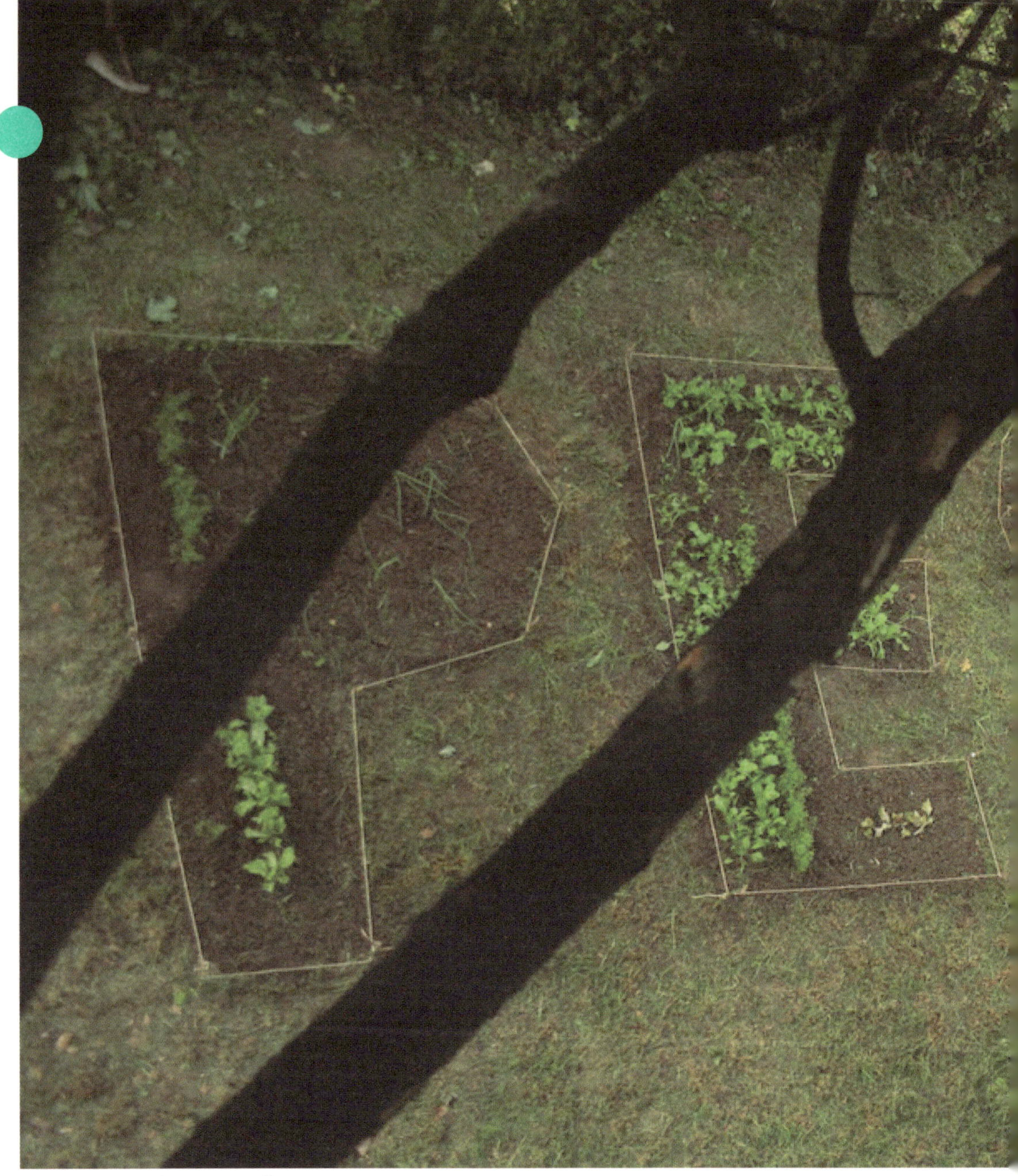

▚ 49. *Let's Grow*

Entgrafting with Martin Bendžela took place mostly in an open landscape by Dúbravica where we in advance mapped and prepared a number of wildly growing fruit trees. These were consequently cultivated by entgrafting them with cultivars from locally well-tried sorts. During the year we followed how these "engrafted ones" flourish in an open landscape where an attack by wild or farm animals or by people is a possibility. A number of trees were actually destroyed by animals, who apparently like young ofshoots of cultivars more than the original wildly growing or self-bred trees, which is an interesting observation.

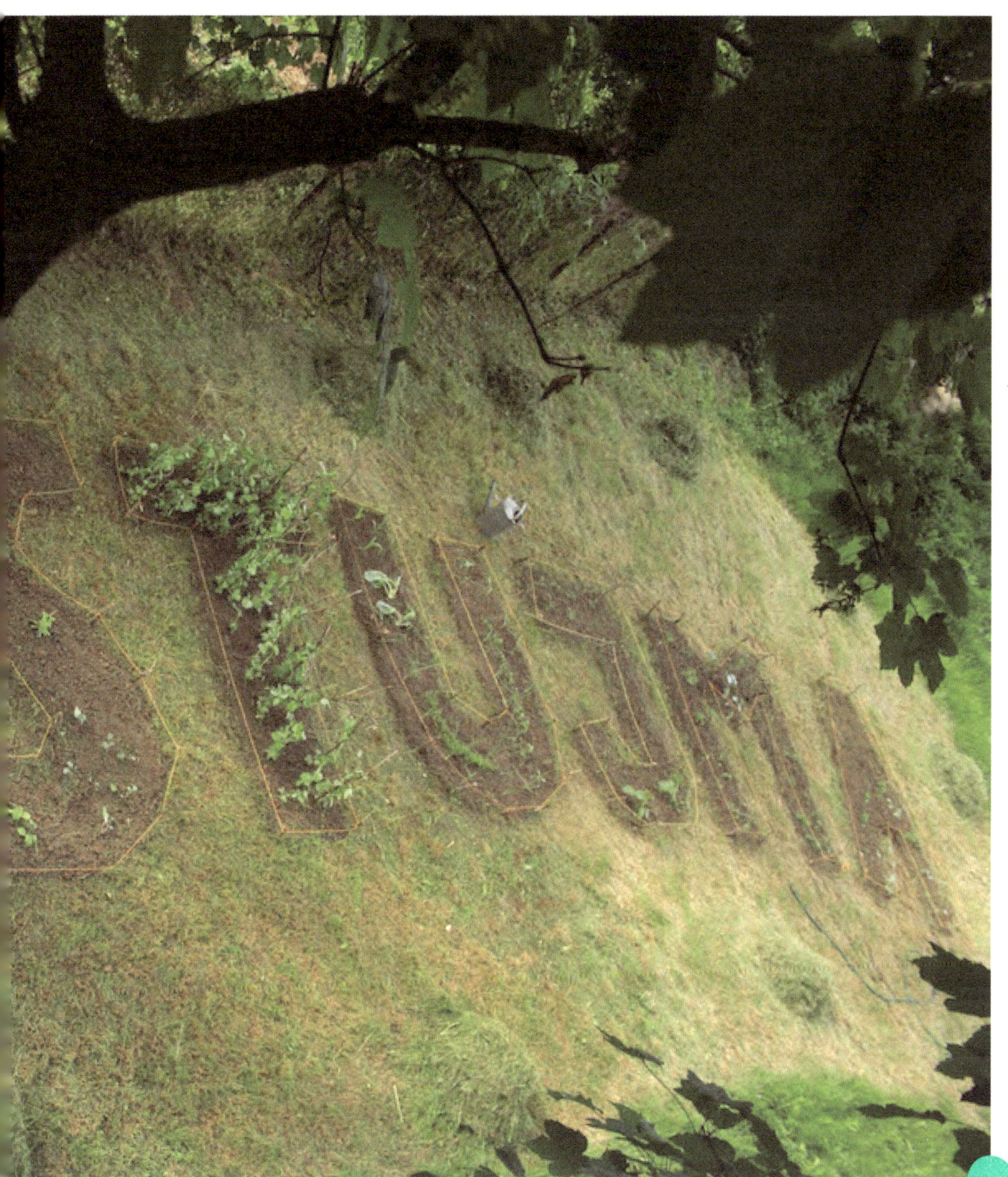

Several of the engrafted young trees were also stolen. We would like to further follow those trees that survived, take care of them, these will serve as objects of artistic interest. Several of them we replanted into the garden of our NGO to breed them there and later replant into local gardens or give to people.

During these first project years we got to know its possibilities. We will certainly continue in 2015. For example we plan to cooperate with architects and continue our cooperation with visual artists.

Florandroid – Garden Heads

Ⓒ *Pavel Havrda, Michal Kindernay, Ondřej Vavrečka,*
In cooperation with:
Jitush Pospíšilová

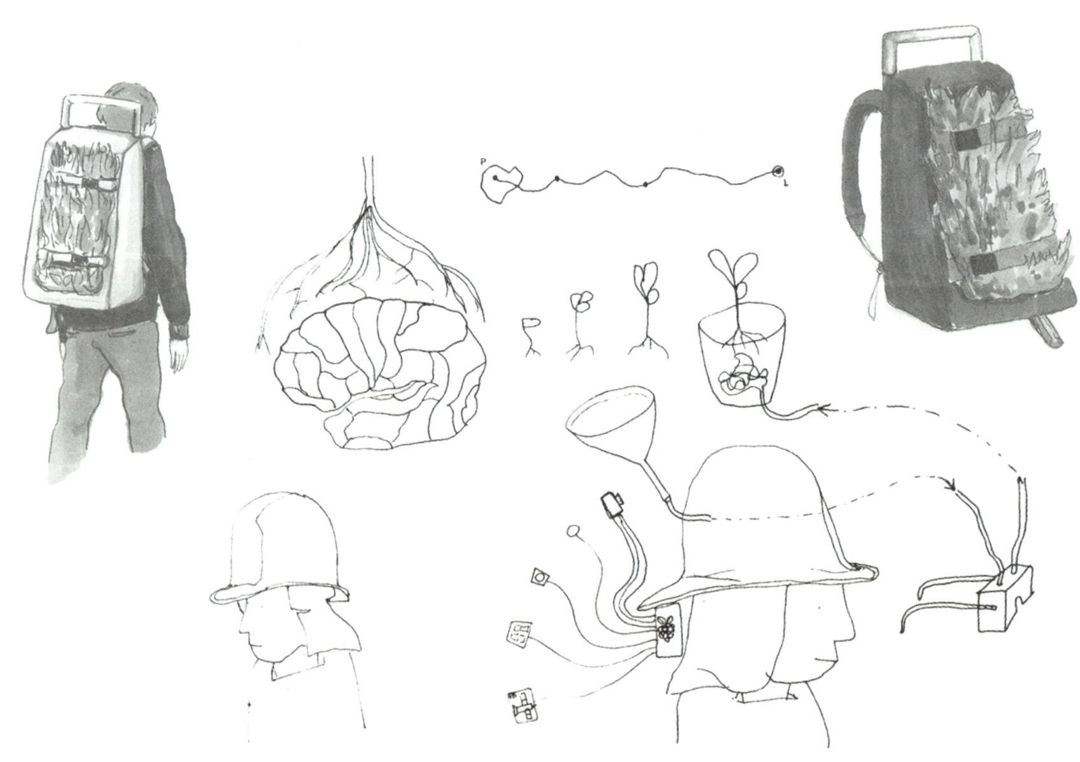

50. Garden Head

#water peephole Transformation into a florandroid

In one of his earthly adventures with Bacchus and his entourage, the god Priapus became infatuated with a beautiful nymph, Lotis. She sought to escape the lustful Priapus, and the gods helped her by turning her into a lotus, but it so happened that Dryope, the daughter of a Greek king, had gone to pick flowers in honour of the water nymphs (sic!), and she also picked the lotus where Lotis was hiding. The gods then punished Dryope by turning her into a tree.

What the myth relates as fate – Lotis the nymph was accidently killed when flowers were picked for the water nymphs – we see as an expression of her free will. What the myth sees as ignorance – the fact that a nymph was hiding inside the plant – we regard as patently obvious. What the myth presents as punishment – Dryope being turned into a tree – we consider a wonderful adventure.

What the myth considers a curse, that a plant cannot move, we turn on its head and lend plants our musculoskeletal system. We give plants the freedom of our legs!

The reason why being turned into a plant is a punishment in the myth – because plants cannot speak – we pay no heed to (though it is always on our minds). Plants can speak. Let us – at least temporarily – lend plants our ears!

What the myth seeks by turning her into a plant – so that others will not recognise her – we see not as a drawback, but as an advantage. Let us grow from plants!

The time has never been more auspicious for germination on our heads than now! The time has never wished life to the roots in our bodies more than now! The weather has never been better for growth from our heads than now!

We imagined that we ourselves are the roots…

And then the plants would be an extension of our bodies.

And so we put them on our heads.

A plant germinates and grows, and we germinate too, we grow, we force our way up to the light.

We are sublime.

Plants!

Our footsteps are free and we want to share this freedom with you. At least as a small way thanking you for what you give us – food, beauty: life!

Each of us will walk with you through the countryside for six days. Where the wind takes us, there the wind will take you. Where we hear our bodies' call, there we will hear your bodies' call.

We will look at the world through spectacles made of what makes you flourish or perish: water.

Water and you: we will collect rainwater in our spectacles to be absorbed by your roots.

In our houses we will plant your brother or sister – our brother, our sister – and we will place you – us – side by side. And we will contrast and compare you with one another. During the week we will be in motion, and on the seventh day of rest we will return home to your brother or sister.

In one of his earthly adventures with Bacchus and his entourage, the god Priapus became infatuated with a beautiful nymph, Lotis. She sought to escape the lustful Priapus, and the gods helped her by turning her into a lotus, but it so happened that Dryope, the daughter of a Greek king, had gone to pick flowers in honour of the water nymphs (sic!), and she also picked the lotus where Lotis was hiding. The gods then punished Dryope by turning her into a tree.

Florandroid

This project combines old and new technologies with art and ecological and societal strategies. It reflects humanity on the brink of the economic and environmental crisis of the Anthropocene, and it responds to questions of sustainable agriculture and individual approaches to food policy. Our portable personal garden is part of the urban ecopolis and an active contribution to urban gardening. It also serves as a natural sensor of water quality, and the quality of the environment as a whole. Our systems include plants with their roots on our heads, and each day we will expose them to the same influences we are exposed to. These peripatetic plants are dependent on local resources, the weather, the individual locations and the chosen route. For a participant the symbiosis of human time and plant time can produce a positive slowing-down, a different state of consciousness. The system includes irrigation and monitoring units and a miniature weather station. [1]

1   Translated by: Adrian Dean

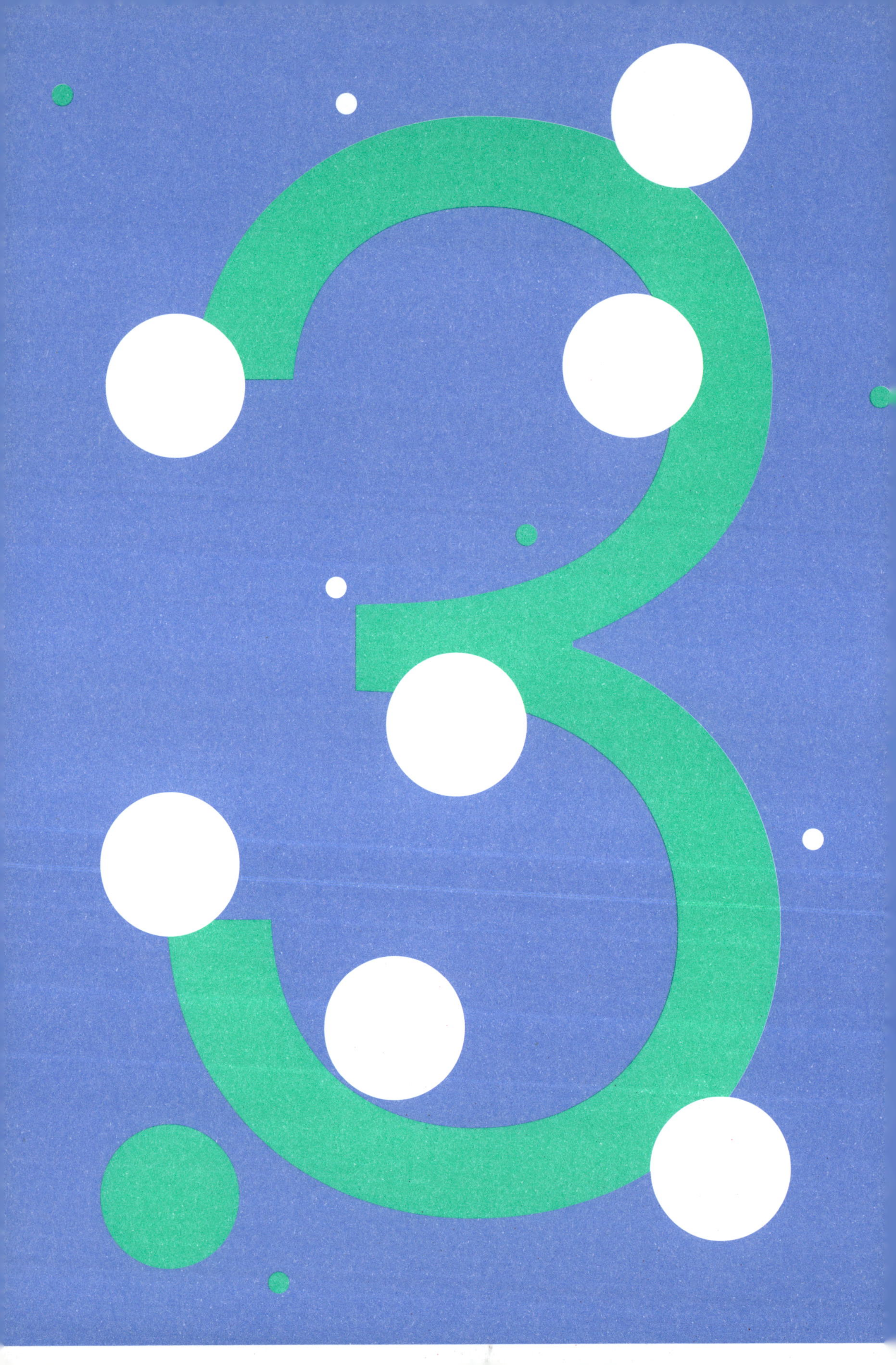

Convergence

A visual journal of the
festival Convergence
            20—27 April 2015
// Brussels, Saint-Nazaire,
Nantes, Praha, Hranice,
and along the Atlantic
coast line.
▓ *Gívan Belá*

*… not the recent summit on art and technology at
banff, not the former media journal, not the science
fiction novel by charles sheffield, not the software,
not a possible phenomenon also known as the
catch-up effect, not the goth festival, not the front
line assembly album, not the political party in mex-
ico, not the 1952 oil painting by jackson pollock,
maybe the property that different transformations
of the same state have a transformation to the
same end state, but what is it really? …*

Convergence was set up as an alternative media
art festival, with artists literally walking out of the

safe settings of room, studio, gallery, to intercon-
nect with what is found outdoors. Between April
20-26, 2015 in 5 different cities, artists were putting up showcases of two years of experimenting
with ecological art, and communicating about it.

For the occasion, a special app PVC was programmed that would allow the participants and audience to stream video and pictures, and comment
on them. On the website all items had an equal
status, and were not critical in time and space.
One should not divide again what is brought together. Let's assume it all happened in the same
space, the wider environment this world is.

—

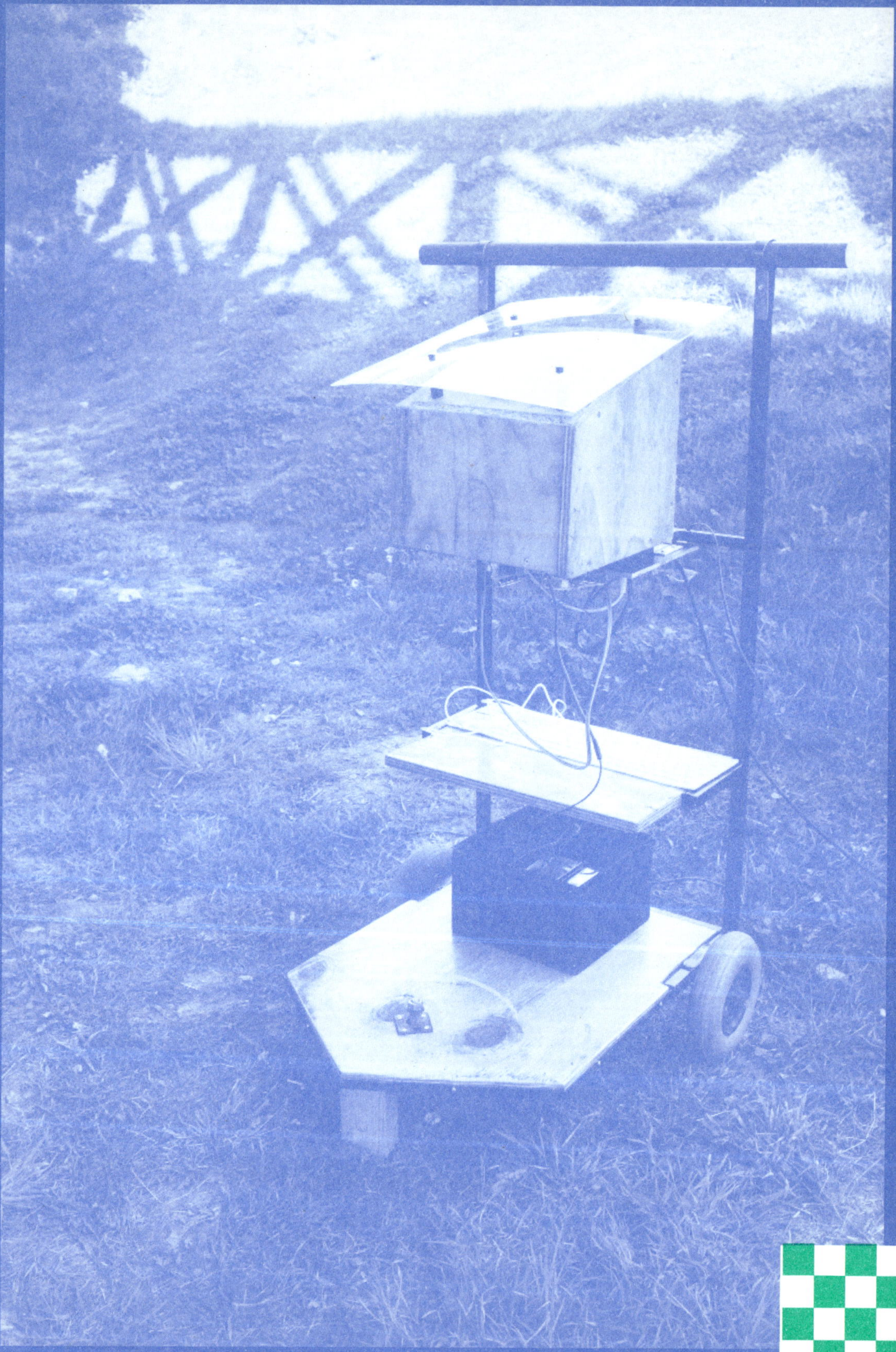

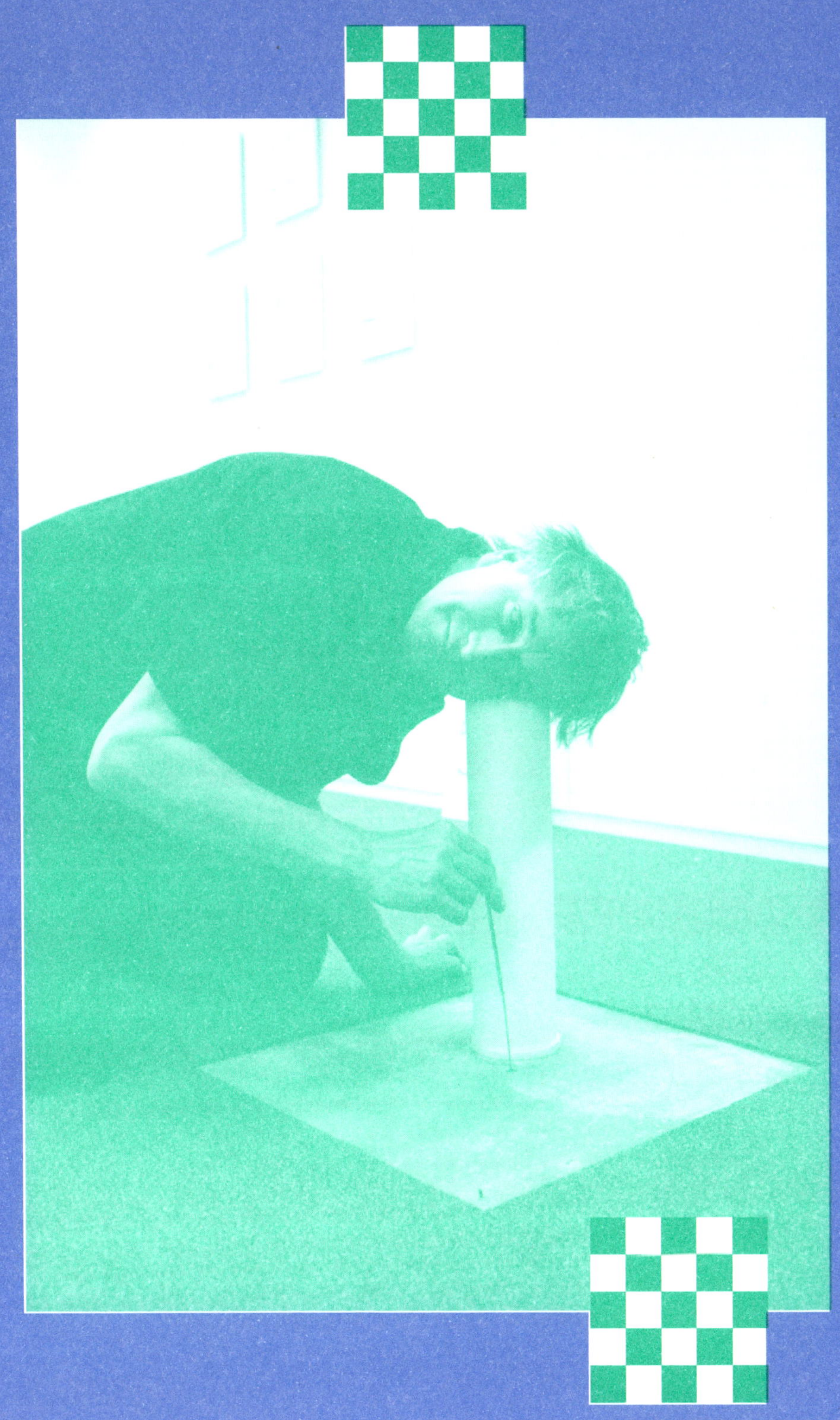

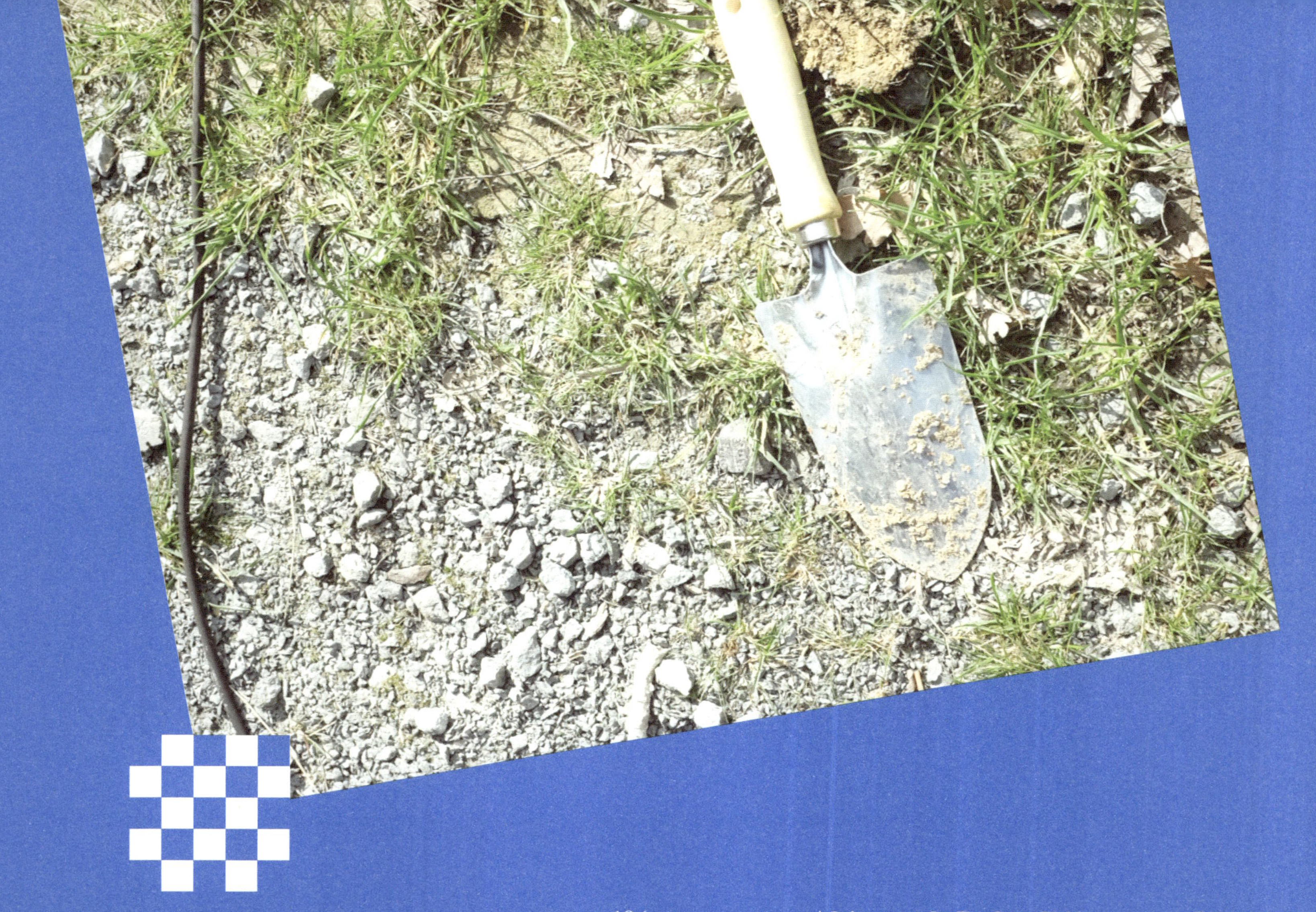

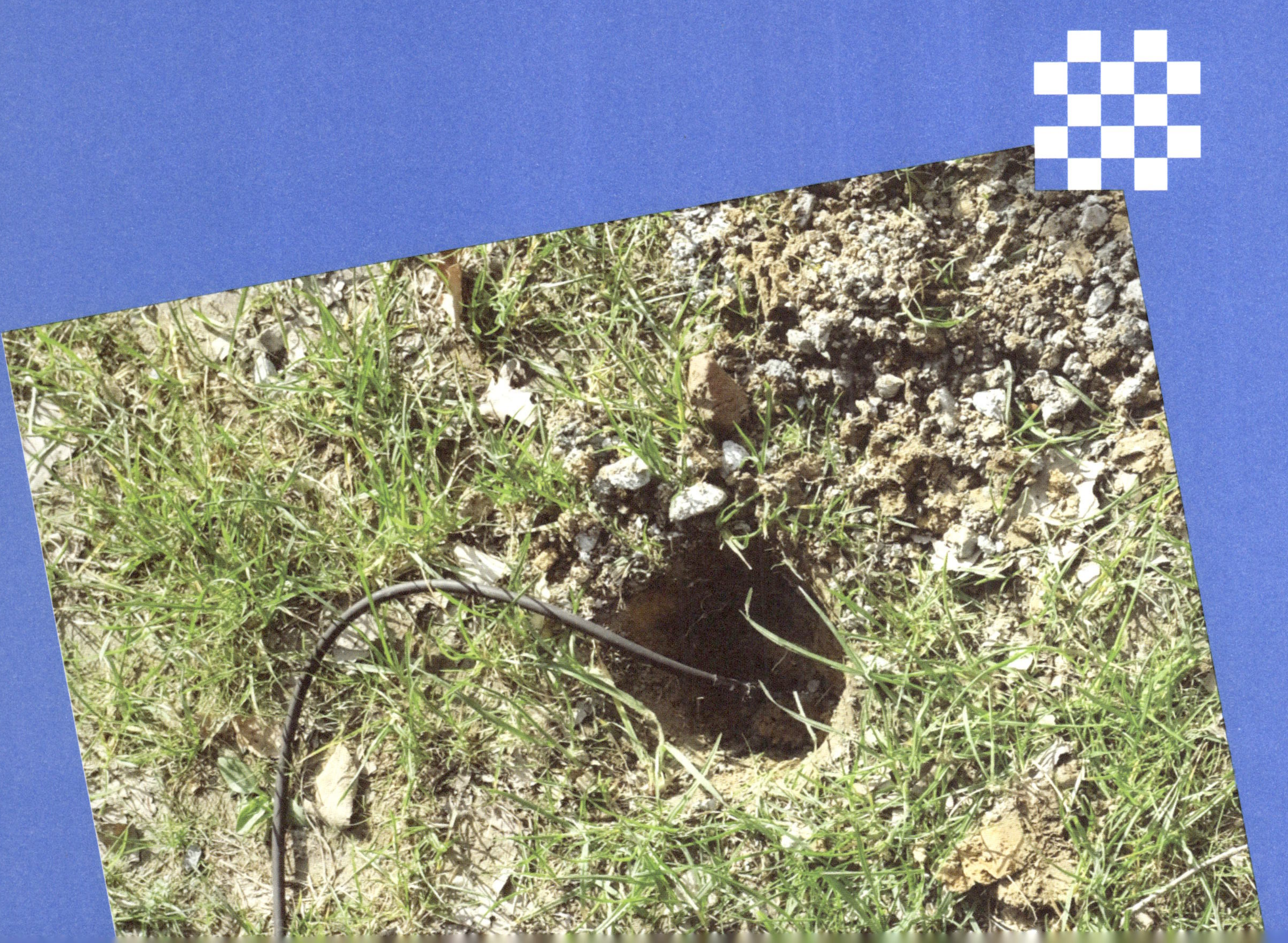

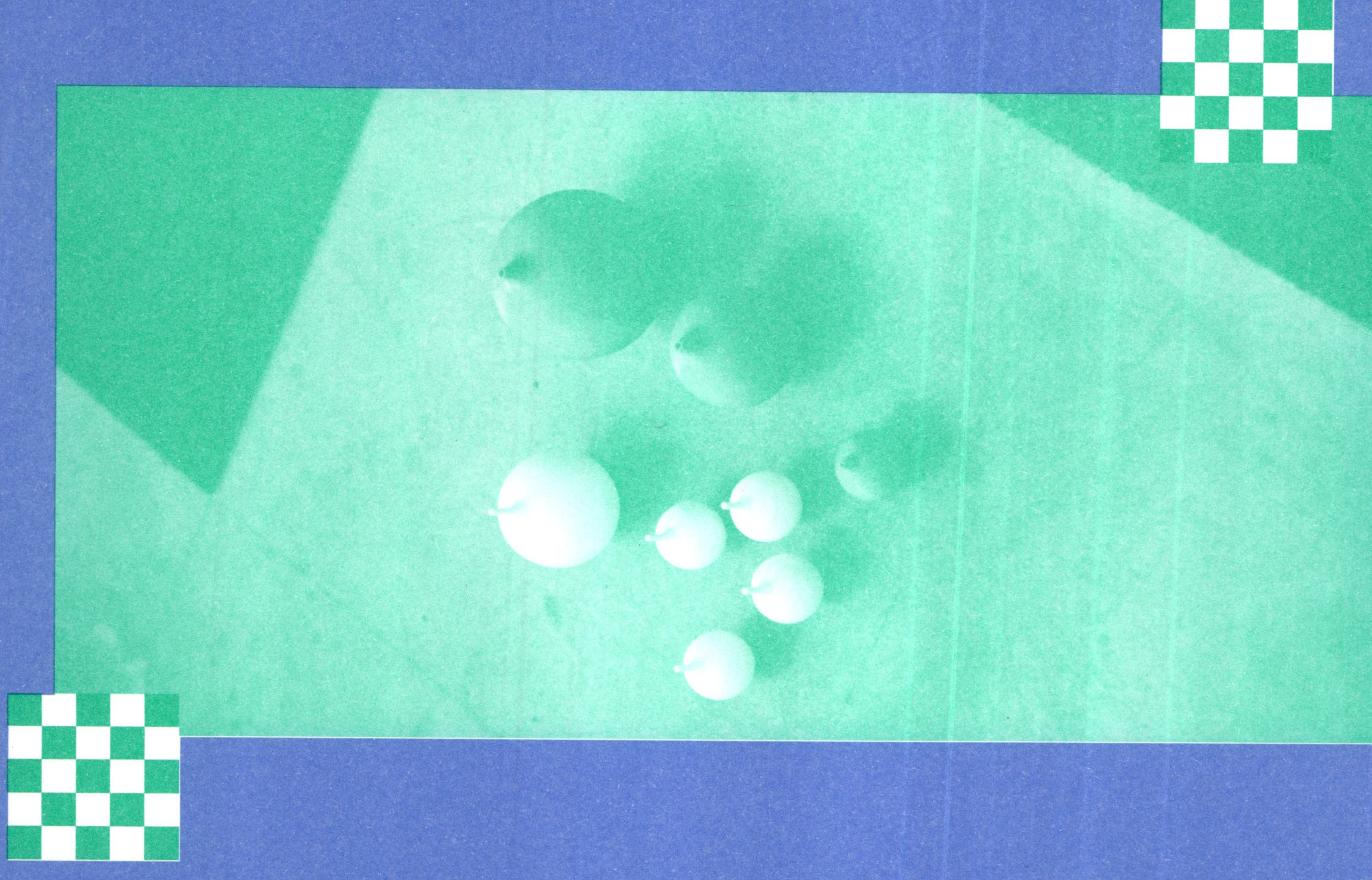

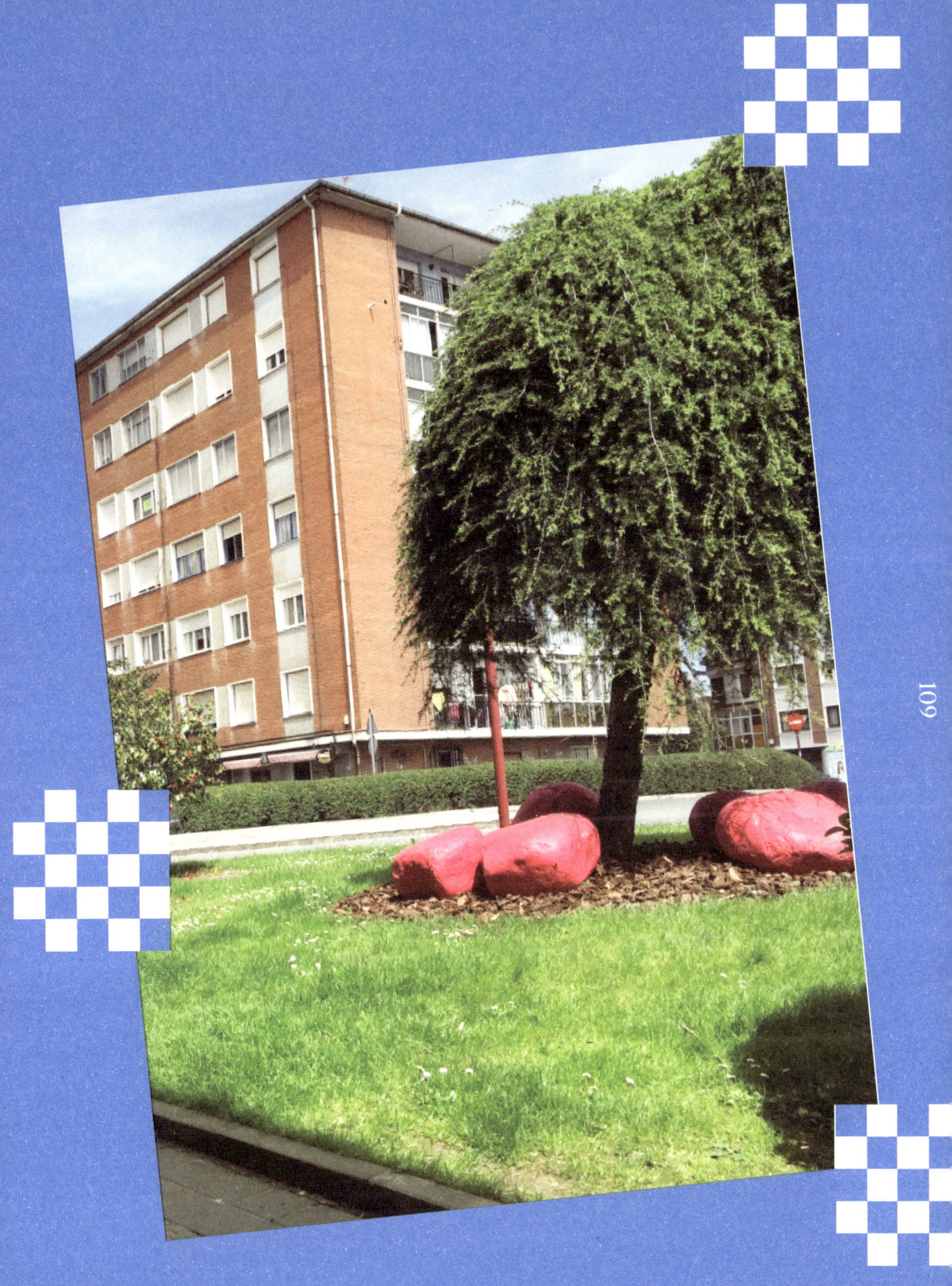

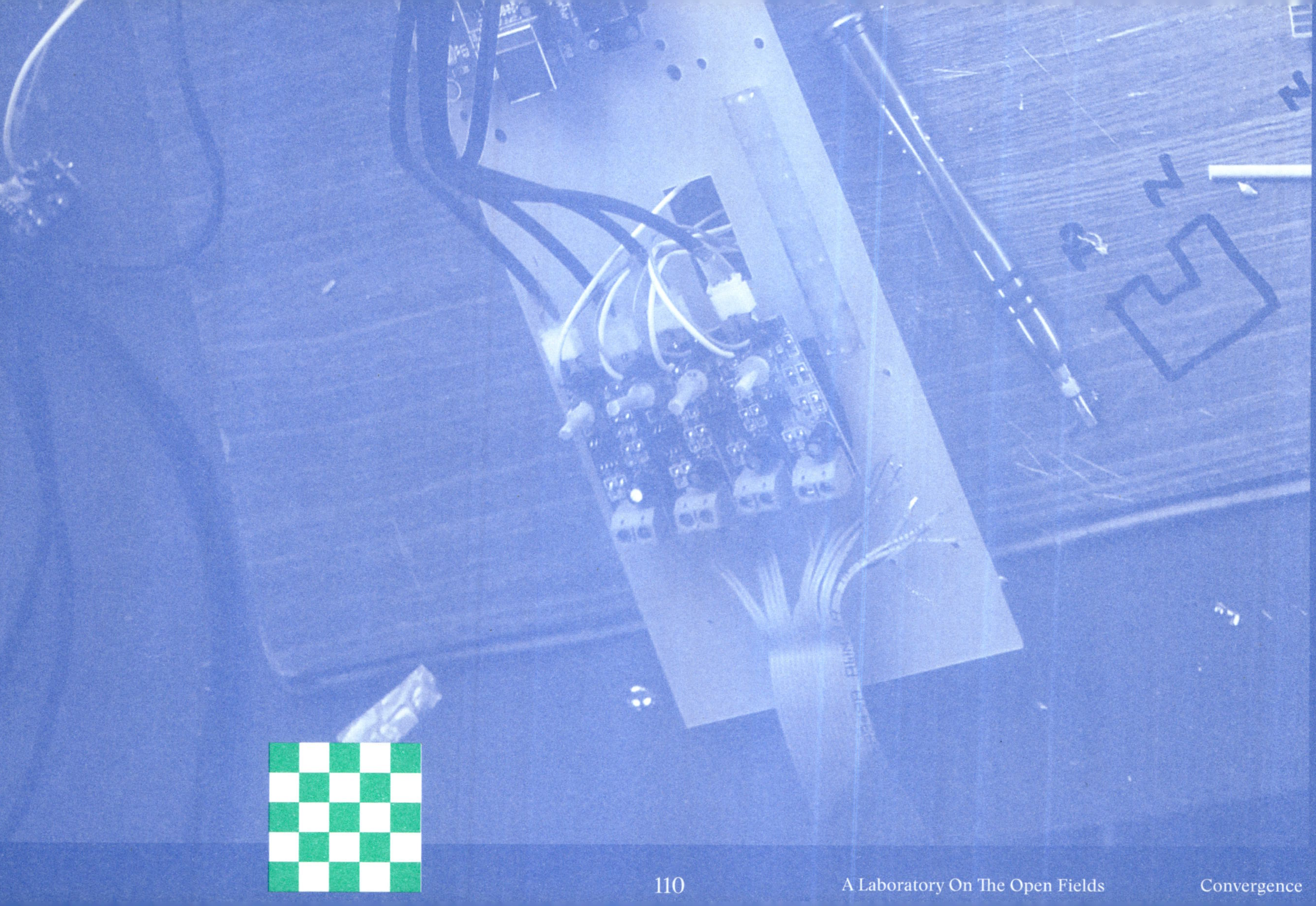

A Laboratory On The Open Fields

Convergence

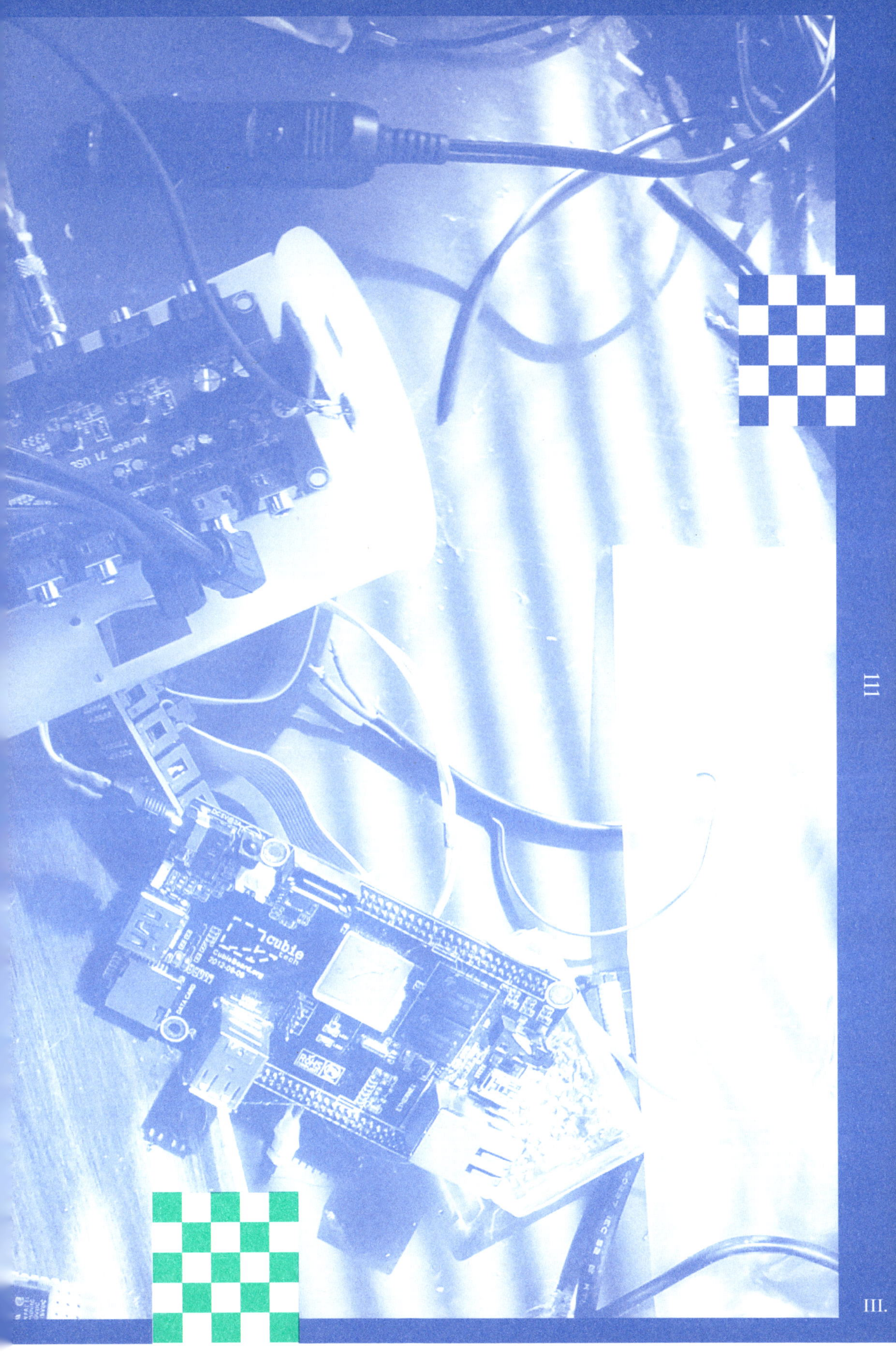

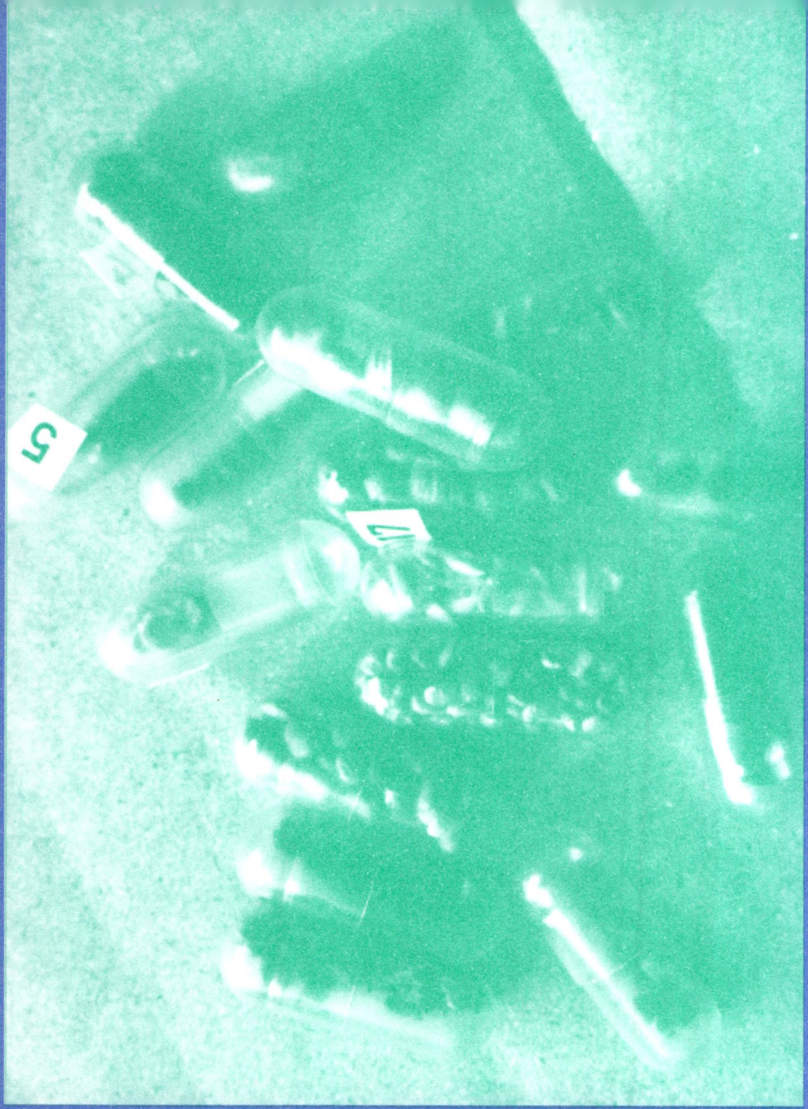

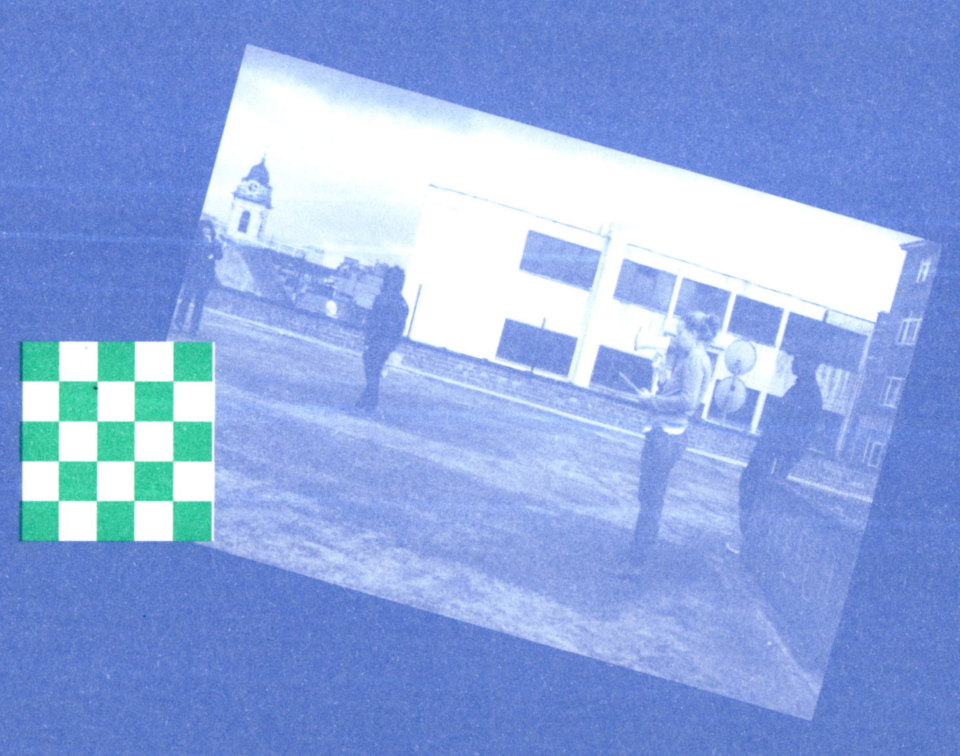

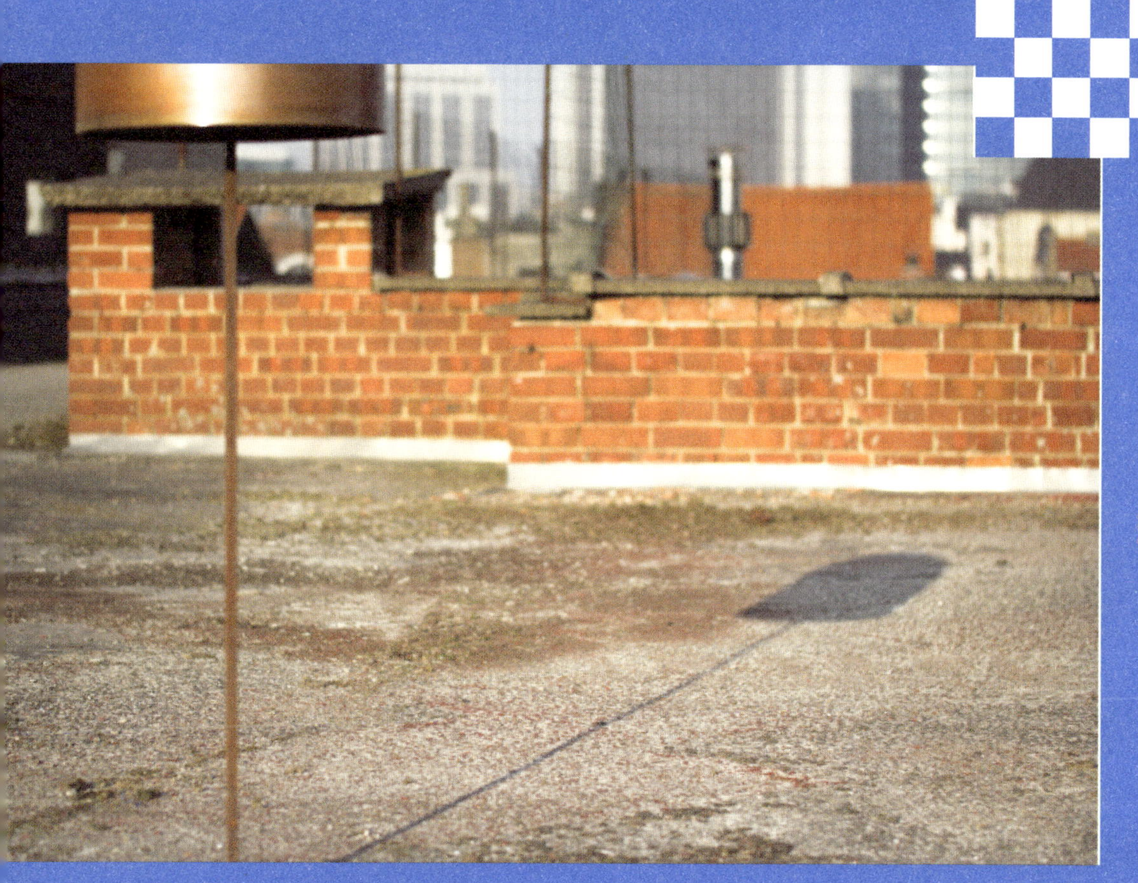

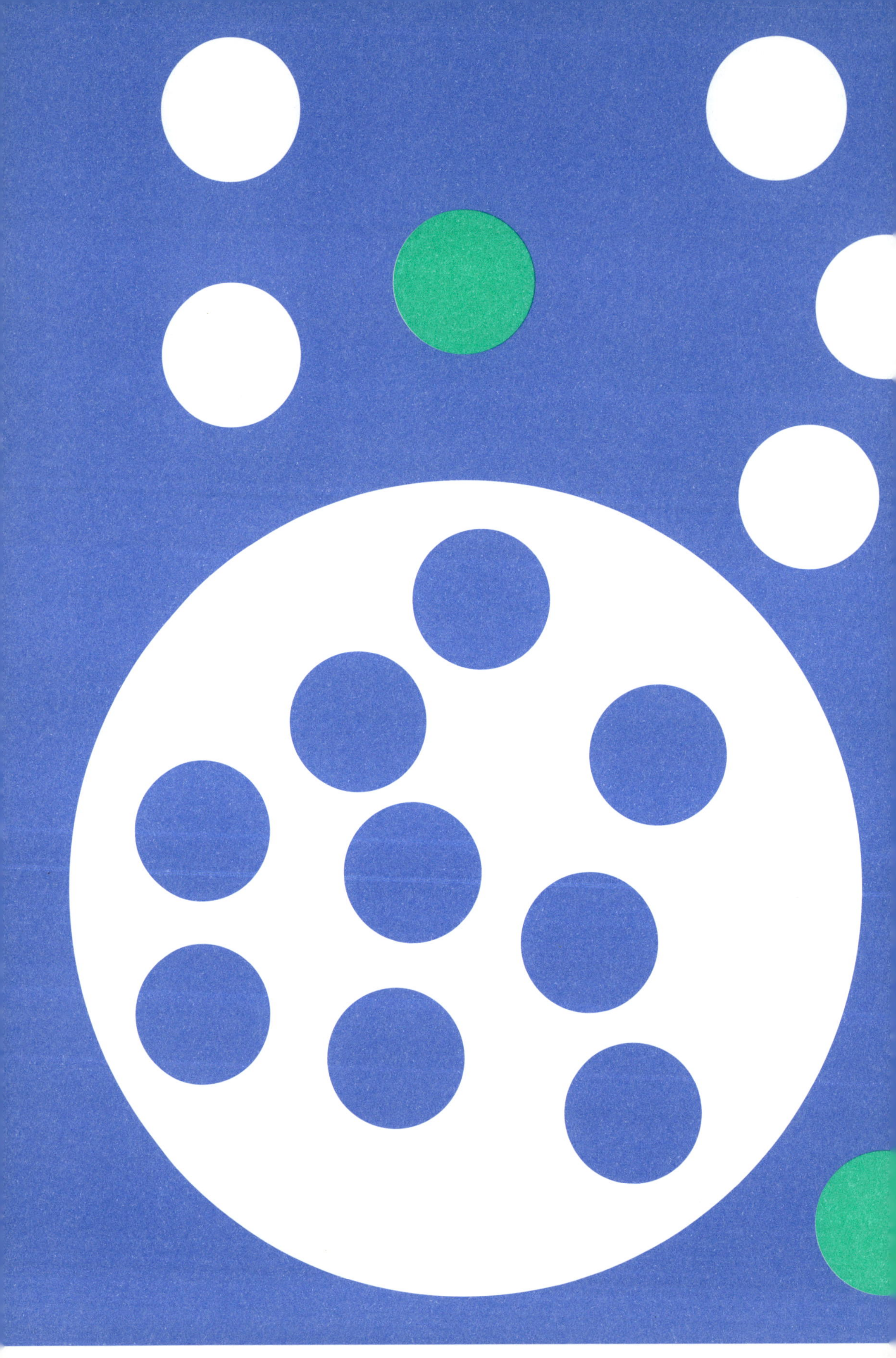

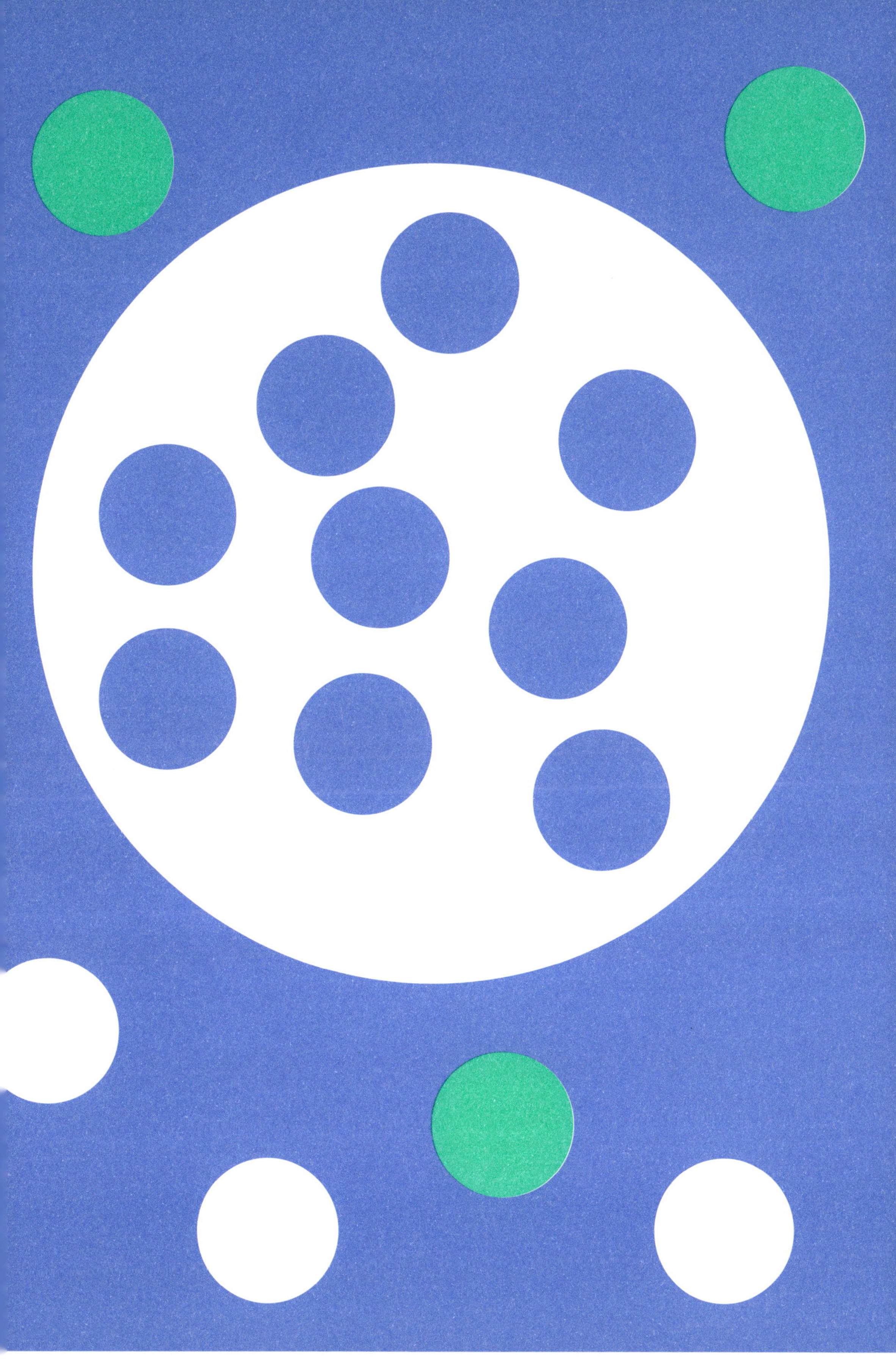

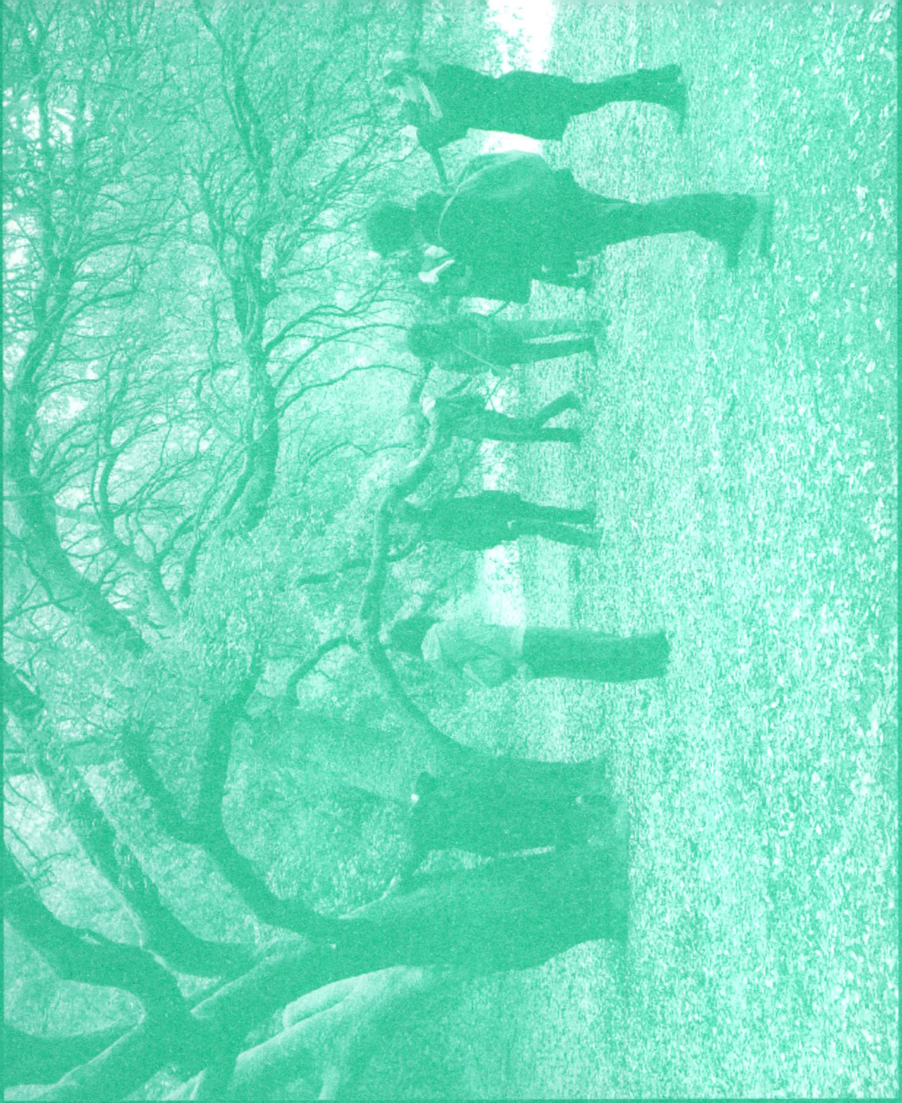

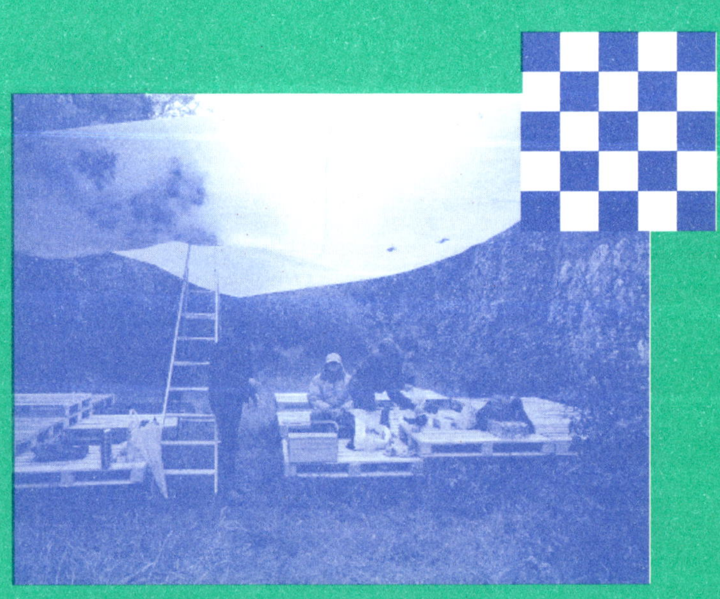

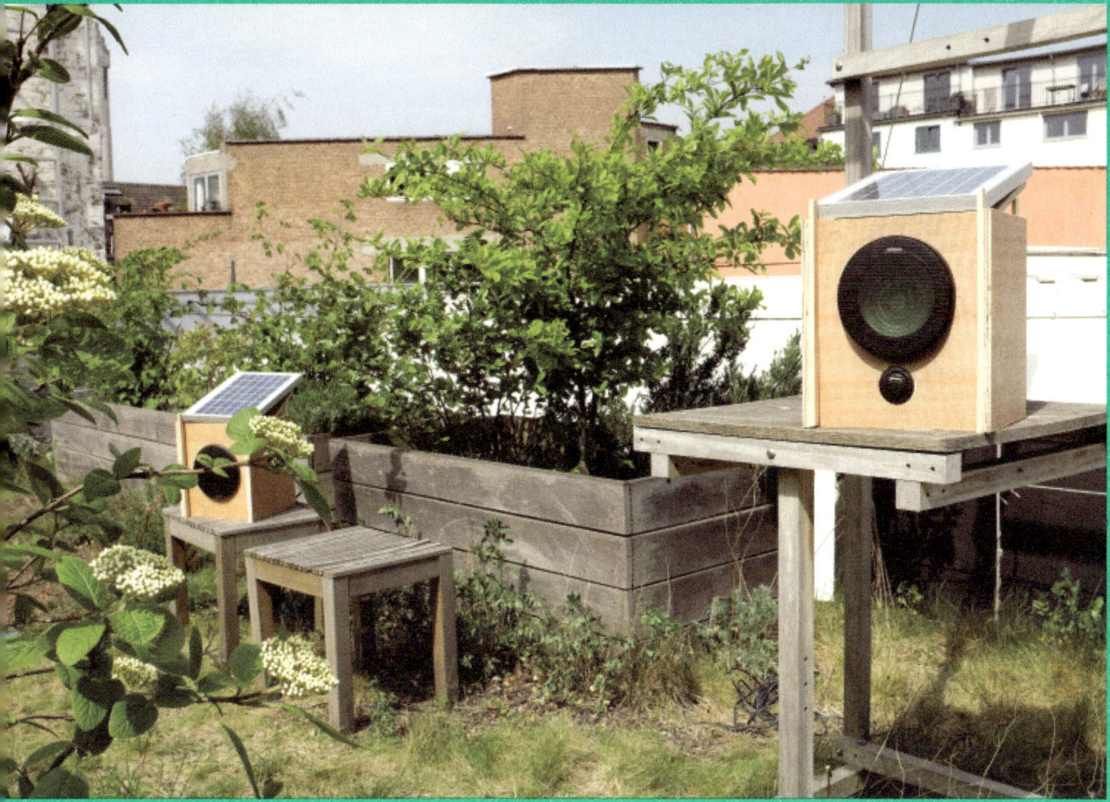

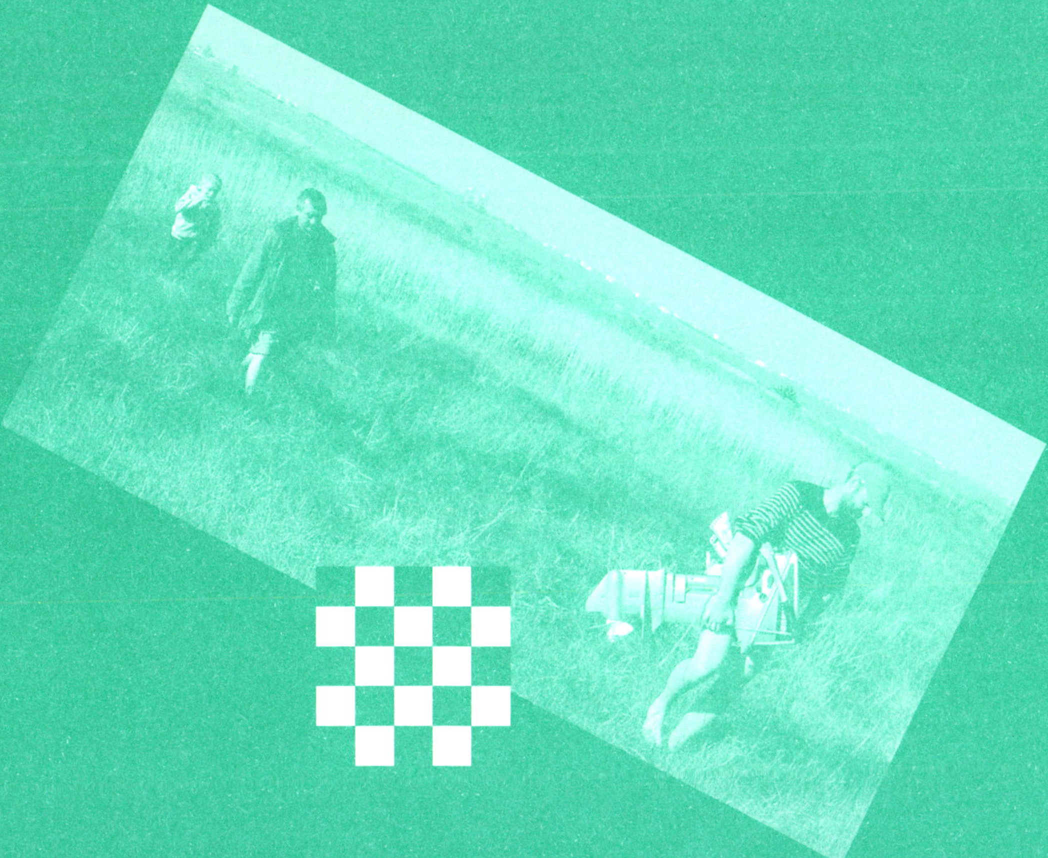

III.

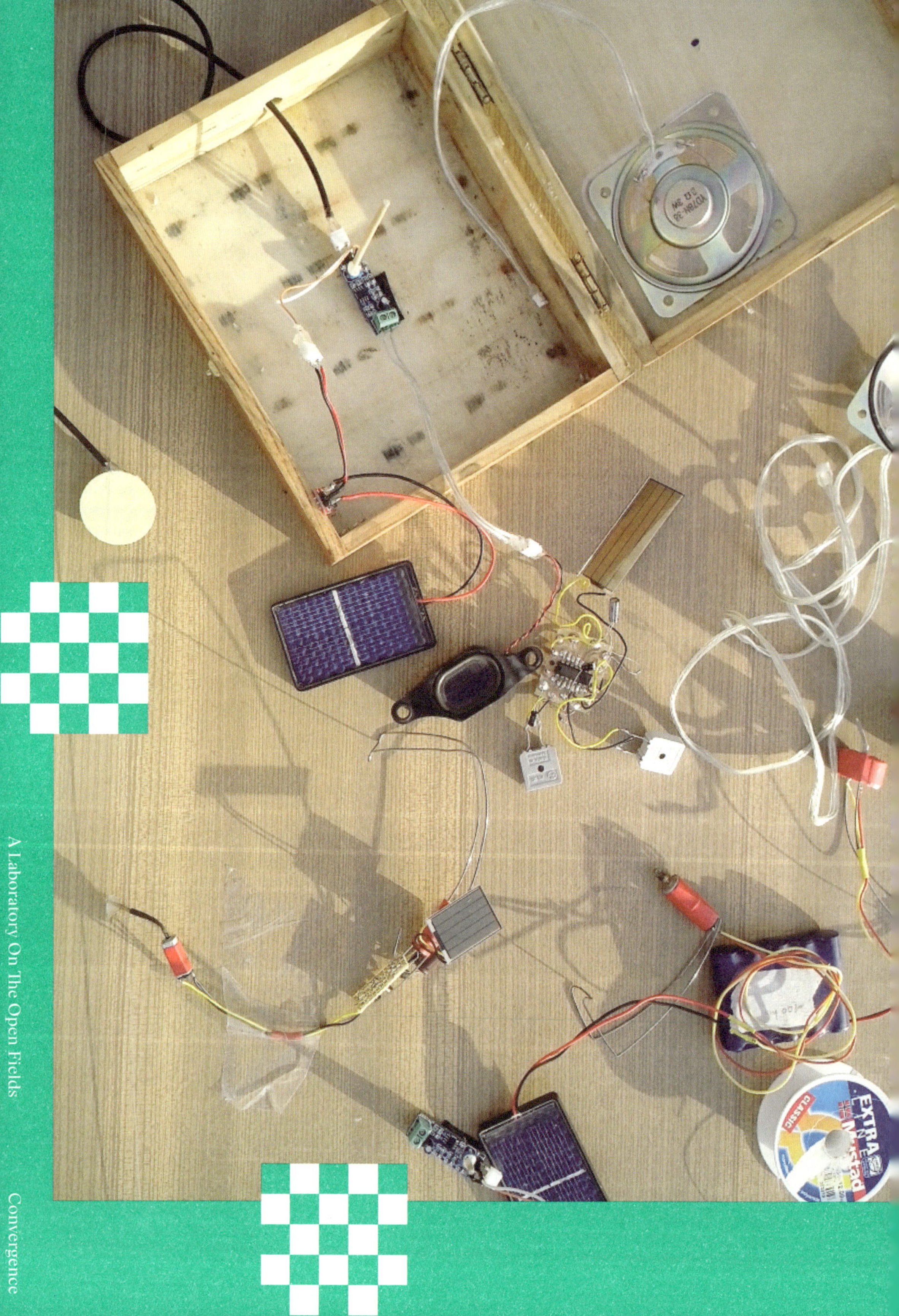
A Laboratory On The Open Fields
Convergence

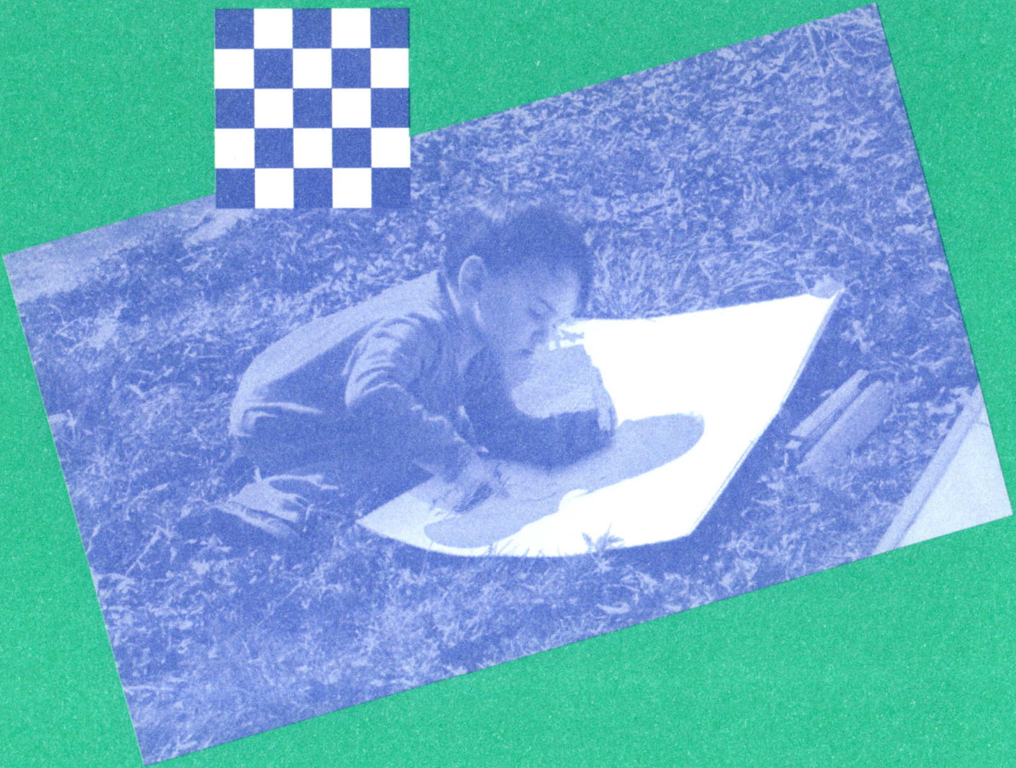

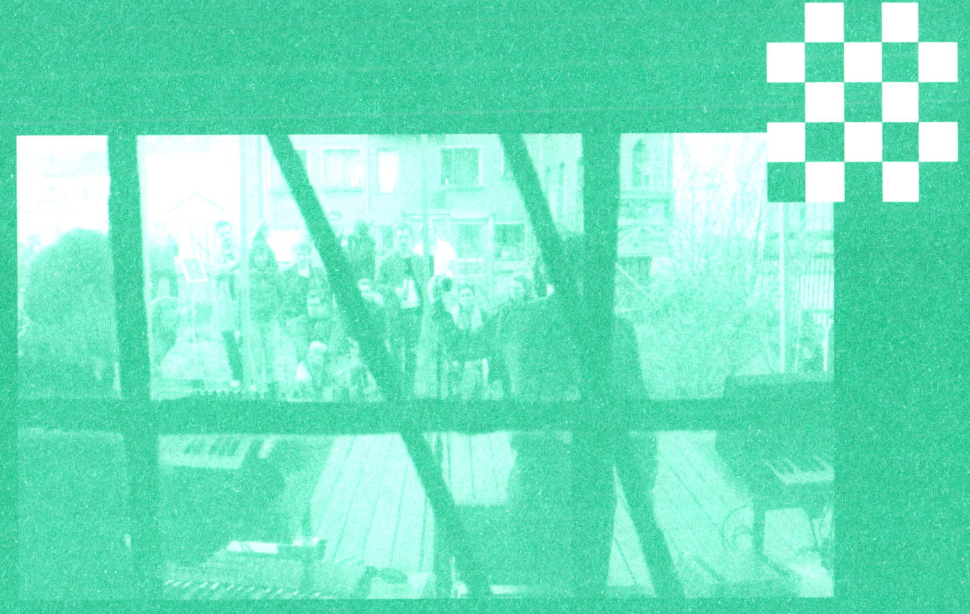

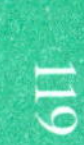

III.

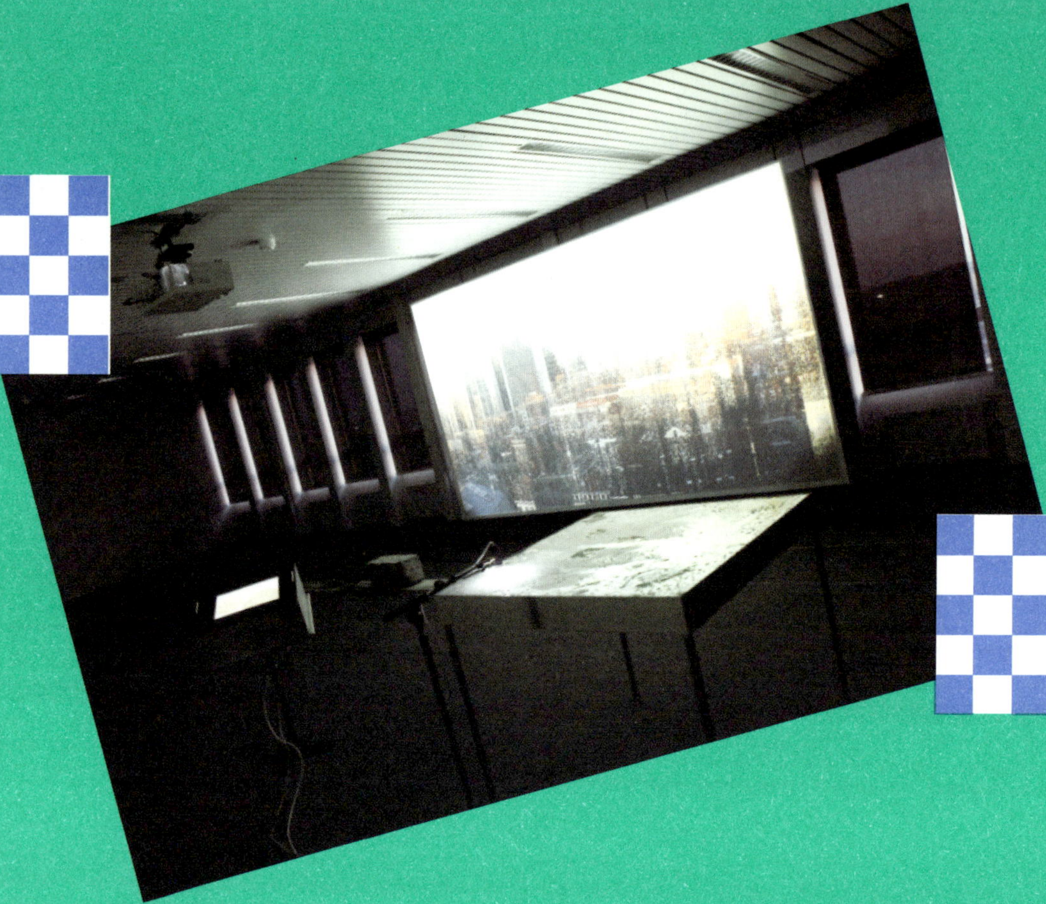

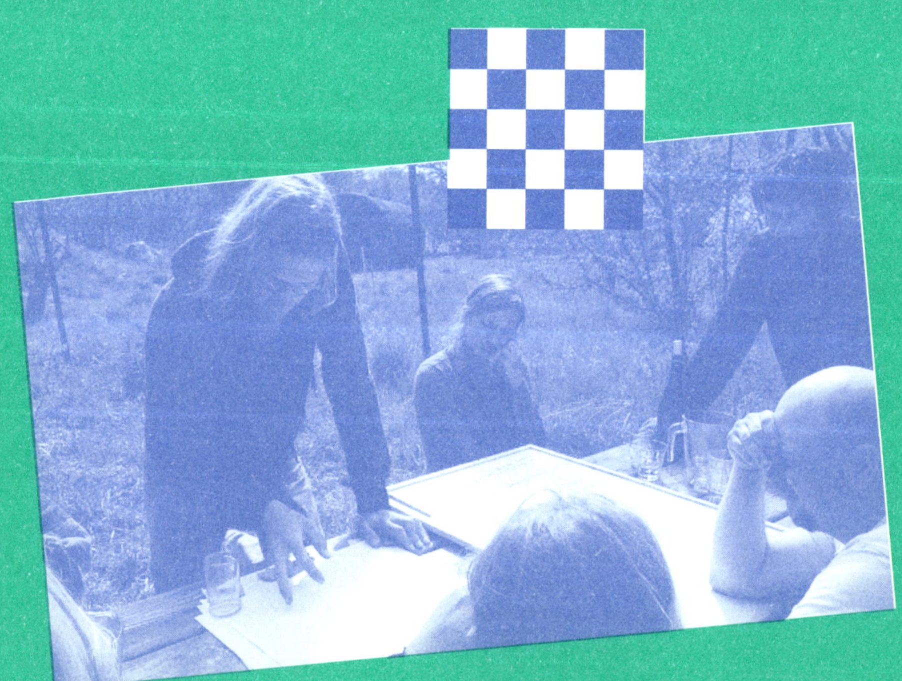

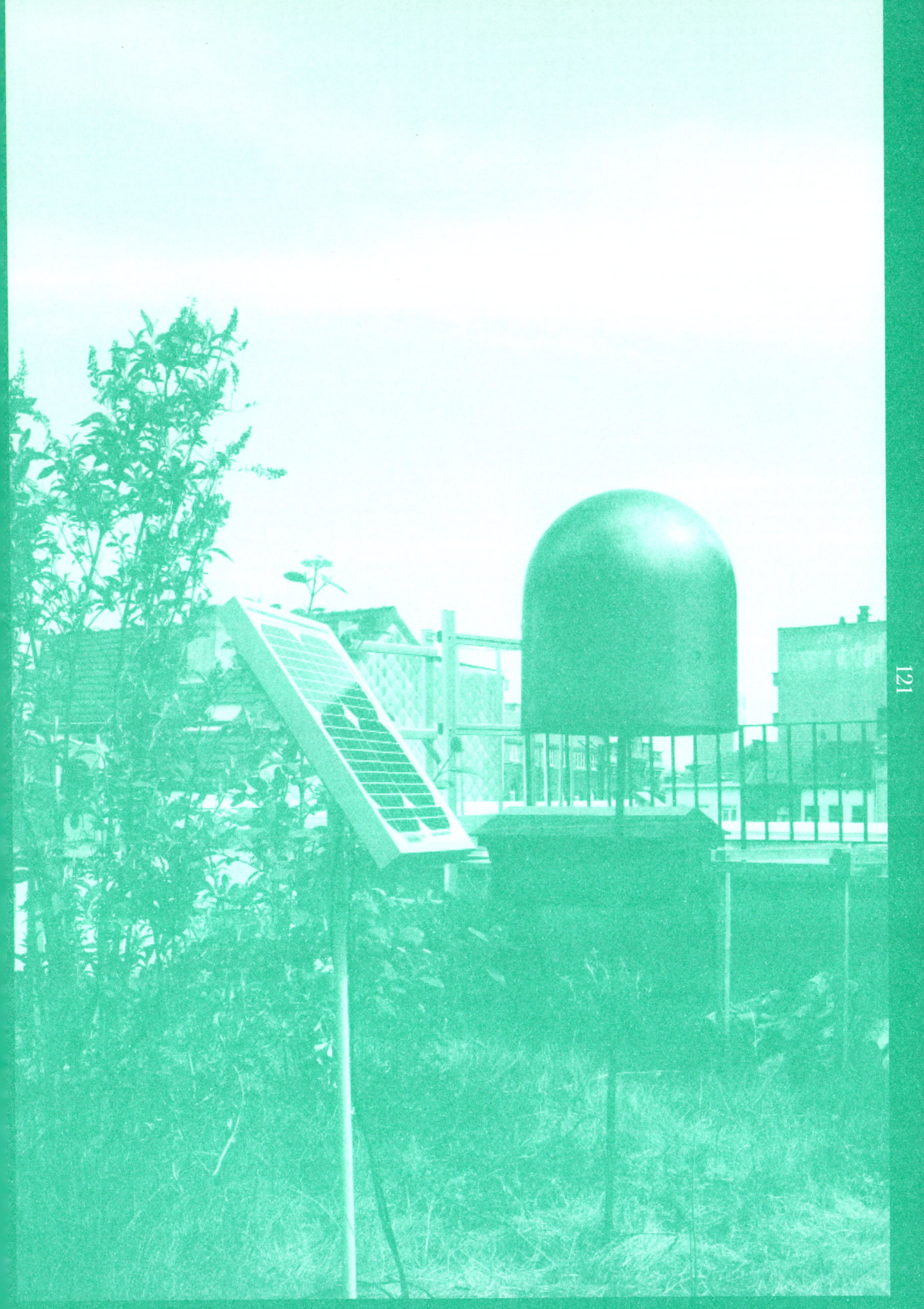

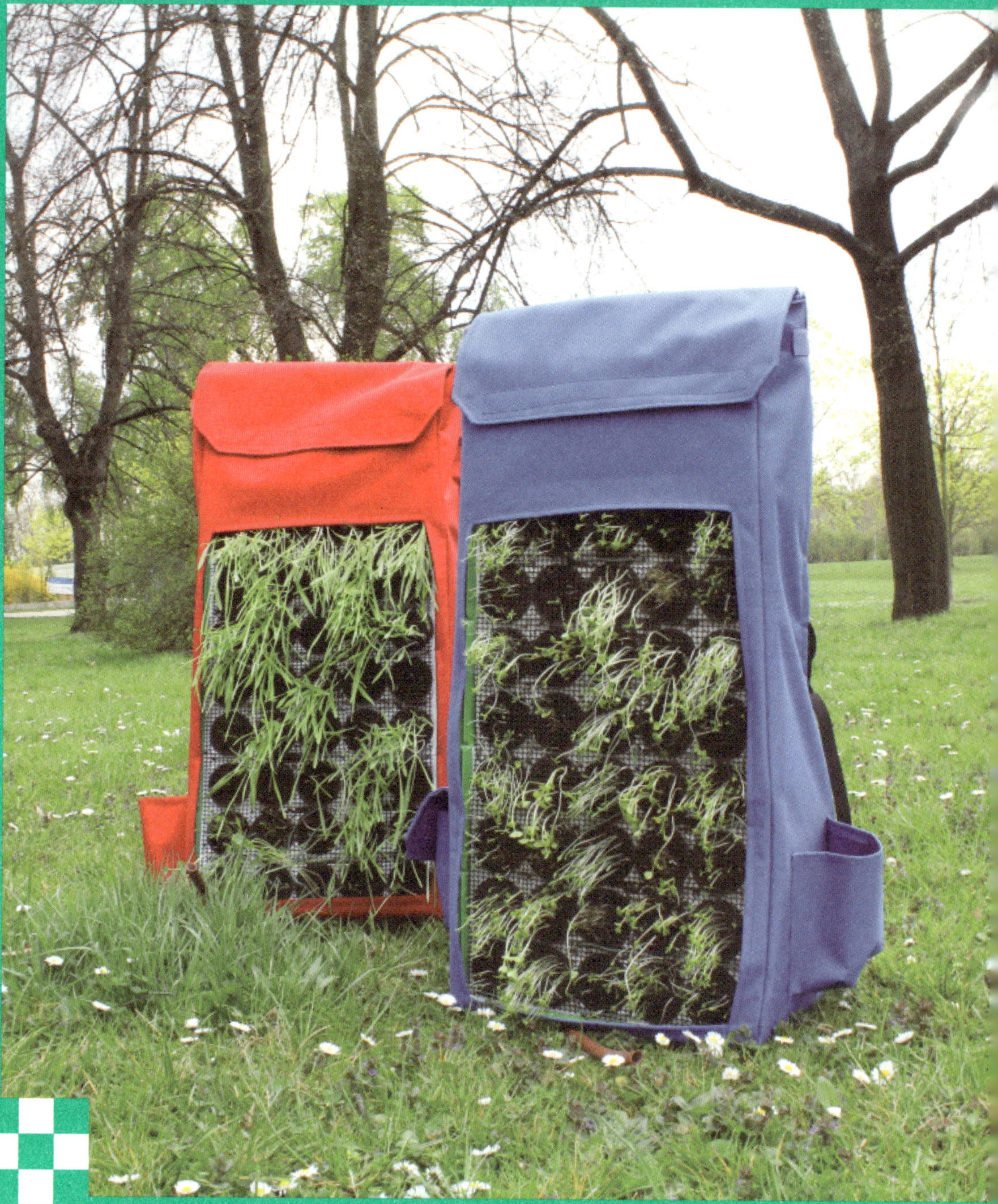

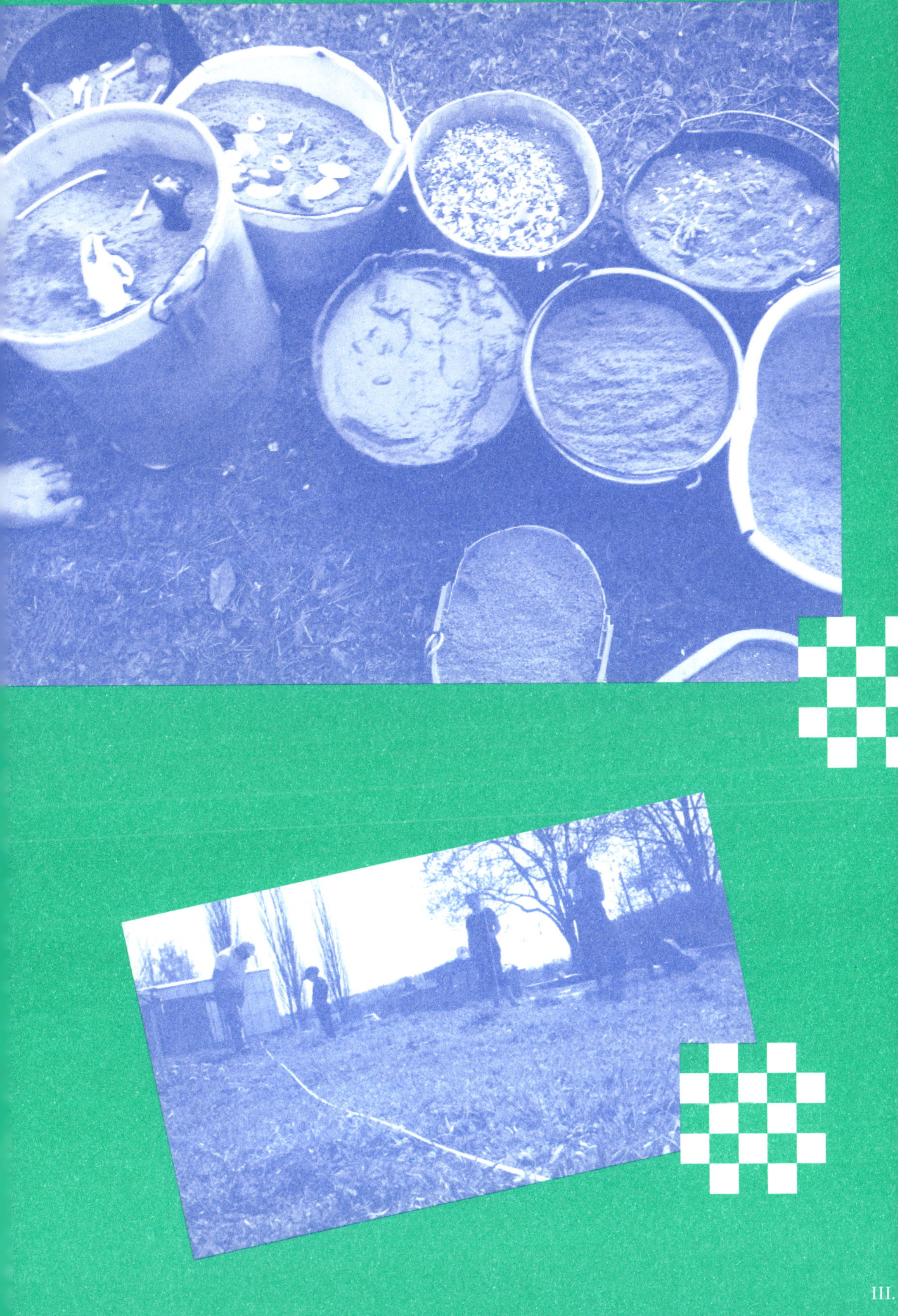

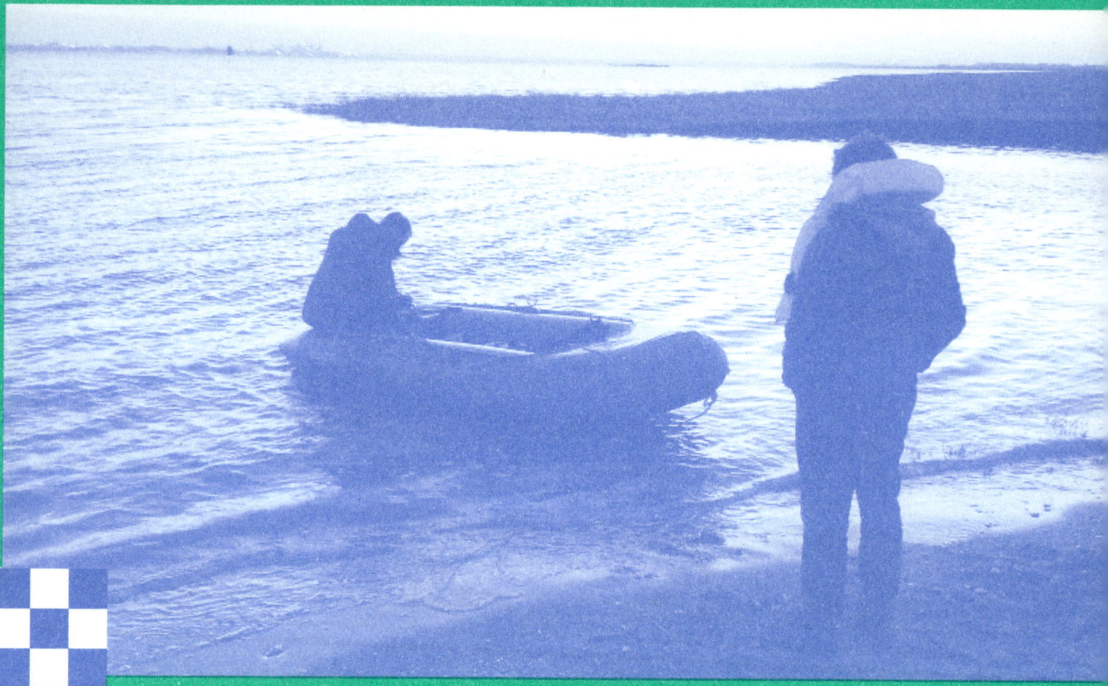

Convergence

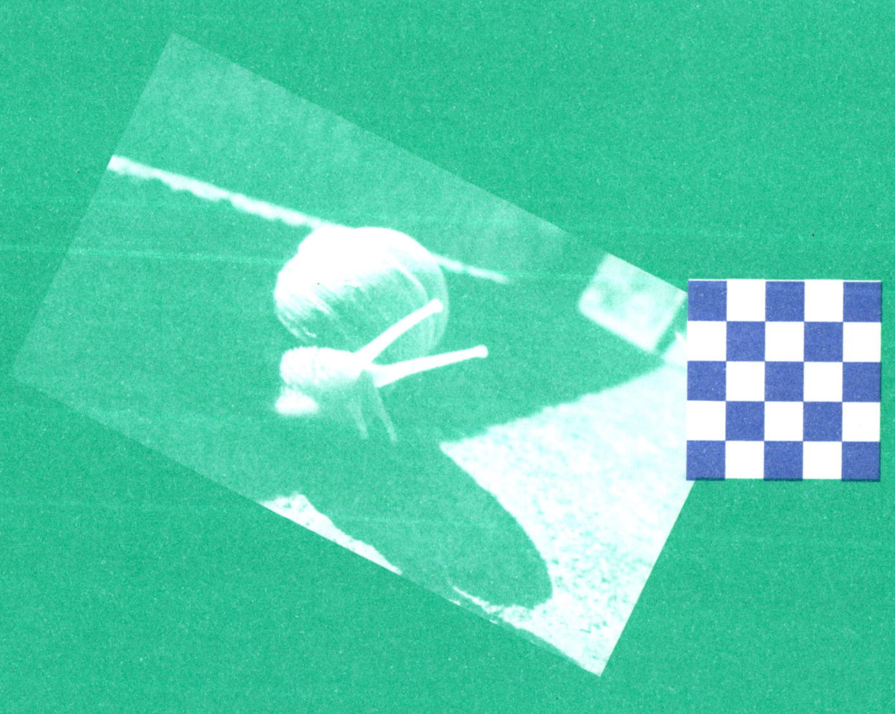

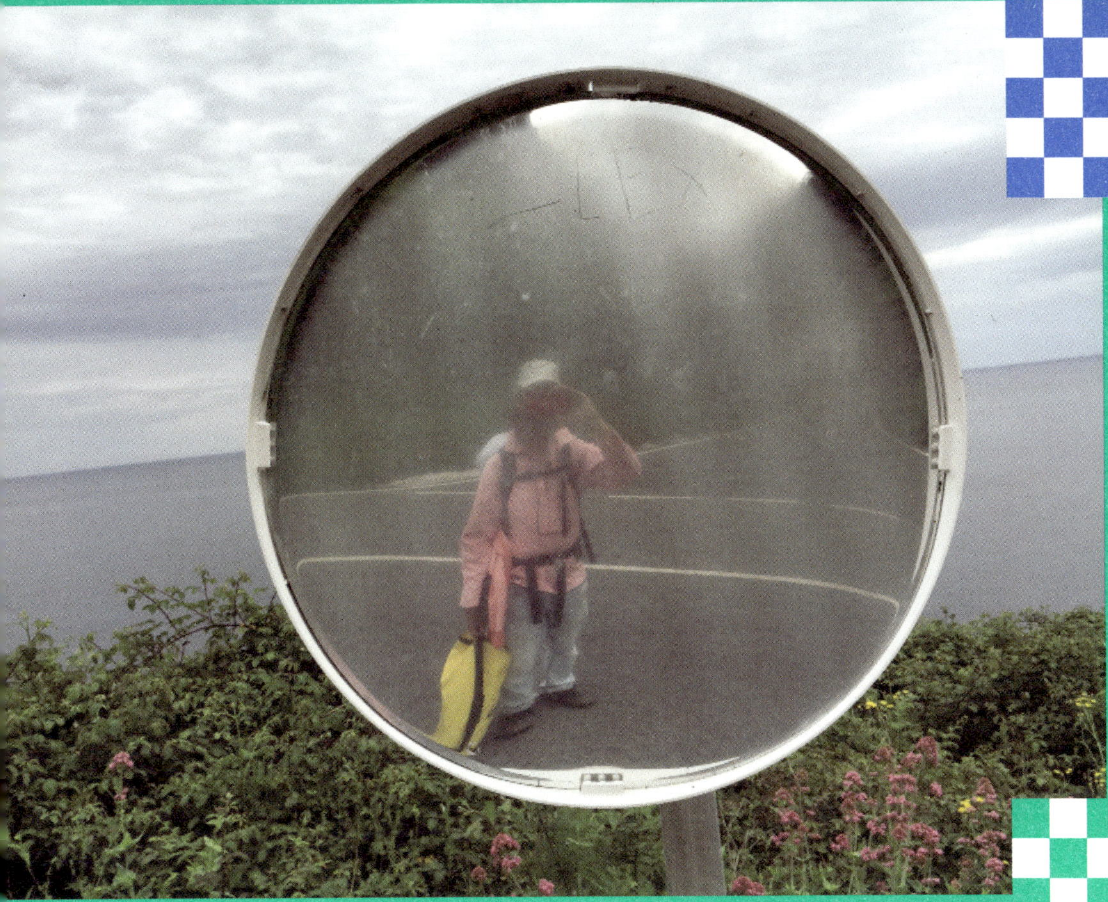

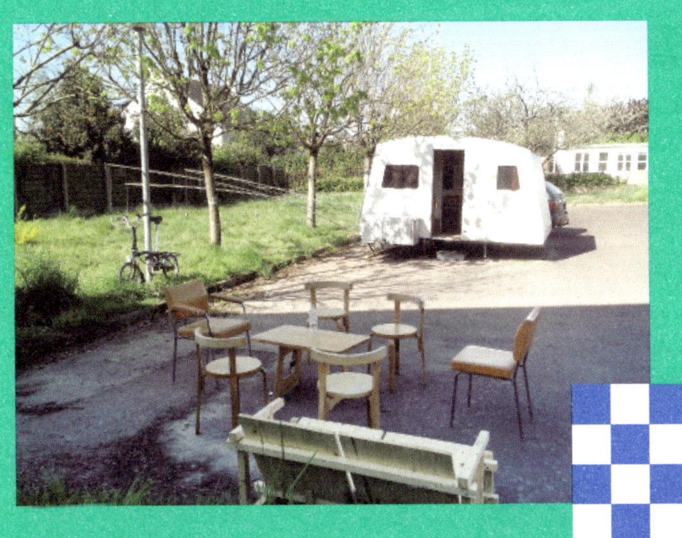

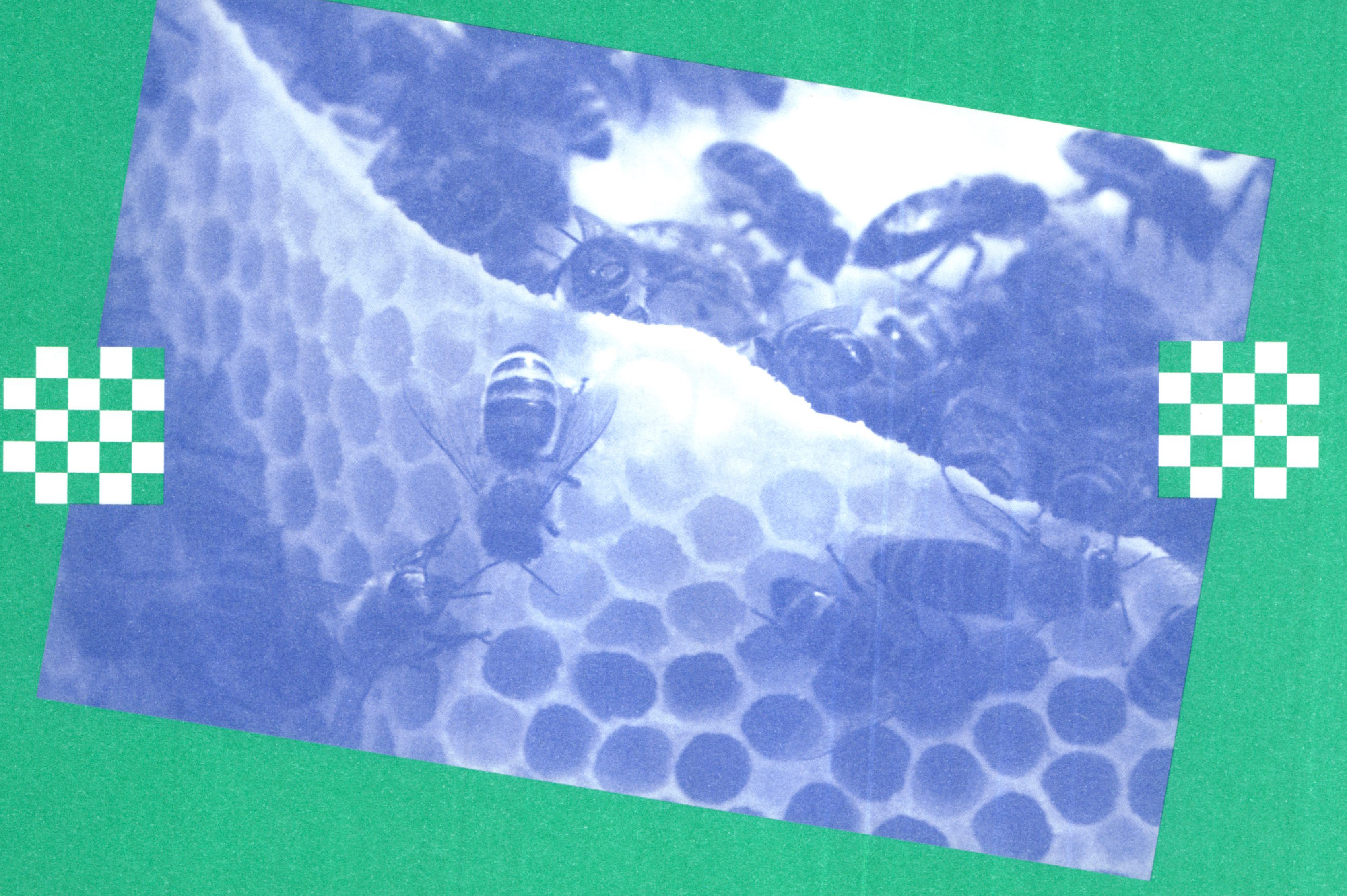

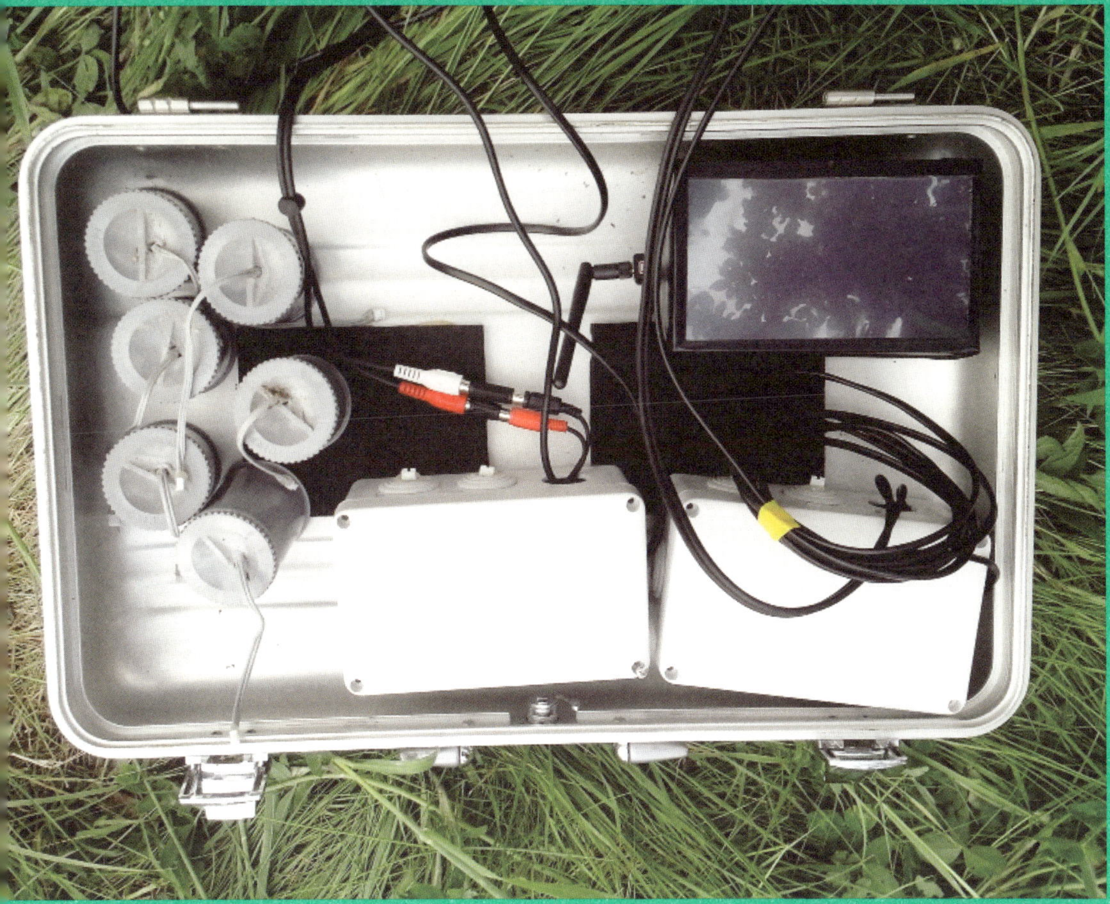

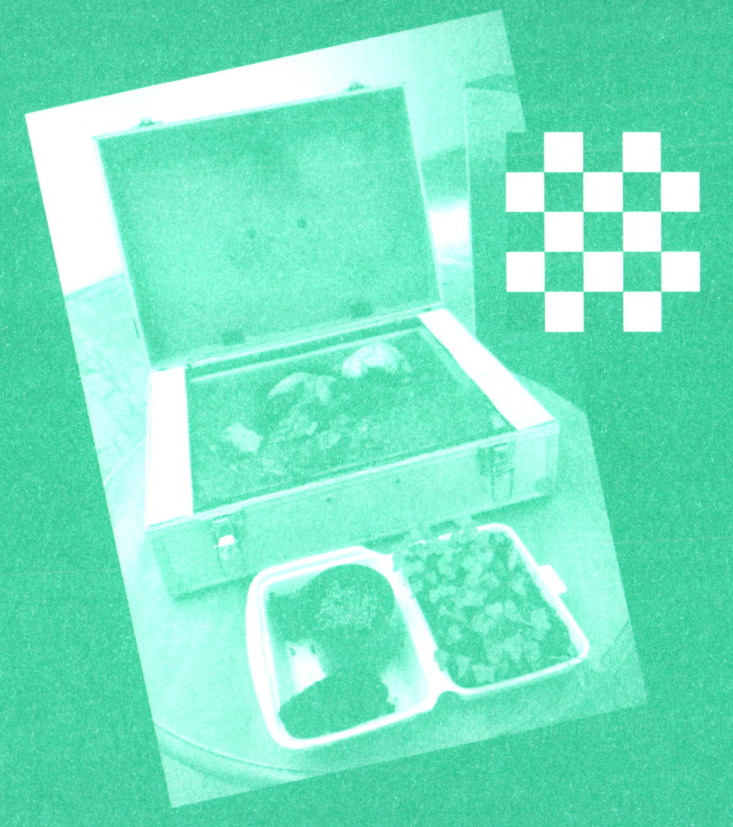

III.

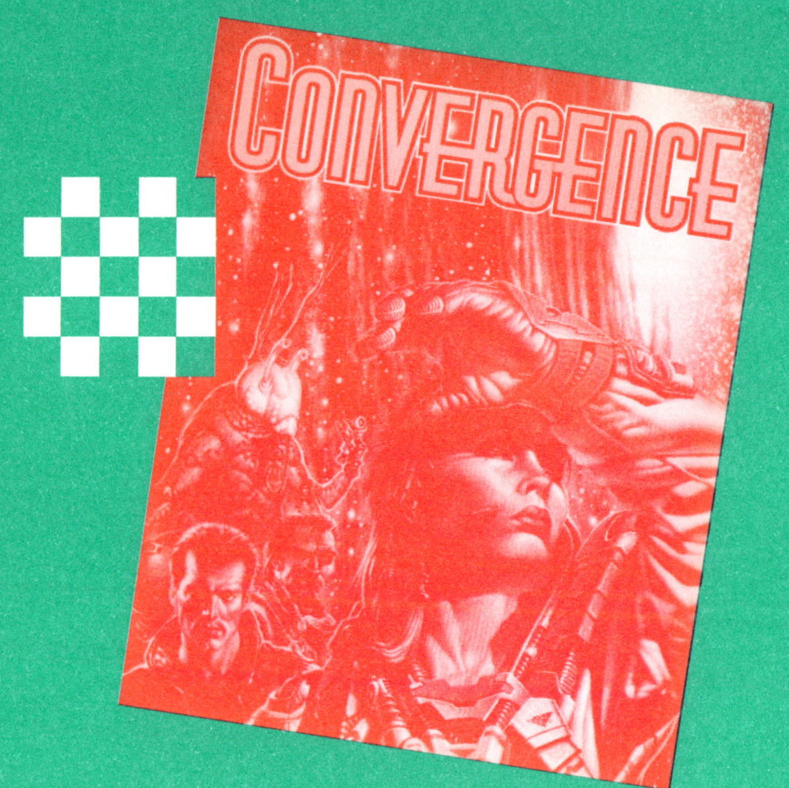

CONVERGENCE

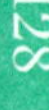
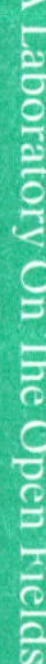
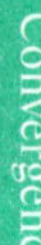

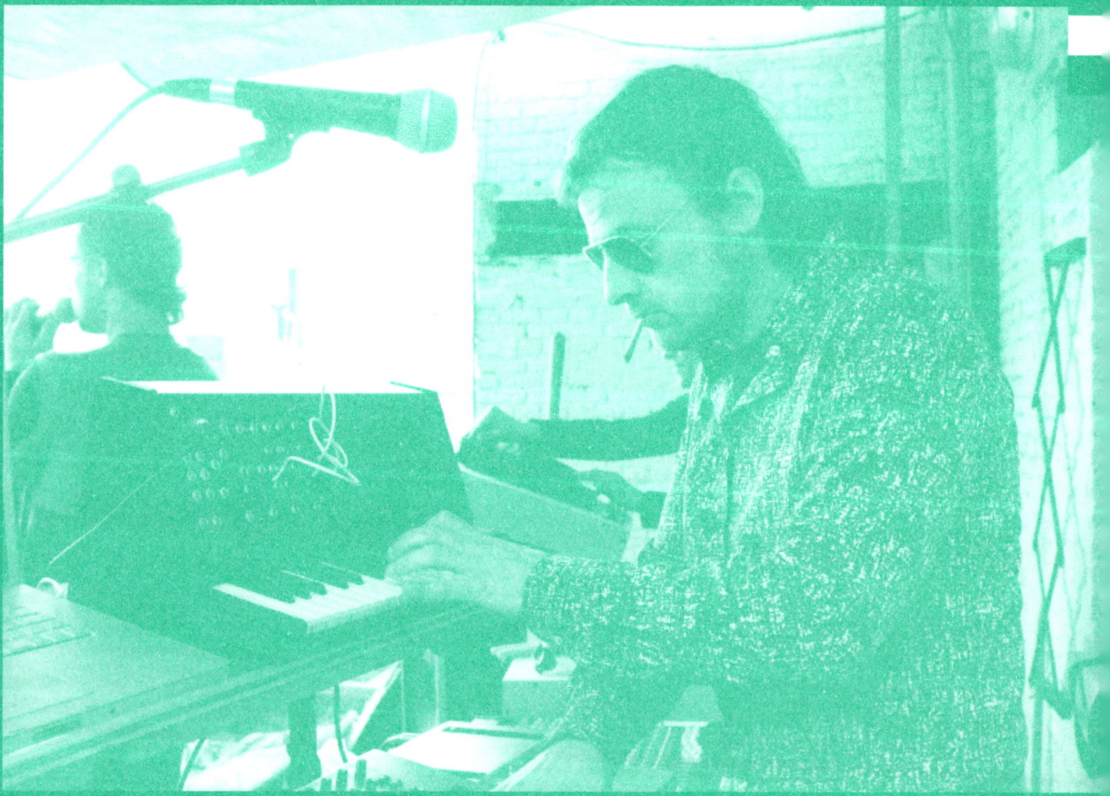

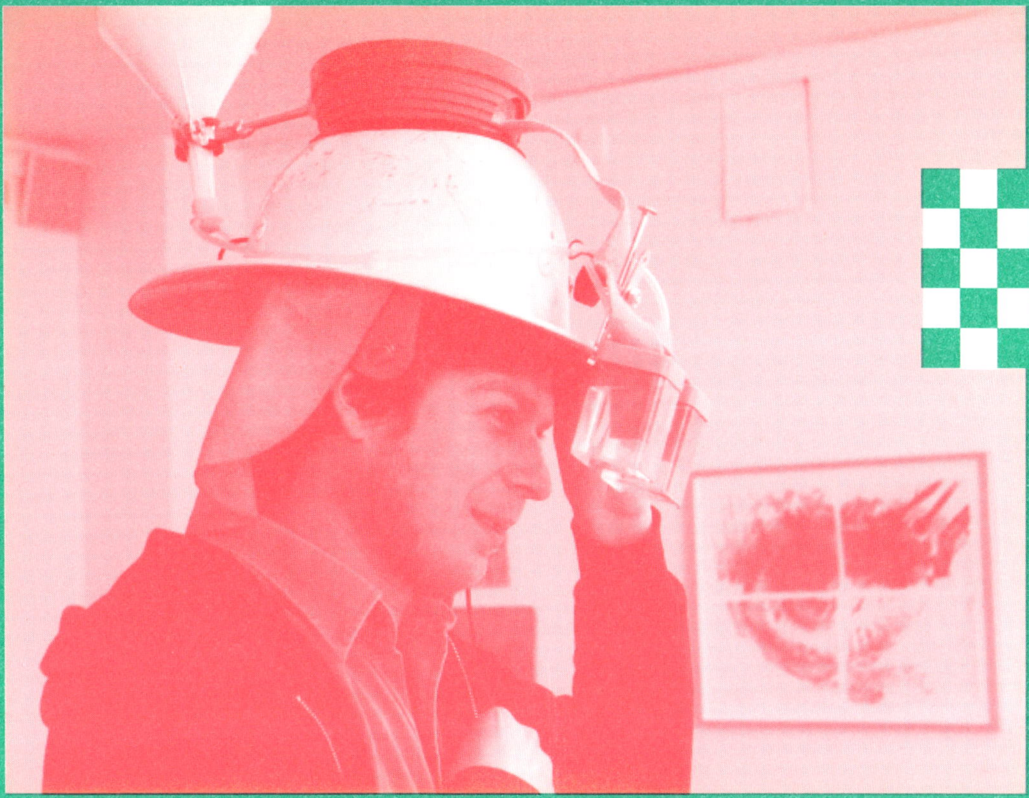

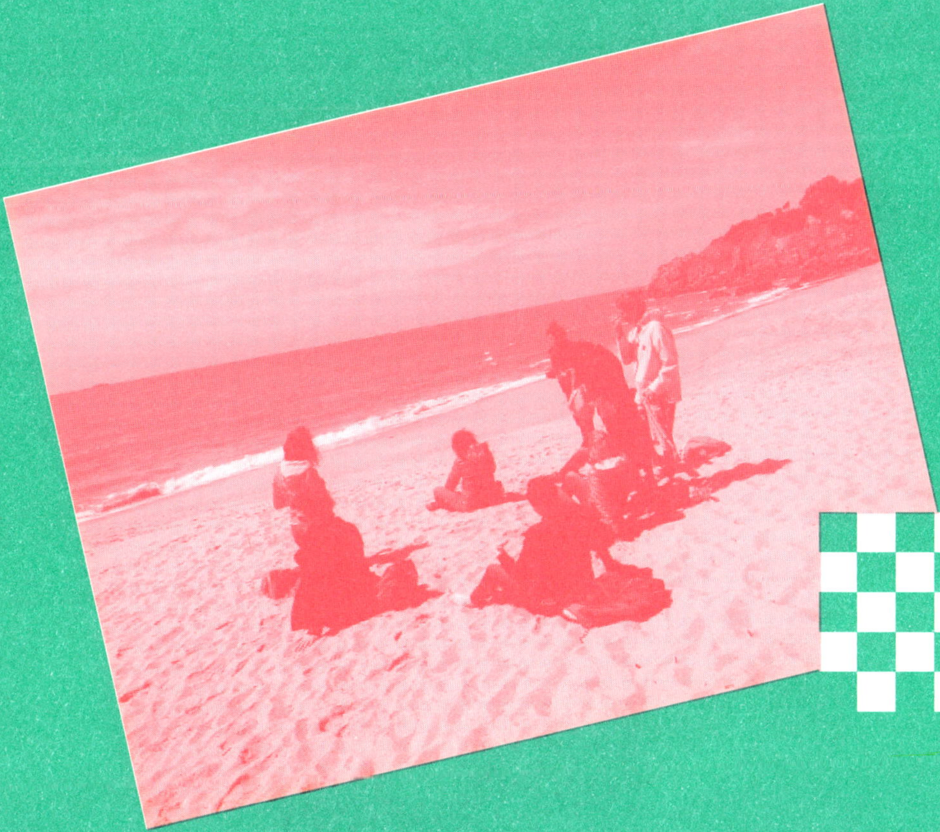

III.

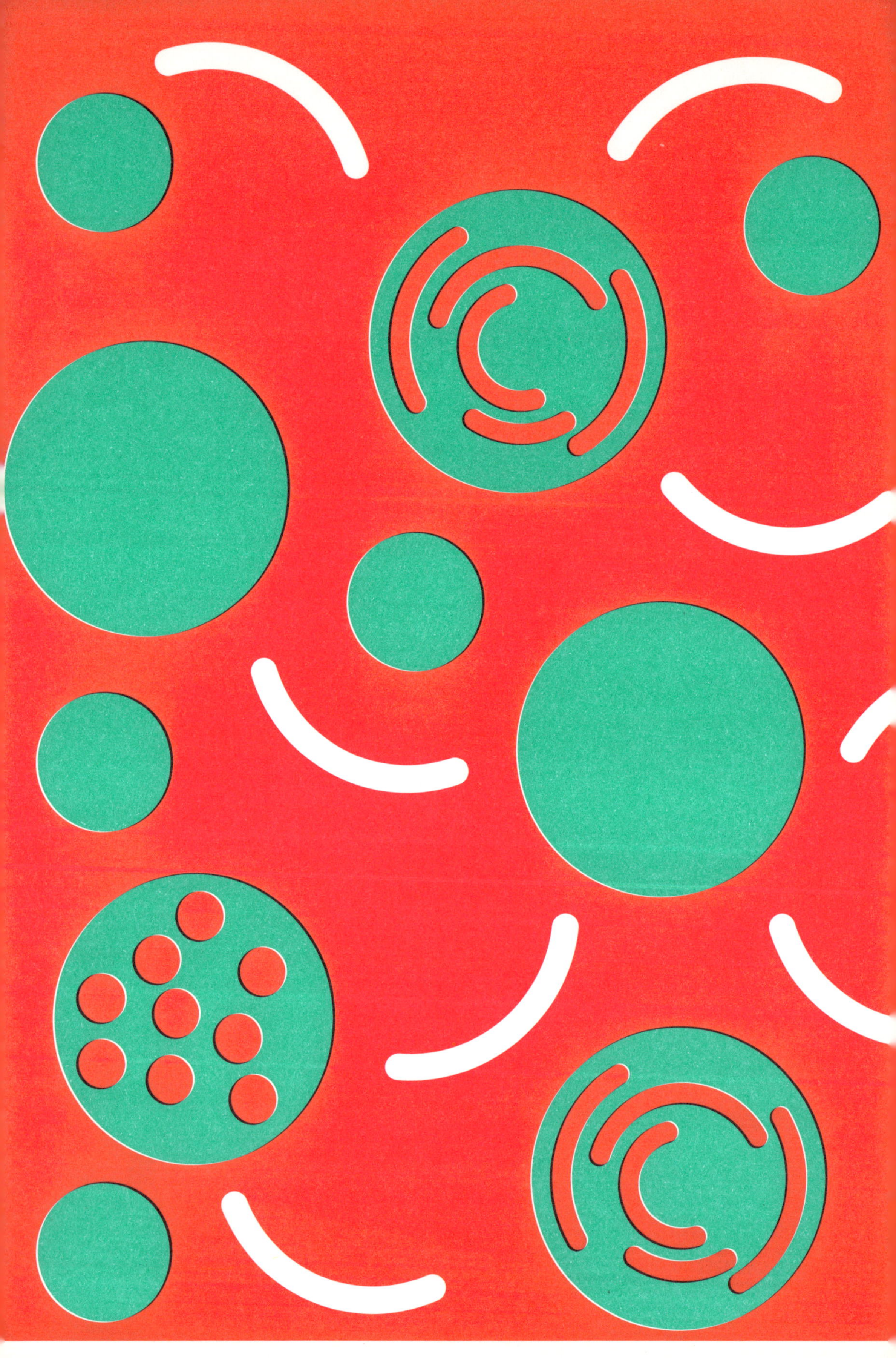

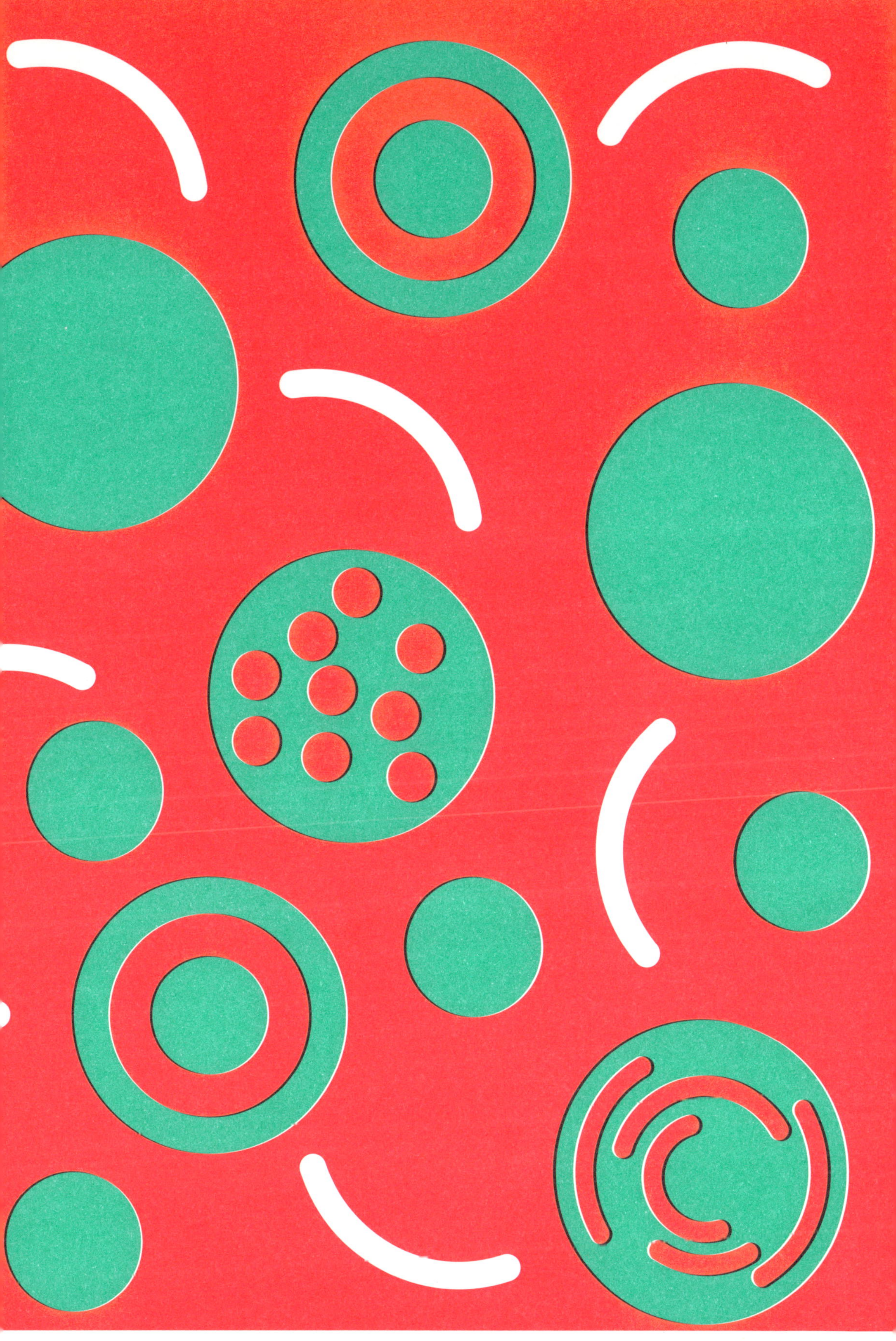

List of *Links*

I. *Art* Structures

OKNO – ALOTOF: Looking Back to Look Forward?
http://alotof.org/w/Article:OKNOalotofMissionstatement

ECOS
http://alotof.org/w/Article:ECOSalotofMissionstatement

Kravín Rural Arts as a Garden Laboratory
http://alotof.org/w/Yo-yo_-_KRA,_a_garden_with_a_bright_future,
_where_things_get_tangled_up

Wandering Arts Biennial: Platform For Artistic Mobility
http://alotof.org/w/Article:NADINEalotofMissionstatement

II. *Art* Works

About the notions Experimental and Ecology
http://alotof.org/w/Article:Experimental

Not Revolutionary
http://alotof.org/w/SolaSoundGarden

The Sound Beehive Experiment
http://alotof.org/w/The_Sound_Beehive_Experiment

Fieldnotes from an Urban Beekeeper
http://alotof.org/w/Article:SoundBeehive

P2P Food Lab
http://alotof.org/w/P2P_Food_Lab

Media Writing, Writing Media
http://alotof.org/w/MediaWriting

Corrosion: a sound lecture
http://alotof.org/w/Corrosion

Listening to Batteries
http://alotof.org/w/Listening_to_batteries

Island
http://alotof.org/w/ISLAND

Fetish
http://alotof.org/w/Article:Fetish

III. Convergence

List of *Contents*

Colophon
Ignorance

**ALOTOF Ignorance is a printed
and online publication**
www.alotof.org
www.alotof.org/w/Ignorance

**Published by OKNO and MER
Distributed by MER**

OKNO
Koolmijnenkaai 30-34
B-1080 Brussel
www.okno.be

MER. Paper Kunsthalle
Geldmunt 36
B-9000 Gent
www.merpaperkunsthalle.org

**ALOTOF is a temporary collaboration
between OKNO, ECOS, Yo-Yo
and Nadine**

All texts and images by the collaborating
ALOTOF artists, unless where mentioned
differently.

Edited by Gívan Belá (fka Guy Van Belle)
and AnneMarie Maes

Proof read by Lloyd Dunn
and Ada Ceuppens

Bioactive graphic design by The Rodina
www.therodina.com

Printed and binded at Tiskárna Didot, spol.
s r.o. Brno, www.tiskarna-didot.cz

Printed on ecological paper Munken Print
White 115gm2 and 300 gm2

Thanks to all artists and other creative
people contributing and supporting.

© 2015

Supported by MER, OKNO, ECOS,
Yo-Yo and Nadine

ISBN 978 94 9177 598 7

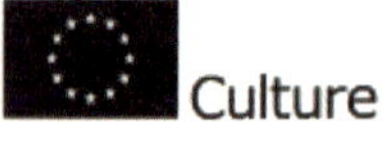
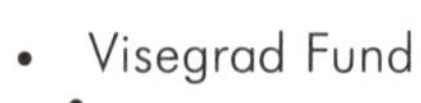
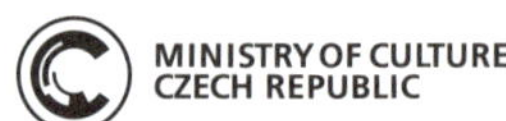
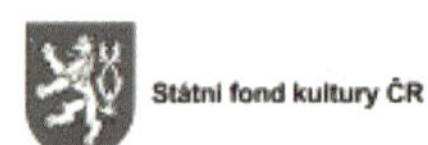
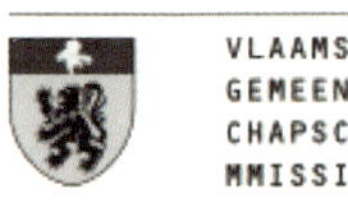
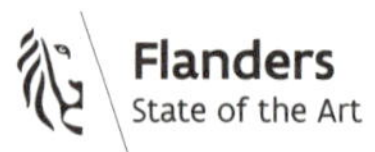
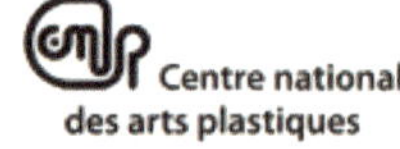
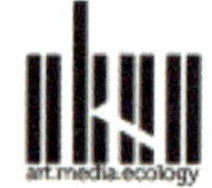
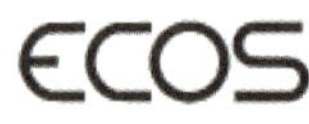
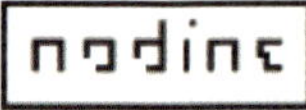

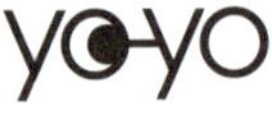

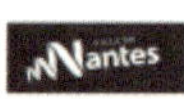
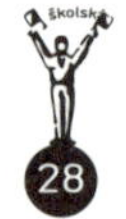